WOMEN AND DEVELOPMENT

The World Employment Programme (WEP) was launched by the International Labour Organisation in 1969, as the ILO's main contribution to the International Development Strategy for the Second United Nations Development Decade.

The means of action adopted by the WEP have included the following:
—Short-term, high-level advisory missions
—Longer-term national or regional employment teams
—A wide-ranging research program.

A landmark in the development of the WEP was the World Employment Conference of 1976, which proclaimed, inter alia, that "strategies and national development plans should include as a priority objective the promotion of employment and the satisfaction of the basic needs of each country's population." The Declaration of Principles and Programme of Action adopted by the conference have become the cornerstone of WEP technical assistance and research activities during the closing years of the Second Development Decade.

This publication is the outcome of a WEP project.

WOMEN AND DEVELOPMENT

The Sexual Division of Labor in Rural Societies

A study prepared for the International Labour Office within the framework of the World Employment Programme

Edited by Lourdes Benería

PRAEGER SPECIAL STUDIES • PRAEGER SCIENTIFIC

Library of Congress Cataloging in Publication Data
Main entry under title:

Women and development.

Bibliography p.
Includes index.
1. Women in rural development. 2. Division of labor.
3. Rural development—Social aspects. 4. Underdeveloped
areas—Women's employment. I. Benería, Lourdes.
HN980.W65   306'.36   82-606
ISBN 0-03-061802-9   AACR2

The responsibility for opinions expressed in studies and other contributions rests solely with their authors, and publication does not constitute an endorsement by the International Labour Office of the opinions expressed in them.

The designations employed and the presentation of material do not imply the expression of any opinion whatsoever on the part of the International Labour Office concerning the legal status of any country or territory or of its authorities, or concerning the delimitation of its frontiers.

Published in 1982 by Praeger Publishers
CBS Educational and Professional Publishing
a Division of CBS Inc.
521 Fifth Avenue, New York, New York 10175 U.S.A.

Copyright © International Labour Organisation 1982

3456789   052   98765432

Printed in the United States of America

PREFACE

Dharam Ghai

The present volume forms part of the program on rural women of the International Labour Office. This program received a major impetus from the conclusions of the World Employment Conference of 1976, which noted that women often constitute the group at the bottom of the ladder in respect to employment, poverty, education, training, and status. Concerning rural women, the conference recommended that measures be taken to relieve their work burden and drudgery by improving working and living conditions, as well as by providing more resources for investment. The Program on Rural Women in our branch has attempted to implement the relevant recommendations of the World Employment Conference as well as those adopted at the World Conferences on Women held in Mexico City and Copenhagen in 1975 and 1980.

In view of the inadequate information on the employment patterns and labor processes, incomes and living conditions, and organizations of rural women, the initial focus of the program in our branch has been on empirical research and studies in these areas carried out by scholars. The general approach of the program is to move gradually from a substantial conceptual and informational base to the dissemination and exchange of information and insights through seminars and workshops, followed by the planning and implementation of pilot projects to assist the rural women in generating more productive employment and higher incomes on a self-sustaining basis, preferably through rural women's organizations.

A significant volume of research has been carried out since the mid-1970s. This research in turn has provided a solid base for advisory services and for evaluation and initiation of action programs designed to benefit the poorest rural women. The studies have covered such themes as the basis and evolution of the sexual division of labor; the nature and terms of participation of rural women in agriculture, rural industry, and rural services; the impact on rural women of agricultural modernization and agrarian changes; and the prevalence, role, and potential of organizations of rural women.

The present volume brings together a number of studies sponsored by our program in recent years. Zubeida Ahmad and Martha Loutfi, who are responsible for the program on rural women in our branch, closely followed the evolution of the research and the preparation of this particular volume. These studies illustrate the range and magnitude of the contribution made by rural women as workers in different sectors. They underline both the underestimation of their labor and contribution to production in conventional analyses and statistics, and the highly disadvantageous and discriminatory terms of their participation in economic activities.

An area illuminated by these studies is the basis and evolution of the sexual division of labor in different sectors, regions, and socioeconomic systems, and at different stages of development. By generating original data or through use of available data, the studies make an important contribution by substantiating or refuting a number of general propositions often made in the growing literature on women and development. A noteworthy feature of most of the studies is that issues affecting rural women are discussed in the wider national and international socioeconomic context. In these and many other ways, these studies make an important contribution to our understanding of the grossly underestimated role of women in the rural and national economies of developing countries, and of the forces that perpetuate their subordination. Through this understanding they also prepare the groundwork for devising policies and action to assist working women in overcoming the specific problems facing them.

Dharam Ghai
Chief, Rural Employment Policies Branch
Employment and Development Department

CONTENTS

Woman of Africa
Sweeper
Smearing floors and walls
with cow dung and black soil
Cook, ayah, the baby on your back
Washer of dishes,
Planting, weeding, harvesting
Store-keeper, builder
Runner of errands,
Cart, lorry, donkey . . .
Woman of Africa
What are you not?

Okot p'Bitek
Song of Ocol

INTRODUCTION

Lourdes Benería

> They say "life brutalizes." That they recognize it
> explains why, for all that has been said to the con-
> trary, they remain painfully human. They are women
> of tremendous strengths, these women of the shadows.
> One of their strengths, and not the least, is their
> silence which outsiders have understood as submis-
> sion (Cornelisen 1977, pp. 9-10).

During the 1970s the growing interest in women's issues
materialized in different directions. For the international community the 1975 International Women's Year represented a turning
point. For many it was the natural outgrowth of the new visibility
of women and their specific problems and concerns that had been
dramatized by the women's movement of the late 1960s and early
1970s. For others it was a way of responding to women's demands
and to the realization that women were speaking of problems affecting more than half of the world's population. The fundamental questions posed by the women's movement could not be disregarded any
longer. An unprecedented amount of research, programs, and policies addressed to specific problems of women have sprung up since
then.

The results have been encouraging even if no dramatic changes
have occurred. We have learned a great deal about the nature and
significance of women's role in different societies. A growing body
of empirical literature and documentation about women's work and
condition across countries has provided the basis for new concep-
tualizations of women's problems. Feminist analysis and feminist
theory remain an exciting area in which fundamental questions are
asked in relation not only to women but also to society in general.
In many countries women are challenging the traditional division of
labor between the sexes and asking difficult questions about how
societies are organized to satisfy basic human needs. More specifically, women's struggle for equality challenges the old tenets of
patriarchal society; in addition, it poses fundamental questions
about the nature of inequality, of exploitation and subordination,
and about the type of social change necessary to eliminate them.

In many countries, programs and policies specifically addressed to women have been set up. In a handful of cases, efforts
have been made to deal with women's oppression on a larger scale

by including its amelioration among basic national objectives. In addition, the dynamics of economic change are affecting women in different ways. The urbanization process experienced to different degrees by most countries has often made women more invisible by secluding them in the household while making them more dependent on men for subsistence; this is especially the case in early stages of development, when urban life generates more employment for men than for women, as in many African countries today. In other cases industrialization is changing the composition of the labor force and contributing to fundamental changes in women's participation in production. Although some of these changes can be regarded as positive, new forms of oppression appear, and women's subordinate position in society remains highly visible and disquieting almost universally. This subordinate position can be observed both at the household level, where women's activities are primarily centered, and at other levels of society. Oppressive institutions and practices are numerous and still commonplace; they are embodied in such basic economic institutions as male-centered inheritance systems, unequal distribution of revenues between the sexes, asymmetry in the sexual division of labor, and discrimination in employment and wages. And they are institutionalized in daily life and in such social institutions as patriarchal religion, female seclusion, wife beating, polygamy, and reduction of women's mobility.

Different explanations of and conflicting views about the nature of the problem exist, even among women themselves. At the theoretical level various approaches and models have been devised that differ both analytically and in terms of their implications for policy and action. But one of the most pervasive themes of the present feminist movement has been the emphasis placed on the role of reproduction[1] and women's reproductive activities as a determinant of women's work, the sexual division of labor, and the dominance/subordination relationship between the sexes. This emphasis has resulted in a penetration of analysis into the household in order to understand the nature of the domestic economy, of domestic work, and of the relations between the sexes within the household.

The implications of this emphasis on reproduction are important in several ways. Traditional analysis (and traditional policy and action) related to "the woman question" had formally focused on the nature of women's participation in the labor market and other issues falling outside the domestic economy. Consequently, the solution to women's oppression was seen as being located essentially in the sphere of paid production—that is, outside the household and independent of it. To use an example applied to industrialized countries, neoclassical economic models have explained women's secondary position in the labor market by using several approaches, such as "overcrowding" of women in low-productivity occupations; differences in educational background and working experience of women (human capital); imperfections in the labor market, such as the existence of monopsonistic hiring of female labor, leading to lower wages for women.[2] These models would suggest that in order to eliminate sex differences in the labor market, the conditions affecting either the demand or the supply side that lead to discrimination by sex would have to disappear. However, they do not explain why these conditions appear and what forces generate them. What remains to be explained, for example, is why overcrowding takes place and what are the roots of the differences in educational background and working experience between the sexes.

On the other hand, the internal labor market model explains women's position by focusing on the hierarchical job structure within the enterprise. This model is more explicit in rooting sexual segregation and wage differentials in the internal structure of the firm, and suggests that the basis for sexual differentiation in the labor market is the productive structure. A hierarchical productive structure, together with the dynamics of the internal labor market, tends to create differences among workers that are related to sex and other factors (Blau and Jusenius 1976).

While these models provide explanations for women's position in the labor market, they pay little attention to the factors located in the household and the sphere of reproduction, and to the patriarchal socialization process to which women are subject. In contrast, the emphasis on reproduction suggests that in order to understand women's position in the labor market, we need to analyze the significance of women's role in the household/reproductive sphere and then to focus on the interaction between reproduction and production. This means, for example, that although the internal labor market model provides an illuminating analysis of the inherent forces within the enterprise that lead to differential treatment by sex, it needs to be complemented by an analysis of how the structure of the household and other socializing institutions, such as schools, provides the bases that channel women toward certain positions in paid production.

This suggests the need to analyze the domestic economy, the sexual division of labor within the household, and the social relations between household members that it generates. It also means that the solution to women's oppression rests both on their full participation in nonhome production under conditions of equality between the sexes, and the transformation of household relations and gender assymetries so that relations of dominance and subordination between the sexes are eliminated. At the policy level this approach implies that any effort to eliminate discrimination by sex in the pro-

ductive sphere cannot ignore other issues related to reproduction—
such as the burden of the "double day" that women face when they
work outside the household, a burden still common in most countries.

In brief, this double focus on production and reproduction does
not invalidate the argument of Engels and the traditional left about
the need to transform and do away with exploitative and hierarchical
productive structures, and about the need for women to participate
in paid production in order to deal with women's oppression; but it
does indicate that this transformation needs to be accompanied by
other fundamental changes in the relationship between the sexes—
beginning at the household and ideological level. This is in fact the
most basic message of the present feminist movement.

Most of the chapters in this volume reflect this double focus.
However, readers will notice that some of them tend to place greater
emphasis on the structure of production to explain women's work and
condition, while others focus more explicitly on the interaction between production and reproduction. These empirical studies have
the common feature that they are, in one form or another, the product of research or consultation sponsored by the Programme on
Rural Women of the International Labour Organisation. For this
reason they focus primarily on rural societies in the Third World.
The objective of this research is not only to increase our knowledge
about how the development process affects women, but also to set
the basis for devising policies and action dealing with specific problems facing them, and to give a direction to women's struggles.

Several basic themes are developed in this volume. First,
some chapters speak to the wide range of variations observed in
rural societies with respect to the sexual division of labor. Although
domestic activities are overwhelmingly performed by women across
countries, what is considered to be women's work in terms of nondomestic production is far from rigidly defined. Women can be
found performing agricultural tasks similar to men's, as well as
tasks that are sex-typed. In the Hausa region of Nigeria, a high
degree of seclusion prevails, but women are still engaged in some
agricultural tasks as well as in processing food for sale and in retail trade (see Chapter 4 of this volume). In the case of the lacemakers of Narsapur, India, described by Maria Mies, a strong
prejudice against women's work outside the household has led to
their concentration in a type of activity—lacemaking—geared to the
international market but carried out within the domestic compound.
Carmen Deere and Magdalena León de Leal describe the performance of different types of tasks by women in agriculture and analyze the extent of women's involvement in market production, depending upon the degree of market penetration in the local economy.
Kate Young describes how, in the Mexican region of Oaxaca, women's

involvement in weaving was replaced by their participation in coffee production, mostly coffee picking on a seasonal basis, when the combination of merchant and local capital led the region to replace traditional crops with the more commercialized coffee production.

This flexibility in the types of activities that women are performing outside the household implies that the sexual division of labor should not be viewed as "a given," but as subject to change. As Boserup clearly pointed out:

> While members of any given community may think that their particular division of labor between the sexes is the "natural" one, because it has undergone little or no change for generations, other communities may have completely different ways of dividing the burden of work among the sexes, and they too may find their ways just as "natural" (1970, p. 15).

Second, most chapters in this volume illustrate the changing nature of the sexual division of labor as a result of changes taking place in the overall economy and as accumulation proceeds. The chapters by Mies, Deere and León de Leal, and Young analyze the connection between capitalist penetration into local economies, the development of national and international markets, and women's activities. Similarly, Noeleen Heyzer's study illustrates how the establishment of labor-intensive multinational industries in Southeast Asia has attracted a high proportion of young rural women and incorporated them into the semiurbanized labor force. The transformation of agrarian structures and the process of land commercialization and concentration contribute to the proletarianization of the labor force, but the effect tends not to be identical for men and women (see Chapter 2 in this volume). In addition, changes in the overall economy have an impact upon the household. This implies that, far from being a static unit of production and consumption, the household is subject to changes—for example, in the quantity and quality of housework and in the intensity of reproductive activities—whose roots are in the sphere of accumulation.

Third, this dynamic process is reflected in patterns of migration. Women may migrate because employment for females is available, a factor analyzed in particular by Heyzer, but also because of a given household structure that tends to make female labor more redundant than male labor. An analysis of both the employment opportunities available to women and the dynamics of the household in terms of labor redundancy constitutes a good example of the need to focus on the interaction between production and reproduction in order to capture fully the process of migration. Young's and Heyzer's chapters are very successful in integrating both aspects.

The subject of migration is highly connected with the transition between the rural and the urban/industrial world. Although this volume focuses on rural women, one chapter—Heyzer's—presents a case study of this transition in which many women in the Third World find themselves today. In this process women may be freed from some of the old patriarchal forms of the more traditional agricultural societies, yet new forms of subordination and exploitation appear in urban/industrial society—tied to the process of proletarianization of the labor force that affects both men and women, and also to the division of labor between the sexes.

Boserup's pioneer work on the role of women in economic development underlined some of the problems facing women in the industrial/urban economy. She pointed out that a process "of polarization and hierarchization of men's and women's roles" can be observed "in the modern, urban economy," whereas it is not usually observed "either in family production for subsistence or in market production in home industries at the village level" (1970, p. 140). She also called attention to basic differences in industrial skills and educational background between the sexes, which result in women's secondary position in the urban labor markets. However, Boserup attributed this process of proletarianization and hierarchization to the modern, urban economy without specifying the type of "modernization" underlying her analysis. A number of studies that have appeared since then, such as Heyzer's in this volume, go one step further; they emphasize the connection between the type of development model behind specific urban/industrial growth and women's place within it (see Benería and Sen, forthcoming). Thus, Boserup's polarization and hierarchization is viewed not as the result of modernization, but as a result of a capitalist development model.

Fourth, a corollary of this significance of the development model is that women's subordination has to do not only with male domination but also with the basic economic and political structures of society—that is, one of the dimensions of women's oppression is the existence of mechanisms of exploitation that feed on and accentuate inequalities related to class and gender. This is a basic theme underlying most chapters in this volume. Thus, Mies's study of Narsapur's lacemakers describes the high degree of exploitation to which women lacemakers are subject as workers producing commodities for the market and as women whose mobility and options are highly restricted by seclusion. We are dealing, therefore, with the economics and politics of class and gender, both of which need to be taken into consideration and the interaction between them analyzed in order to fully understand women's position in the economy. Thus, despite the conditioning influence that women's concentration in reproductive activities exercises upon their work, class differences among them are easily observable, as pointed out by Longhurst and by Deere and León de Leal. Since class differences speak again of inequalities, they lead us to ask questions about the reasons for their existence and about the possibility of doing away with them.

Fifth, these questions lead to the subject of institutional change and its effects on women. If private ownership, unequal distribution of resources, and a capitalist organization of production result in fundamental class differences—affecting women in a variety of ways—we need to ask whether any institutional change addressed to altering these factors will do away with gender-related mechanisms of subordination affecting women. Elisabeth Croll and Zenebeworke Tadesse address themselves to this question in regard to China and Ethiopia respectively. Both studies show that institutional change toward a more egalitarian distribution of economic resources sets up favorable conditions for effective struggle against the oppression of women. Yet both speak also about the contradictions that can appear when policies aimed at attaining equality between the sexes are implemented while patriarchal forms—expressed through tradition or law—still prevail.

Finally, one of the most pervasive themes in these chapters is the extent to which women's economic activities are underestimated in labor force and national income statistics, and are undervalued in general. Specific case studies of women's work show that the degree of women's involvement in economic activity other than domestic work is high, even in cases where women are secluded, but official statistics do not often capture the degree of their involvement (see Chapters 1, 3, and 4 in this volume). In addition, conventional statistics and the theoretical concepts that feed them are biased in the direction of excluding a good proportion of the activities in which women are involved. Dealing with these biases requires an effort to redefine the concept of economic activity so that it includes not only tasks directly related to commodity production but also tasks that contribute to human welfare (see Chapter 5 in this volume). In what follows, I will deal with the contents of each chapter in more detail.

Mies raises some fundamental questions about the economic and social foundations of the inequality between men and women. In her introductory remarks she points out that biological determinism is the deepest-rooted obstacle to the analysis of the causes of women's oppression. Women themselves, she states, "find it difficult to establish that the unequal, hierarchical and exploitative relationship between sexes is caused by social—that is, historical—factors." On the other hand, the tools of analysis themselves, such as the basic definitions and concepts, are affected by biological determinism. As a response to these problems she suggests, first, transforming and revising the tools of analysis in such a way that we can look at them "from below"—that is, from the perspective of women's oppression. Second, our search for the origins of women's oppression should include the analysis of how "history in the making" has affected women and placed them in a subordinate position throughout history. As a result, she states, "We should no longer look at the sexual division of labor as a problem related to the family, but as a structural problem of a whole society."

The second part of Mies's study includes an empirical analysis of this "history in the making." It refers to women lacemakers in Narsapur, Andhra Pradesh, India—engaged in a putting-out industry affecting 150,000-200,000 women. The proceeds from the handmade lace and lace products, sold in the national and the international markets, have been increasing rapidly since 1970; its expansion, Mies argues, has led to a greater class differentiation within local communities as well as to a greater polarization and differentiation between men's and women's tasks. In the process of describing the nature of women's participation in this industry, Mies raises some very interesting questions about the origins of seclusion and purdah, the transmission of dominant values in a stratified class system, the division of labor between the sexes, the process of industrialization required by the industry's organization of production, and the effect of pauperization on women's work.

A second study on India, included in Chapter 2, focuses on a very different subject: the effect of the transformation of agrarian structures and of technological change on labor requirements in agriculture, and their impact on women in particular. More specifically, Gita Sen focuses on the changes introduced by the Green Revolution in two regions—Haryana/Punjab, a region with a powerful group of middle farmers, and Thanjavur, a region dominated by large landowners and with a long history of landless labor. Historically women's participation in agricultural work has been lower in Haryana/Punjab than in Thanjavur.

After analyzing in detail the overall process of agrarian change and its effects on land concentration, the proletarianization of the labor force, and labor requirements in the agricultural sector, Sen focuses her analysis on the impact that the process has had on women. In Haryana/Punjab land reform and the new technology have narrowed the range of tasks done by women and placed them at the bottom of the hierarchy of permanent and casual labor. In addition, a decline in farm size and the attempts by small farmers to adopt the new technology have led to a greater participation of women from small landholding households in casual wage labor. Sen describes a more widespread proletarianization process in Thanjavur, "with many conversions of landed into landless households." This process has affected women to the extent that those who previously were family workers are now coolies, having lost their land. Women workers have also been pushed out of their traditional tasks as the result of the increase in "surplus" labor caused by land concentration and the introduction of capital-intensive methods of cultivation. The pattern that emerges in both regions is that of a process by which agrarian and technological change has a differential impact on agricultural workers by sex—women tend to be placed in the lower echelons of the labor hierarchy.

Chapter 4 is an anthropological study of a Moslem Hausa village in northern Nigeria, a polygamous society where seclusion of married women of childbearing age has been on the increase as a predominantly urban phenomenon during this century. As a result of the reduction of women's mobility enforced by seclusion, Longhurst describes a very rigid sexual division of labor. Women's role in farm work is not very significant, but they do perform some seasonal work, such as picking cotton. Seclusion, however, does not prevent them from processing food for sale, an activity that forms "an important part of the cash economy of a Hausa village." From the seclusion of their homes, women also trade in goods they have not processed, such as condiments and seasoning. Therefore, they remain, as Longhurst puts it, "very active economic entrepreneurs" despite the constraints of seclusion. However, he estimates that the return for their work is much lower than that of men's.

A relatively high degree of economic independence exists between men and women of the same household. Longhurst points out that one implication for economic development programs of the separation between men's and women's work is that the programs are likely to have different impacts on the two sexes. For example, agricultural projects aimed at improving land productivity will help the men, but might not help women, because men "are under no cultural obligation to pass the proceeds along to women." Therefore, economic aid should be addressed to specific family members rather than be assumed to affect all of them equally. Otherwise the unequal distribution of resources among household members is likely to continue or to be intensified.

The issue of underestimation of women's economic activities at the concrete level is raised in the four first chapters. Chapter 5 focuses entirely on this question at a more general level. After reviewing the concepts behind labor force statistics, the chapter discusses the reasons why women's participation in the labor force, as conventionally defined, tends to be grossly underestimated, especially in predominantly agricultural areas. Although underestimation is an issue that also affects the male labor force, women's primary concentration in domestic activities underlines the reasons behind the specific underestimation of the female labor force. Consequently, studies of women's work must use a great deal of caution in drawing inferences from official statistics. In addition, the disparity in female labor force participation rates reported across countries is likely to be exaggerated, and international comparisons are likely to be misleading unless standardized data collection is adopted.

The second part of Chapter 5 argues that the underestimation of women's work is even more pronounced if we question the conventional definitions of labor force. These definitions have tended to focus on participation in commodity production—that is, in the production of exchange values rather than use values. Ultimately they are intended to measure the degree of direct involvement in a given process of growth and accumulation. The argument presented in this chapter is that participation in the labor force should include use value production as well. In order to elaborate this argument, the chapter discusses the contributions made by recent literature on the economic significance of use-value production in subsistence agriculture and in the household sector. While efforts to estimate labor force participation in subsistence agriculture have been made, domestic activities have normally been viewed as outside the economic realm, and unpaid domestic workers as outside the labor force. In order to account for all use-value production, some practical implications for data collection are drawn. The objective of this exercise is not only to develop more accurate estimation of women's participation in production, but also to counteract the ideological undervaluation of women's work that is so prevalent across countries. An additional objective is to define economic activity in such a way as to relate it to human welfare rather than to a given process of growth and accumulation.

Of the two chapters focusing on migration, Young's discusses the reasons behind female migration from a rural area, while Heyzer's analyzes an example of the pulling factors that attract migrants to industrial employment. In the first case the analysis is based on the transformation of some rural communities in the mountainous area of Oaxaca, Mexico, since the 1940s. Young describes the changes generated by the introduction of cash crops, particularly coffee, into the area, and by the establishment of ties with the national and international markets. The ensuing changes in agrarian structures and technology created a "surplus" population, which led to out-migration; the flow reached such proportions that by 1970 an absolute population decline was registered despite high birth rates. Women migrants, mostly young daughters, outnumbered men for reasons ranging from the fact that subsistence production fell upon men to the undermining of women's activities by technological change and by the industrially produced goods available in the market. An additional reason was the greater availability of employment for young women in the urban economy. Thus, Young's approach constitutes an interesting example of the usefulness of analyzing migration by focusing on the interaction of forces whose roots lie in the structure of production as well as in the sexual division of labor at the household level.

Although Heyzer's approach is quite similar to Young's, she focuses mainly on the employment side: her study of young migrant women in Singapore's labor-intensive industries provides an illuminating picture of young women in transition from the more traditional rural society to an urban environment where they have become wage workers in multinational industries. The migratory flow of women is the result of a background of poverty in the Chinese New Villages and the kampongs of West Malaysia; young women rather than men migrate because they can be "spared from the land without the loss of that land." Migrant workers make up 51 percent of the total manufacturing work force in Singapore, and about 45 percent of workers in the manufacturing sector are women. The large majority (81 percent) of women workers are located at the bottom of the wage distribution.

On the basis of her fieldwork as a semiskilled trainee in a factory, Heyzer describes what the transition from traditional life to industrial employment implies for migrant women. She also analyzes their participation as unskilled and semiskilled workers in a fragmented labor process where technology and the division of labor reduce each worker's control over her work to a minimum. Overall, she presents a picture of alienated work, as viewed from inside the factory, and describes some of the workers' responses to what she calls "an atmosphere of compulsion." The transitional attitudes and values of rural workers and their contrast with the more urbanized and "modern" workers are described. Heyzer's conclusion is that women's participation in this type of wage labor does not necessarily create "a stable female work force integrated into a system that allows the improvement of women's position"; instead, "We witness what seems to be a permanent migrant sector that lives within a limiting framework of compulsion." In the process a basic problem is raised again: that new forms of subordination can appear in the face of some positive change, such as greater economic independence and freedom from traditional patriarchal forms.

This takes us to the even more basic question of what structure of production and what model of development can best eliminate both the forms of exploitation that affect men and women and those that are specific to women. The last two chapters of this volume deal with this subject by focusing on the effects of institutional change on women.

Zenebeworke Tadesse's analysis of the impact of land reform on women in Ethiopia illustrates the positive aspects of radical change and the contradictions that can appear while patriarchal forms are still maintained. Her discussion focuses on three issues: women's access to the means of production, law and customs regarding property rights, and the role of women in political organizations. The Land Reform Proclamation of March 1975 has brought about significant changes—from the abolition of private ownership and hired labor to the implementation of peasants' possessory rights over cultivated land. In regard to women, Tadesse states, the proclamation is egalitarian in intent although, given that land is allotted to a family unit, it is "internally contradictory when counterposed to the Ethiopian family structure." Because there is no complete break with the preexisting patriarchal barriers to women's emancipation, women's economic role has not been redefined, and their status within the family and the community has not changed. As a result the land reform has left women economically dependent on men rather than making them equal partners in the new agrarian structure. In some cases it has created new problems; given that the proclamation is based on the assumption of the monogamous family, problems have appeared in the polygamous areas, where men have been registering one wife and leaving the others without access to land.

The last chapter provides an analysis of how rural development strategies in the People's Republic of China affected women. A number of policies and measures to encourage women "to take a full and wide-ranging part" in the agricultural labor force were introduced during the 1940s and 1950s. Elizabeth Croll analyzes the impact of these measures from the point of view of women's quantitative participation in production, of changes in the sexual division of labor, and of the political involvement of women at different levels of rural society. She emphasizes that important changes took place in the degree to which women participate in agricultural production and in the sociopolitical realm. Yet some problems persisted, and these changes were not accompanied by a redefinition of tasks within the domestic sphere. As a result women have faced the typical dual demands of the "double day," and this has had a negative repercussion on the extent and nature of their involvement in activities outside the household. Important efforts to socialize domestic labor in the areas of child care, processing food grain, meal preparation, and sewing clothes were introduced during the Great Leap Forward. Croll analyzes the factors that led to the decline of such an interesting experiment. Ultimately, she concludes, the important progress reached definite limits because any redefinition of the sexual division of labor was assumed "to primarily derive from the entry of women into the waged labor force."

Thus the Chinese experiment suggests that the radical reorganization of society along more collectivized productive and distributive lines facilitated the efforts to overcome many of the obstacles facing women in the traditionally patriarchal Chinese society. Yet the strategy reached its limits because it did not deal with the problems in the sphere of reproduction adequately or for long enough. This is still the fundamental challenge of any development strategy that would include the emancipation of women as a basic objective.

NOTES

1. By "reproduction" I mean not only biological reproduction and daily maintenance of the labor force, but also social reproduction, the perpetuation of social systems. Thus I subscribe to the view that in order to control social reproduction—such as through inheritance systems—most societies have developed a variety of forms of control of female sexuality and of women's activities, and this control is at the root of women's subordination (Benería 1979).

2. For a detailed analysis of these models and of the internal labor market model, see Blau and Jusenius 1976.

REFERENCES

Benería, Lourdes. 1979. "Reproduction, Production and the Sexual Division of Labor." Cambridge Journal of Economics 3, no. 3 (September):203-25.

Benería, Lourdes, and Gita Sen. "Accumulation, Reproduction and Women's Role in Economic Development: Boserup Revisited." Signs, forthcoming.

Blau, Francine, and Carol Jusenius. 1976. "Economists' Approaches to Sex Segregation in the Labor Market." In Martha Blaxall and Barbara Reagan, eds., Women in the Workplace, pp. 181-99. Chicago: University of Chicago Press.

Boserup, Ester. 1970. Woman's Role in Economic Development. London: George Allen and Unwin.

Cornelisen, Ann. 1977. Women of the Shadows. New York: Vintage Books.

Women replanting the rice in the paddies in Northern Iran.
Photograph courtesy of the International Labour Organisation.

Work and childcare: washing the "cabuya," which will be used to make ropes and sandals, Imbabura province, Ecuador. Photograph courtesy of the International Labour Organisation.

They call it handloom, but this young woman from rural India uses hands and feet to produce cloth at a rate of about two yards a day. Photograph courtesy of the International Labour Organisation.

A woman combining childcare and hand-glazing of earthenware pots, Twante, Burma. Photograph courtesy of the International Labour Organisation.

In the Middle East, women are commonly employed on tobacco farms. Photograph courtesy of the International Labour Organisation.

Nimble fingers at work, Indonesia. Photograph courtesy of the International Labour Organisation.

Making clothes for family consumption while men and children are watching, Iran. Photograph courtesy of the International Labour Organisation.

1

THE DYNAMICS OF THE SEXUAL DIVISION OF LABOR AND INTEGRATION OF RURAL WOMEN INTO THE WORLD MARKET

Maria Mies

INTRODUCTION

The Problem of Biased Concepts

When women began to ask about the origins of the unequal relationship between the sexes, they soon discovered that none of the explanations put forward by social scientists for several hundred years was satisfactory. This is because in most explanations, whether they stem from an evolutionist, a positivist-functionalist, or even a Marxist approach, the problem that needs explanation is, in the last analysis, seen as biologically determined and, hence, beyond the scope of social change. This is mainly because the concepts that emerged in the context of particular historical circumstances were universalized and rigidified in a dogmatic way. Thus, they were no longer flexible enough to explain social change and the concreteness and dynamics of historical processes.

This covert or overt biological determinism, paraphrased in Freud's statement that anatomy is destiny, is perhaps the most deeply rooted obstacle to the analysis of the causes of women's oppression and exploitation. Although women who struggle for their emancipation have rejected biological determinism, they find it very difficult to establish that the unequal, hierarchical, and exploitative relationship between men and women is caused by social—that is, historical—factors. One of the main problems is the fact that not only the analysis as such but also the tools of the analysis, the basic definitions and concepts, are affected (or, rather, infected) by biological determinism.

This is largely true for the basic concepts that are central to our analysis, such as the concepts of nature, of labor, of productive labor, of the sexual division of labor, and of the family. If these concepts are used without a critique of their implicit biases—and that means ideological biases—they tend to obscure rather than to clarify the issues. This is true above all for the concept of nature.

Too often this concept has been used to explain social inequalities or exploitative relations as inborn, and hence beyond the scope of social change. Women in particular should be suspicious when this term is used to explain their status in society. Their share in the production and reproduction of life is usually being defined as a function of their biology or "nature." Thus, women's household and child-care work are seen as an extension of their physiology; they give birth to children because "nature" has provided them with a uterus. All the labor that goes into the production of life, including the labor of giving birth to a child, is not seen as the conscious interaction of a human being with nature—that is, a truly human activity—but, rather, as an activity of nature, which produces plants and animals unconsciously, and which has no control over this process.

This definition of women's interaction with nature—including their own nature—as an act of nature has had, and still has, far-reaching consequences. The definition of women in terms of nature has affected other concepts in their relation to women—for instance, the concept of labor. Because of the biologistic definition of women's interaction with nature, her work both in giving birth and in raising children, as well as the rest of domestic work, does not appear as work or labor. Today the concept of labor is usually reserved for activity that produces surplus value, a definition that tends to exclude a large proportion of women's activities. (For an elaboration of this point, see Chapter 5 in this volume.)

The same hidden asymmetry and biologistic bias that we can observe with regard to the concept of labor also prevails with regard to the concept of sexual division of labor. Although this concept seems to suggest that men and women simply perform different tasks, it hides the fact that men's tasks are usually considered as truly human ones (that is, conscious, rational, planned, productive), whereas women's tasks are seen as basically determined by her nature. The sexual division of labor, according to this definition, could be paraphrased as one between "human" and "natural" labor. Furthermore, this concept also obscures the fact that the relationship between male ("human") and female ("natural") laborers or workers is a relationship of dominance and even of exploitation.[1] When we try to analyze the dynamics of this division of labor, we have to make clear that we mean this asymmetric, hierarchical, and exploitative relationship, and not a simple division of tasks between equal partners.

The same obfuscating logic prevails with regard to the concept of family. This concept is used and universalized in a rather Eurocentric way—presenting the nuclear family as the basic and timeless structure of all institutionalization of men-women relations—and hides the fact that the structure of this institution can be a hierarchical, inegalitarian one. Phrases like "partnership within the family" may serve to veil the true nature of this institution.

This brief discussion of the androcentric and biologistic biases inherent in some of the important concepts has made clear that it is necessary to systematically expose the ideological function of these biases, which is to obscure the asymmetric and exploitative social relations.

This means that with regard to the problem before us—the analysis of the dynamics of sexual division of labor—we are not asking "When did a division of labor arise between men and women, and how is it changed?" (such a division is the necessary consequence of all human interaction with nature); our question is, rather, "Why did this division of labor become a relationship of dominance and exploitation, why did it become an asymmetric, hierarchical relationship?" This question still looms large over all discussions on women's liberation.

Suggested Approach

What can we do to eliminate the biases in the above-mentioned concepts? Not use them at all, as some women suggest? But then we would be without a language to express our ideas. Or invent new ones? This is what others feel is better. But concepts summarize historical practice and theory, and cannot voluntaristically be invented. We have to accept that the basic concepts we use in our analysis have already been "occupied"—like territories or colonies—by dominant sexist ideology. Although we cannot abandon them, we can look at them "from below" (Mies 1978), not from the point of view of the dominant ideology but from the point of view of the historical experiences of the oppressed, exploited, and subordinated, and their struggle for emancipation.

It is thus necessary, regarding the concept of productivity of labor, to reject its narrow definition and to show that labor can be productive only in the sense of producing surplus value as long as it can tap, extract, exploit, and appropriate labor that is spent in the production of life, or subsistence production, which is nonwage labor done mainly by women. Since this production of life is the perennial precondition of all other historical forms of productive labor, including that under conditions of capital accumulation, it has to be defined as work and not as unconscious, "natural" activity. This is because human beings do not just live; they produce their life.

In what follows, I will call the labor that goes into the production of life "productive labor." The separation from and the superimposition of surplus-producing labor over life-producing labor is an abstraction that leads to the fact that women and their work are being "defined into nature."

The search for the origins and the dynamics of the hierarchical sexual division of labor should not be limited to the search for the moment in history or prehistory when the "world-historic defeat of the female sex" (in the words of Engels) took place. Although studies in primatology, prehistory, archaeology, and anthropology are useful and necessary for our subject, we cannot expect them to give an answer to this problem, which is basically a conceptual one. This means that the juxtaposition between man and Nature—that is, man's (productive) and woman's (nonproductive) labor, referred to above, has to be understood as a result of thinking that systematically ignores the concrete, material base of its own existence, and thus becomes a mystification.[2] In addition, we should not search for a single factor or a prime mover in history that is responsible for the downfall of women. Rather, we should try to develop a materialist and historical concept of women and men and their relations. This would enable us to understand the real historical forces that led to the subordination of women. Women who are serious about their emancipation cannot afford to confine themselves to an idealistic and contemplative attitude toward their own oppression. It would amount to mere cynicism if they analyzed their situation without wanting to change it. If we use this approach, we need not speculate about the sequence of the various stages of human development in a history that is difficult to reconstruct.

We can learn much about the actual establishment of sex hierarchies if we look at "history in the making"—that is, if we study what is happening to woman bearing the impact of development processes in the West and in Africa, Asia, and Latin America, where poor peasant and tribal societies are being "integrated" into a so-called new national and international division of labor under the dictates of capital accumulation. In both spheres a distinct sexist policy was and is used to subsume whole societies and classes under the dominant production relations. Developmental strategies devised for women usually appear in the guise of "progressive" or "liberal" family laws. By the very fact that such laws are made, the family as an institution is separated as a "private" sphere from the "public" sphere of "social production." And the ideological biases referred to above are being reproduced. It will be seen later in this chapter that these ideological biases assume the character of an almost material force regarding women. This also means we should no longer look at the sexual division of labor only as a problem related to the family but, rather, as a structural problem of a whole society.

INTEGRATION INTO THE WORLD MARKET AND CHANGES IN THE SEXUAL DIVISION OF LABOR

The Lacemakers of Narsapur*

As was made clear in the introduction, the question of the social origins and the dynamics of the sexual division of labor is not only a question of fixing a date in history or of trying to establish a chronology of stages in the development of this division, but also a question of developing a new concept of women and their history. This history is still going on.

Although very little research on the actual processes of change of the sexual division of labor has as yet been done, I think we can formulate a few hypotheses:

1. Changes in the sexual division of labor are related to changes in the social division of labor within a system—that is, changes in production relations and class relations.

2. The change processes affecting women and men in many parts of the world bearing the impact of the expansion of a world market system continue to be based on an asymmetric division of labor between the sexes.

3. The maintenance of this asymmetric division of labor and women's ongoing responsibility for the production of life or subsistence production forms the base upon which production of surplus value and mainly male productive labor can be built. In this process the sexual division of labor is changed.

4. These changes, however, do not mean that old forms of the asymmetric sexual division of labor are abolished and replaced by egalitarian ones. They are only redefined according to the

---

*This case study is part of a study, carried out under the sponsorship of the ILO, on women in the subsistence sector in India in 1978-79: Maria Mies, "Housewives Produce for the World Market—The Lace Makers of Narsapur," ILO, Geneva, 1980.

requirements of the new production system. Female (subsistence) productivity still constitutes the base of male (surplus-producing) productivity.

5. Production for the market, particularly for the world market, leads not only to pauperization of small peasants and petty commodity producers, but also to class polarizations among them.

6. Because of the preservation of the basic structure of the asymmetric division of labor between the sexes in the ongoing processes, these changes do not lead to greater equality between women and men of the pauperized classes, but, rather, to a polarization between them. The social definition of women as housewives plays a vital role in this polarization.

If we look at the processes that are going on both in the industrial centers and at the peripheries, we can find enough evidence of these changes. In the following I shall give a brief account of such changes as they occurred in a house industry, the lace industry, around Narsapur in the West Godavari District, Andhra Pradesh, India. The fieldwork was carried out in 1978-79 in the town of Narsapur and in the village of Serepalem. The lacemakers of Narsapur are mainly poor Christians and women of the Agnikulakshatriyas, originally a fishermen's caste that has now turned to other work. The lacemaking women of Serepalem belong to the Kapus, a caste of agriculturalists. All of them are poor, and the majority are illiterate.

This case is mentioned here because it shows the classic way in which capitalist production relations are being built upon the backs of women as workers and housewives. One of the methods by which capitalism is trying to solve its global crisis is the introduction of production diversification and of forms of production organization that are believed to belong to the stage of early capitalism, in which women and children work under inhuman conditions in household industries (Marx 1974, chs. 8, 22).

In the villages around Narsapur, 150,000-200,000 women are engaged in the production of handmade lace. This lace industry— or, rather, the technique of crocheting—was brought by missionaries around 1860. Some informants say that lacemaking was introduced by the wife of a Scottish missionary who wanted to help converts, mostly untouchables (or Adi Andhras),[3] during a time of famine. According to another report, lacemaking was taught to the early female Christian converts because their families were socially boycotted after conversion and their men did not get work as agricultural laborers or shoemakers. The missionaries gave the women thread, taught them the technique of crocheting, and sent the finished lace goods--such as table mats and doilies—to their friends and relatives in England and Scotland, who would sell them. The money thus received was sent to Narsapur, where part of it was kept to buy more thread and the rest was paid to the lace workers.

Thus, the beginning of this industry seems to have been purely a women's affair. A woman was the initiator, the producers were poor women, and the marketing was done by women in Scotland and England, who did this voluntary charitable work to support the missionaries. None of the women involved were working for profit or living on the labor of the primary producers. In 1900, however, the situation changed. Two brothers, Jonah and Josef, who belonged to the same community of converted Adi Andhras and had been teachers in the school of the Brethren Mission, started to export lace goods as a regular business. At the same time they organized the production of lace along the lines of the putting-out system and with an extensive division of labor. Whereas formerly women had made a whole tablecloth or a whole doily or a whole lace collar, now the work process was split into a number of components: some women would make one type of "flower"; others, another pattern; others, lace ribbons. All these parts would be collected by agents—usually women—who had the confidence of the exporter. They would bring the parts to other women, who would join them into finished articles. These agents would also give the thread to the lacemakers and pay them the wages on a piecework basis when they collected the finished goods. The joining of component lace parts or attachment work was usually done in the house of the exporter, and supervised by him or his wife. In the course of time other firms were set up to export lace. There are now more than 60 lace exporters (or "manufacturers," as they call themselves) in Narsapur.

Around 1970 the lace industry and lace exports experienced a rapid expansion. This expansion was partly due to the new demand in European and American markets for cheap handicrafts and handmade or handwoven goods from Asia, Africa, and Latin America, but it was also partly a result of the development of capitalist farming in the rich district of West Godavari. But first let us look at the growth of the lace exports between 1970 and 1978.

Up to 1970 the amount of lace exported and the number of exporters had been fairly constant; after 1970 exports rose steeply and the industry experienced a virtual mushrooming of exporters, traders, and middlemen, a process accompanied by strong monopolistic tendencies on the part of the biggest exporters. Although it was difficult to get exact figures for the total volume of exports, and even more so for profits, Table 1.1 gives an indication of the rapid growth of this industry.

TABLE 1.1

Exports and Internal Sales of Lace Negotiated Through State Bank of India: 1970–78

(thousands of rupees)

Month	1970	1971	1972	1973	1974	1975	1976	1977	1978
January	21	29	33	33	59	88	112	153	99
February	25	13	38	102	121	98	112	375	259
March	8	14	88	99	89	94	153	651	223
April	53	102	70	104	87	167	42	255	384
May	30	58	59	120	137	154	99	352	226
June	10	31	86	61	166	132	125	229	62
July	41	60	48	162	52	194	164	298	116
August	54	76	86	152	112	187	156	108	275
September	45	104	96	157	125	150	130	448	137
October	37	145	72	144	140	235	167	314	357
November	42	61	100	91	120	183	97	251	288
December	37	65	80	136	140	165	110	295	235
Total	403	758	856	1,361	1,348	1,847	1,467	3,729	2,661
Internal Business	15	25	33	48	42	56	132	223	267

Note: The relative unit value of manufactured export index decreased from 100 in 1970 to 86.7 in 1977 (Verghese 1979, Table 1). When one compares this with the increase in the value of exports of lace negotiated through the State Bank of India, we see that the volume of exports of lace greatly increased over the period 1970–77.

Source: State Bank of India, Narsapur, D/o 2-1979.

These figures cover only the exports recorded by the State
Bank of India at Narsapur. Many exporters negotiated their bills
through banks in Madras, Kakinada, and other cities. Even the
State Department of Industries at Hyderabad had only estimates of
the total volume of exports of lace from Narsapur.

In 1970, 1–1.5 million rupees' worth of lace goods were exported from Narsapur to Australia, the Federal Republic of Germany, Italy, Denmark, Sweden, the United Kingdom, the United
States, Ireland, and the Netherlands. In 1976–77, the exports had
risen to 5 million rupees, and in 1977–78 they totaled approximately 8 million rupees. Lace worth 1–2 million rupees was sold in the
major Indian cities, mainly to tourists. According to an official
statement, 95 percent of the foreign exchange earnings from the export of handicrafts from the state of Andhra Pradesh came from the
lace industry of Narsapur.

If one looks at the turnover of one of the big exporters, the
above figures appear to be somewhat underestimated. According
to the Directorate of Industries of Andhra Pradesh, the son of one
of the main exporters, who is also a thread stockist (wholesale
agent), stated:

> After I came here, I developed the Indian market
> also. . . . My father's turnover was Rs 300,000–
> 400,000 in thread business, now it is 4 million. In
> lace business it was also Rs 300,000–400,000, now
> it is 4 to 5 million.

The father of this young man had been a middle-level peasant
who owned six acres of land. He started as a middleman in the lace
business, then invested some money, got addresses of lace importers, and in the course of ten years rose to a monopoly position as
thread stockist. He exports lace to big department stores in the
Federal Republic of Germany, the United Kingdom, and other
Western countries.

Since lace export proved to be a profitable business, the
caste and class composition of both exporters and lace workers
changed. Whereas the early lacemakers and exporters came from
the community of Harijan Christians, the majority of the lacemakers
are now Kapus, a caste of agriculturists.

Most of the exporters also are Kapus. Some of them were
middle-level or rich peasants who had made substantial profits during the Green Revolution (West Godavari is one of the main areas of
the Green Revolution in India) in the 1960s and early 1970s. But
now, because of the stagnation of the Indian economy, the relative
overproduction of rice, and the lack of markets resulting from the

low purchasing power of the Indian masses, the large farmers no longer know where to invest their surplus profitably. Therefore, many of them have begun to invest in business. The lace industry, with its export orientation and the very limited need for fixed capital, together with the extremely low wages, offered a very lucrative area for investment. Anyone who had or could obtain 5,000-10,000 rupees to invest—many of these new exporters got loans from the banks—and had access to some of the most popular patterns could become a lace manufacturer. All he needed was the address of an importer overseas. The consequence of the Kapu farmer class entering this industry was that the Kapu women were favored as lacemakers. The latter were mostly from the poorer strata of the Kapus, landless or poor peasants. The Christian women were gradually pushed to the periphery of the production process.

It goes without saying that all the exporters are male. But with the rise of the Kapus and a few other communities in the lace business, the agents, most of whom had been female, also became predominantly male. Asked why they now mostly employed male agents, the exporters answered that the men were more mobile. They could go to the villages on bicycles, visit the women producers, give them thread, and collect the finished goods in a much shorter time than had been needed by the female agents, who had to walk from village to village or go by bus. Moreover, the biggest of the new firms also employ men exclusively for the finishing of the lace goods in their houses. This work is still done only by women in the old firm of Jonah and Josef.

The expansion of the lace industry and its integration into a world market system lead not only to class differentiation within particular communities (Christians, Kapus) but also to the masculinization of all nonproduction jobs, especially of trade, and the total feminization of the production process. The dividing line between men and women is the integration of their products into the market. Men sell women's products and live on the profits from women's work.

This process of the men taking control even of such a delicate women's production as lacemaking (taking control means appropriating the products) is closely connected with the process of general expansion of this industry.

The lacemaking industry is a classical case of the putting-out system. The crocheting is done entirely by girls and women of all ages. The mothers teach their daughters around the age of five to six years how to make simple patterns, and then they continue until they are old or their eyes are ruined, because they continue to make lace in the evening, by the light of a dim oil lamp. Many women complain of bad eyesight, headaches, and muscle pains. I met an

80-year-old widow who was still working late at night in a small, dimly lit hut. She said with some pride that she could still earn her livelihood with the work of her own hands and was not dependent on her sons, who were too poor to support her.

The women get the patterns and the thread from middlemen or agents, who also collect the finished lace goods and pay the women their wages. In some cases half the amount of the wages is advanced by the exporter and the other half has to be invested by the agent. The agents, therefore, need some money of their own, and try to get the better of both the exporters and the women. The women are paid piecework rates. For lace made of 2,000 meters of thread, they get Rs. 4 (there are approximately 8 rupees to the U.S. dollar). A woman usually needs a week to use up 2,000 meters. This means she earns Rs. 4 per week, and her daily earnings average Rs. 0.56. (Women work on Sundays and holidays.) This amounts to less than one-third of the official minimum wage for female agricultural laborers.

The manufacturers and local officials argue that these women are "sitting in the house" and are not used to working in the fields, and that crocheting is just a way for them to pass their leisure time. We found, however, that the women were engaged in lacemaking for six to eight hours per day. Whenever they found time before or after their housework, they began crocheting. Thus, they had practically no time for themselves.

It was obvious that the extreme exploitation of these women—about which they all complained—was made possible only by the organization of the production process—the individualized form of the household industry—and, more important, the maintenance and propagation of the housewife ideology, the "woman sitting in the house." The male exporters, as well as the women themselves, saw the lacemakers mainly as housewives and not as workers. Although many of the women were the actual breadwinners of their families because the men had lost their land (due to indebtedness or because they were jobless), the men did not change their ideas; they said that the women of their community did only housework, and had always been confined to the house.

It is not clear whether this statement is a reflection of historical reality or a rationalization of present practices. The Kapus are agriculturists like the Khammas and the Reddis, the economically and politically dominant peasant castes of Andhra Pradesh. In the whole of Andhra Pradesh, women of poorer levels of these castes have worked in the fields. To clarify this point I tried to find out from anthropological records when the Kapus, or a level of them, had begun to keep their women under purdah[4] or seclusion and excluded them from agricultural work. A level of the Kapus had

claimed and obtained the status of warriors (Kshatriyas), and had
held a monopoly over arms in the service of the kings in that area.
The warrior castes in various parts of India kept their women under
purdah and seclusion, particularly the princely families of these
castes. Thus, it seems possible that the seclusion of the Kapu
women has been a result of an earlier process of class differentiation among the Kapu agriculturists.

According to Thurston (1915), the Kapus are from the same
stock as the Reddis, the main caste of agriculturists in Telengana.
Their origin dates back to the beginning of the Christian era, and
they used to be the largest caste in the Madras Presidency. The
Reddis (Irattu, Iretti, Radda, Rathos, Rathaur, Rashtra-Kuta,
Ratta) date their origin back to the Ratti tribe that ruled the Kongu
Kingdom from the beginning of the Christian era to the ninth century. (Reddi means "king," and Kapu means "waterman," according to H. A. Stuart, writing in the Madras Census Report of 1891.)

The Kapus split into many subdivisions, some of which keep
their women gosha (secluded). Since some of these Kapu subdivisions trace their origin back to Ayodhya, the capital of the mytho-
logical Kshatriya king Rama, it is possible that the practice of keeping their women gosha is to be understood as a means of demon-
strating their higher status as Kshatriyas (warriors). The Kshatriyas in the north, particularly the Rajputs of Rajasthan, had this
custom of secluding women long before the Muslim rule in India.
The exclusion of women from field and other manual work is, of
course, linked to the conquest and subordination of other tribes and
communities, who then could do this work. A story reported by
Thurston reflects this connection between seclusion of Kapu women
and the subjection of other castes to their service:

> In the Kapu community, women play an important part,
> except in matters connected with agriculture. This is
> accounted for by a story to the effect that, when they
> came from Ayodhya, the Kapus brought no women with
> them [that is, they were warriors], and they sought the
> assistance of the gods in providing them with wives.
> They were told to marry women who were the illegiti-
> mate issue of Pandavas [the five Pandava brothers of
> the Mahabharata], and the women consented on the
> understanding that they were to be given the upper
> hand, and that menial service, such as husking paddy
> (rice), cleaning vessels, and carrying water, should
> be done for them. They accordingly employ Gollas
> and Gamallas as domestic servants. Malas and
> Madigas (untouchables) freely enter Kapu houses for

the purpose of husking paddy, but are not allowed into
the kitchen, or room in which household gods are
worshipped (Thurston 1915, p. 245).

This story may be one of the legends of the origin of the higher status of the Ayodhya Kapus. But it also shows how class differentiation by means of conquest is accompanied by domestication
of some of the women of the conquered peoples, who then also rise
above their original status. The illegitimate daughters of the
Pandavas surely are the daughters of the soil, of tribes that were
subjected.

The warrior castes are the ones who appropriated new lands
for the kings. In order to keep their own stock "pure" and to protect their own women or the women they had appropriated from re-
taliatory attacks by subjected peoples, they put them under purdah.
Moreover, since their pay was a share in the booty, there was less
necessity for their domesticated women to work in the fields or to
do other menial work. Thus, purdah and seclusion of women became a sign of a higher caste and class status (Mies 1973; 1980).

In a stratified class system the dominant strata are always
the ones who define the dominant values. It is probable that even
the poor women of the Kapus had to follow the caste rules of purdah
and seclusion. The tenacity with which women cling to these oppressive norms, because they are symbols of a bygone higher status,
even when they are virtually starving is the ideological and psycho-
logical base on which a new phase of exploitation can be built, this
time in the service of surplus accumulation on a world scale.

The maintenance of the ideology of seclusion is very important
for the extraction of surplus value by the exporters (and their anonymous international counterparts, the lace importers), since lacemaking is tied to the concept of the "woman sitting in the house."
Although domestication of women may be justified by the older forms
of seclusion, it has definitely changed its character. The Kapu
women are no longer gosha—women of a feudal warrior caste—but
domesticated housewives and workers who produce for the world
market. In the case of the lacemakers, this ideology has become
almost a material force. The whole system is built on the ideology
that these women cannot work outside the house. When we tried to
explain to them that female agricultural laborers were earning much
more than they did, they replied that these were Harijan (untouchable) women. They could not do their work.

This specific work organization and the accompanying housewife ideology prevents the lacemakers from organizing. The sexual
division of labor between "man the breadwinner," the poor peasant
or agricultural laborer, and the "woman sitting in the house," even

where it is only fictitious, provides the basic structure for the
various forms of horizontal and vertical divisions among the lace-
workers, and thus for their exploitation by the male agents, the
male exporters, and the importers in Europe, Australia, and
America.

What is so striking about this industry is the fact that the primary producers have become virtually invisible. Only when one
enters their houses in the villages around Narsapur does one find
them with their children and neighbors. Even in Narsapur many
people did not know about the existence of these lacemaking women,
but they knew the big bungalows of the "manufacturers," the Association of the Lace Manufacturers of Narsapur, and the government's quality marking officer, who is related to an exporter. Thus,
it is not surprising that about 150,000-200,000 women working in
what is called a household industry were nowhere to be found in the
census statistics of the district. For the census operators only the
male head of the household counts. Although the definition of a
household industry used in the census of 1971 would allow for the
registration of lacemaking as a household industry and the lacemakers as workers, this obviously had not happened. According to
the Handbook of Statistics West Godavari District (1977, p. 28),
only 6,449 workers, male and female, were recorded in the whole
Narsapur taluk (a subdivision of a district) as engaged in manufacturing, including household industry. Thus, officially, these women
do not exist as workers. No wonder, therefore, that the nonproducing "manufacturers" appear to be the initiators and active agents
of the lace industry. Their capital accumulation seems to be a
miraculous process, since they do not have to invest in factories
or equipment. The actual producers, however, have been reduced
almost to an anonymous mass of atomized natural forces that can
be tapped whenever the "manufacturers" get orders, then left to
fend for themselves in their "natural" setting when orders decline.

Change in the Division of Labor Between the Sexes

We saw that the domestication and seclusion of women formed
part of a process of class and caste differentiation, and that the lace
merchants used and reinforced this feudal domestication of women.
From the social definition of women as housewives follows the definition of the men as the breadwinners; the separation between the
private sphere of the house and the public sphere, the spheres of
reproduction and production, respectively; and the subordination of
the former under the latter. These separations and definitions are
typical for industrial societies. One may wonder what function they

have in a rural society where the subsistence of the people is not fully covered by their wage income.

The political-economic function of the separation of the sphere of production from the sphere of reproduction and the definition of women as housewives seems to be to create a readily available and readily disposable labor force whose day-to-day reproduction and unemployment are not the responsibility of either the capitalist farmer or the merchant. In contrast with feudal relations, where the laborers are not only tied to the soil but also taken care of by the feudal lord, in this case the laborers are "free" from such care. But they are not "freed" to such an extent that they can become wage laborers in the full sense of the word, able to move to the cities and to get industrial jobs, in which case their wage would have to cover all their reproduction costs. Rather, the agricultural laborers, small artisans, and subsistence peasants are only semi-proletarianized, and similarly the women who make lace are only semidomesticated. This means that in their social appearance they are housewives, but in reality they are wage laborers, fully integrated into a system oriented to the world market.

It is important to understand that this semi-proletarianization of the men and the semidomestication (or "housewifization") of women is not a transitional mode that will evolve into full-fledged proletarianization and "housewifization"; the present system only makes possible the rapid accumulation of capital by both rich peasants and merchants. Therefore, the social definition of women as housewives serves mainly to obscure the true production relations and to consolidate their exploitation, both ideologically and politically.

This function of the social definition of the lacemakers as housewives becomes evident if one looks at the women of other castes and classes in this area. We saw that no Harijan (untouchable) women were involved in lacemaking. Harijan women are mainly agricultural laborers who perform most of the labor-intensive tasks in rice cultivation. They are not domesticated or defined as housewives; rather, they are workers both in their own perception and in the perception of the other castes. Although their wages are lower than those of the male agricultural workers, they earn considerably more in the course of a year than the lace workers. This fact and the fact that they work collectively in the fields have given them more boldness and self-confidence. They talked with contempt about the women who sit all day in the house and make lace for a few paisa. The Kapu women complained that the Harijan women no longer showed respect and fear toward them.

But although the Kapu lacemakers knew that they would earn more as agricultural laborers, they all said that they could not work in the fields. "We Kapu women cannot work in the fields, only Harijan women do this work" and "We have no other skill, we can only make lace" were typical comments. However, it was not so much the lack of skill that prevented the Kapu women from working in the fields, but the fear of being declassed, of losing their social identity in a higher and more respectable caste. Although most of them belonged to agricultural laborer families or were poor peasants who had lost their land, the women were not prepared to work or move outside the house, to give up their status as respected gosha women. This shows that caste divisions are defined along the lines of domestication and nondomestication of women. Although the lacemakers and the agricultural laborer women de facto belong to the same class of pauperized peasants and agricultural laborers, they are separated because members of one category conceive of themselves as housewives, and the other as workers.

To understand this mechanism of separation, it is necessary to see that in India a rise in class status has always been accompanied by contempt for and rejection of manual labor and by domestication of women. Upper castes and classes usually do not allow their women to do manual work outside the home.[5] It is obvious that this separation of women who de facto belong to the same class, and the social value attributed to the domestication of women are mechanisms by which the exploitation of these women can be perpetuated. The main beneficiaries of this separation are the upperclass men, in this case the exporters and traders.

Sexual Division of Labor Within the Family

When production for the world market was introduced in this area, older forms of the sexual division of labor were not abolished but, rather, were used, reinforced, and reinterpreted. Thus, the female labor force was divided along the lines of (despised) agricultural workers and (respected) housewives. Similarly, the overall hierarchical division of labor along sex-specific lines, dating from earlier stages in the history of these communities, was preserved in a transformed way. To understand the nature of this division and its transformation, it is necessary to look at the relationship between women and men within the family, partly because the basic division of labor between productive and reproductive work, which came about under the impact of capitalist production relations, made the family the main arena of women's work. But this work is not autonomous work. If social division of labor means that some men control the means of production, and thus the labor of other men and women, then sexual division of labor means that men in general control the means of reproduction—that is, their women and their productive and reproductive work. Domestication or "housewifization" is the main mechanism by which this control is achieved. (For an analysis of how men were able to gain this control over women's productive and reproductive work, see Mies 1979.) We have now to ask how this division of labor is organized or, more concretely, what are men's jobs, what are women's jobs, and how is this division of labor affected by production for the world market?

The basic division is, of course, between women, who do housework, and men, who work outside the home. The men do not do any work in the house. This was confirmed by all women. All the services in the household—such as cooking food, fetching water, washing clothes—were performed only by women. But many of these reproductive tasks involved a series of production processes. Thus, cooking means not only the preparation of food but also such tasks as the collection of firewood, the processing of certain foods, the making of a stove, and the gathering of cow dung for fuel. While analyzing a woman's working day, we saw that reproductive and productive tasks were closely interwoven, and that the women performed a great variety of different activities during the day.

The arena of women's activity was the house and the courtyard. The men returned to this arena only for eating and sleeping. Except for the old men, the men usually were not seen around the house during the day. But when they returned, they had immediately to be attended to by the women. The women had to prepare the bath water for them. They even had to wash their husbands' backs, which some of the women found outrageous. They had to give food to them before the children or they themselves could eat, and they had to sit next to them and serve them the food on their plate. Many of the women complained that their husbands did not allow them to visit other women. All services of the domesticated woman to her husband were legitimized by the definition that he is the head of the household and the main breadwinner. The women provided this service even when this role was purely fictitious—that is, when the women were the de facto breadwinners of the family, and the men depended on their women's lacemaking to support the family.

The sexual division of labor within the household and sex segregation appeared to be sharper in the Kapu families in Serepalem, where patriarchy and caste played a more important role than among Christians and Agnikulakshatriyas. Since the Kapu women still defined their superior social status by the fact that they could do only housework—in contrast with Christian or Agnikulakshatriya women, who were more mobile in this respect—they still took it for granted that they had to serve and obey the man. They laughed when we asked them why they did not teach their boys lacemaking. "It does not look nice when a boy makes lace," they replied.

Pauperization and Changes in the Social and Sexual Division of Labor

It was not the division of labor between men and women as such or the fact that the women worked longer hours than the men that aroused the women's criticism. It was the experience that more and more men were no longer properly fulfilling their task as breadwinners. In particular the poor peasant women in Serepalem complained about the men's laziness. Here are a few examples of how they saw this situation:

> The men in this village are lazy. They don't even have the patience to build bathrooms with partitions for women. How can you expect them to make kitchen gardens.

> Sometime back we could not get loans in this village. So we went to Vijayawada. I told my husband to work in the betel-leaf gardens. I am more intelligent than he is. This village is no good. The men are not clever enough to live in this world. They do not know how to do other work. So they had to come back with their boxes on their heads. We then went to my mother's house. There he was driving the bullock cart. But we did not have enough money to buy grass for the bullocks. He was ashamed to say in his village that he was living in his mother-in-law's house.[6] He went to his village without telling anyone. Then I learned lacemaking and took him back to my mother's house to clear our debts. That time I pawned my mangalasutram [marriage chain] and earrings. Now Rs. 25 still have to be paid. He also does not want to take land on lease. Therefore I took Rs. 200 on loan and started the lace business. Then he fell ill. He got malaria, so I took a loan of Rs. 1,400 from the chitfund [a kind of village-based lottery] at a loss of Rs. 700. My son is now working as a coolie. Our house fell down, so I made a small hut where we are living. . . .

This case explains why some of the men in Serepalem are considered by their women to be "useless." They were small farmers or agricultural laborers who lost their land or had no work. But it is against their pride to go out and look for other work. They say they cannot work except on the land. Those who had land before do not like to do coolie work, and would rather roam about the village.

The women, however, have to find ways and means to keep the household going. If there is no income from the men, they start making lace. In spite of the rigidity with which they stick to the ideology of the respected housewife, in reality they seem to be more flexible than the men in changing the old pattern of the division of labor if necessity arises.

This flexibility is, of course, more a result of pauperization than a real change in cultural values. Of the 150 families we studied at Serepalem, 110 were in debt. We found that quite a number of Kapu women have become lace agents or subagents. This means that in practice they have to violate the professed gosha norms of their caste, and go out of their house, even to other villages. At the weekly market we even met a poor old Kapu woman who was trying to sell her lace in the open marketplace. This confirms what has been observed about the contradiction between theory and practice in the case of middle-class Indian women: they may deviate widely from the accepted norms in practice, but they never attack these norms directly (Mies 1973; 1980).

Pauperization leads not only to parasitism in the case of men who then try to live off their women's subsistence work (Mies 1980), but also to class polarization and changes in the men's class positions. Another mechanism by which pauperized peasants tried to solve the problem of their survival was by entering the sphere of petty trade (in lacemaking they typically became lace agents or petty traders). The fact that their material interests were inseparably linked to the women's social definition as housewives shows that it is not merely "backward" ideology that keeps women domesticated but, rather, material forces. The following example can serve to illustrate this linkage between a change in the class position of a man and the "housewifization" of his wife.

Whereas pauperized men try to do "business," they keep their wives at home to produce lace. A small thread hawker told the following story:

> I am 56 years old. I was a cultivator before. We had four acres of land. I have six children. My family went into debt and I lost my land. Then I started this thread business. I had losses in agriculture and could not repay the debts. So I lost all my property. Now I do this and get some money. If we don't have any income, what can we do? I started this business one year ago. . . . Now we have neither debts nor property. We had debts before selling the land. . . . I sold my land to a Kapu. Some Kapus have a lot of land. There are plenty of people like me who sold

their land. Some have started a lace business and
some have gone to other villages. The women in our
village make lace. My wife also makes lace. Women
cannot go out of the house.

He had rented a bicycle, and said he could earn Rs. 10 per week.
His family depended totally on his business and his wife's lace work.
Although this man was not a Kapu, he subscribed to the "housewife"
ideology of women because it provided the base for his new business.

This example shows the close connection between processes
of pauperization of peasants, intensification of class differences,
and polarization between men and women. Pauperized men tend to
become traders (nonproducers), whereas their women have to continue subsistence work (housework and other productive work).
Men are able to rise to the class of traders on the base of the ongoing subsistence production of their women.

The Christian women who were most affected by pauperization have less difficulty in moving out of the house and searching
for other jobs if the need arises. They have even gone to work as
agricultural laborers in the rice transplantation and harvesting
season. Also, several of the Agnikulakshatriya women have gone
back to their old occupation of selling fish. Poor Christian women
are engaged in making bricks or working as servants. This confirms that the ideology of domestication of women, preached by the
missionaries and conveniently used by the lace merchants, is dis-
carded in practice if economic necessity forces women to work outside the house to secure the family's subsistence.

These women were also more critical than the Kapu women of
the sexual division of labor within the household. The Agnikulakshatriya women complained that the men did not do any work in the
house:

Our men do not do any work at home. When we are
menstruating the men refuse even to take water from
the well. They will not even serve themselves the
food, but another woman has to come and serve them.
No man helps a woman. Even when the wife is busy
making lace, when her husband comes home, she has
to get up quickly and make tea for him. It is not correct on the part of the men. . . . Even if the girl has
gone to school and studied up to the tenth grade or done
B.Sc., she has to do the same work in the house: cooking for the husband and making lace. Here in our area
there are few girls who work outside the house. With
lacemaking alone we could not run the household, but

it is a great help. We don't give the lace money to our husbands, we spend it all on the consumption of the family. . . . Our men make nets. They do not have much work. They don't like to do any other work, and during their free time they roam around.

The Introduction of "Capitalist" Relations
Between Men and Women

Some of the Agnikulakshatriya women at Narsapur were doing independent lace business for the exporters. They did attachment work, collected the "flowers" from the surrounding villages, and made bedspreads and similar items at a profit of Rs. 10 per piece. One of them expressed their bitterness about the fact that their men did not recognize their work as work:

Our men feel that we just sit in the house and eat, doing nothing. They think that we are investing their money and then show Rs. 10 as our earnings. As if we had won it by playing cards. We say that we are also working along with them. . . . Even pregnant women and women in their postnatal period and old women do this work. One woman of 100 years, Kappanathi Mangamma, used to make lace. . . . We get up early in the morning, go to the villages and come back in the afternoon. If I have to go to far-off places, then it takes two or three days. For 10 gross [of thread] it takes three days. I'll have to go four or five times. If the merchant says it is very urgent, then we have to go for at least six times. It would be better to go for transplantation and harvesting. . . .

This statement shows that the lacemakers' work, and the time spent on it, is "invisible" not only to the exporters or the outside world, but also to the husbands under whose noses this work takes place. Even they define it as nonwork. The money earned by the women appears as something miraculous or natural. In any case, men refuse to do this "nonwork." As one middleman put it: "Women are normally free, so they do this work, and even if they get Rs. 10, it does not make much of a difference. If men also have to start and live on that, then you do not have to look for any future."

What is even more interesting in the above statement is the clue it gives to the relationship between men and women. The men seem to imitate the role of the exporters or businessmen vis-à-vis

their women. They feel that they are investing their money in the
working women, and they also want to get control over their income. But this the women generally do not allow, because they
spend all their earnings on family consumption. They even feed
their men during the time when they have no work, and unemployment is very high among the Agnikulakshatriya men in Narsapur.

This "capitalist" relationship between men and women was
even more pronounced in the case of the Christian women whose
husbands were lace hawkers in the big Indian cities. Here the men
de facto invest the money in the work of their women and sell their
products at a profit. Sometimes the first investment is taken as a
loan, and sometimes the men start this business after their retire-
ment from some other job.

The latter was true in the case of Mariamma, whose husband
had been in the army. Now he is retired, and with his small pen-
sion he started a lace business. She stays in their house in Narsapur, makes lace, and sends it to him in Calcutta, where he tries to
sell it. She says: "I am dependent on his business; if he does not
sell anything or if he does not send money, I have nothing." She
does not see that he is de facto dependent on her work. She has
already internalized the mystification that he who controls the marketing of the product and the capital "gives" work to the actual producers. She has no control over the profit he makes or over the
share he sends back to her.

In the last analysis it makes no difference to this relationship
whether it is Mariamma's husband or a trader or exporter who controls the marketing and the profits. The difference between these
men is only a quantitative one, as between small and big merchants
who try to squeeze each other out of business. In this process the
small Christian hawkers are being rapidly pushed out by the large
merchants, as was seen earlier. Since the reproduction relations
in these families are identical with the social production relations—
those between merchant capitalist and housewife producers—the
breaking down of the latter (the men giving up the lace business)
also means breaking up the former (the reproduction relations).
For example, many of the Christian men had left their families and
gone to Kuwait. Previously most of them were hawkers. Many of
their wives were now absolutely destitute and virtually beggars.
They said:

Before the men went to Kuwait, we used to have work.
Our condition is bad. We can't do anything. We don't
get any work from others, nor can we do our own business because we don't have money for that. If we are
able to sell anything in the shandy [the weekly market],
we can eat; otherwise we go to bed without food.

According to Mariamma, 40 percent of the youth are unemployed. They wander idly around, waiting for a chance to go to the Persian Gulf countries. But the women are left behind with their now useless skill of making lace. They desperately try to sell lace on their own at the weekly market, where they have to compete with the male traders, or to traders who come to their house.

Lace Production and Changes in the Sexual Division of Labor

From the above analysis it is clear that the division of labor between men and women has been by no means static, though always following the same stereotyped patterns. If we look at the actual behavior of people and do not restrict ourselves to recording the professed social norms, we find that the division of labor between the sexes underwent a number of changes after lace production started on a commercial basis. The dynamics of this change are usually obscured by the repetition of certain sex-role stereotypes that serve to maintain and legitimize the asymmetric and unequal relationship between women and men.

Let us now have a closer look at these changes and ask whom they benefited. The first change to occur with the introduction of lacemaking as a house industry was the domestication of Christian convert women, who formerly had been agricultural laborers, and Agnikulakshatriya women, who had sold fish. By their being now exclusively defined as housewives, and thus sharing the prestige of women of other castes that do not allow their women to work outside the house, they have been excluded from other productive activities outside the house and separated from those women of their class who had to continue outdoor productive activity, such as the Harijan women. In the case of the Kapu women who became the main lace workers at a later stage, the sexual division of labor also underwent certain changes. Their domestication and seclusion dated from an earlier stage in the social history of their caste, but when they became lace workers, they became de facto wage earners.

Among the small Kapu peasants this process was connected with the overall process of pauperization affecting them severely since the 1960s. For small peasants, therefore, lacemaking and lace trading are linked to losing their former status of independent cultivators and becoming semi-proletarianized and declassed. In the house, however, the Kapu men still cling to the role of the lord of the house, land, and women, even when they are not able to provide the daily subsistence of the family, and depend on the women's income.

This shows that the dynamics of change in the sexual division of labor coincide with changes in the class structure. The rise of the middle-level and rich peasants under the impact of the Green Revolution led to a polarization among the peasantry; some became rich in this process, and some lost their land and had to emigrate, to become agricultural laborers, or to go into the lace business. The lacemakers' husbands in Serepalem all belong to the pauperized class of former medium-level or small peasants. In this process, however, women have to shoulder the ongoing subsistence production, and are now deliberately defined as housewives. Only as long as women are actual producers as housewives and workers can men become nonproducing traders.

For the Christian converts, lacemaking initially was linked to an improvement in their class position. The men had already lost their connection with the land, but the women's lacemaking enabled them to become small merchants and hawkers. This process was facilitated through the education they had received in the missionary schools. They could move out of the area and do business in far-off cities. But, as was seen, the class polarization taking place generally in this area also affects them. They are no longer able to compete with the newly risen large merchants, who invest the surplus gained through capitalist farming in the lace business. Therefore, they give up their work as petty traders, try to find employment outside the area and the country, and often leave their women destitute.

This process of class polarization has also led to a polarization between men and women. Production for the world market has made the sexual division of labor both in society and in the family not more equal but more unequal. In this process the women seem to be the losers on all fronts. Through their productive and reproductive work they enable the family to survive. Their work enables some men to free themselves from productive work altogether and to become lace agents, lace traders, lace hawkers, and even lace exporters. We have to remember that all lace producers are female and that all lace traders are male.

Summary

If we try to summarize the changes in the social and sexual division of labor resulting from lace production for the world market, we can distinguish three stages. The first stage could be called that of primary accumulation, based exclusively on use-value production. The charitable work of the wives of missionaries, their fund-raising activities in England and Scotland, and the "leisure time" work of impoverished Harijan Christian women were its base. In this stage a new skill was taught to the women, and the organizational and ideological changes took place that made these women into housewives and workers at the same time. On the other hand, the first market links were established with lace importers abroad. Yet, the whole production process and the marketing were still in the hands of women.

These conditions provided the base for the "takeoff" of the second stage. Surplus-value production became the driving force of the production process, and some men acquired a new class status by the exploitation of women's labor. They became traders and merchants—nonproducers who live off the productive work of the women. In this process some men were able to rise to the capitalist class through their control over the market channels. They were now able to transform the whole production process into surplus-value production, although they carefully retained the old form of labor organization and labor control, that of individualized "leisure time activity" of housewives. This process led to a class differentiation in their own community, with capitalist exporters on the one side and the poor members of their community on the other. In this stage women still had a function as agents and even as small traders. The number of big exporters was limited, and they did not compete with the poorer male traders or hawkers who catered for the home market. They still had a somewhat paternalistic attitude toward the lacemakers.

The third stage is characterized, as has been seen, by the rise of the large merchants, and the increase of male merchants and exporters in the wake of the Green Revolution and the new expansion of the world market in handicrafts. Hand in hand with the increase in the number of male exporters went the rise in the number of male agents. The use of "modern" technology—the bicycle—served as an excuse to push women agents out of the trading sphere altogether. The availability of bank credit had the same effect, because the poor, illiterate women could not provide the necessary security to the banks. This phase coincided, as was seen, with monopolistic tendencies of the biggest and most modern of the newly risen merchants, and the merging of large farmers and merchant capitalists into one and the same class. The pauperized peasants, as the result of a lack of industries in the area or other opportunities to do productive work, also tried to join the swelling army of nonproducing petty traders and agents. They pushed the women out of this sector altogether.

If we examine our hypotheses in the light of the analysis of the dynamics in the sexual division of labor among the lace workers of Narsapur, we can come to the following conclusions:

1. Changes in the sexual division of labor were linked to changes in the overall division of labor in the area. These changes were due to the introduction of capitalist farming and to the integration of housewives into a production system oriented to the world market.

2. Capitalist farming and production for the world market have led not only to pauperization of poor peasants but also to growing class differentiation among the peasantry.

3. There seems to be a conjuncture between class polarization and polarization between women and men. Because pauperized peasants are only semi-proletarianized, their women are only semi-domesticated. Not only do they remain responsible for the reproduction of the labor force—as housewives—but their labor power is tapped for production for the world market.

4. Women are not simply "left behind" while men monopolize the new and more profitable areas of the economy; they are deliberately "defined back" into the role of housewives. Only if women remain outside the organized sector and are socially defined as housewives can the double exploitation of their labor go on.

5. Not only the big exporters, but also the husbands of the lace workers, are benefiting, as nonproducers, from the ongoing subsistence production of the lacemakers.

6. Thus, we can conclude that men can raise their class position on the base of the exploitation of women's ongoing subsistence production.

The integration of their work into a world system of capital accumulation has not transformed, and will not transform, the women into free wage laborers. It is precisely this fact—their not being free wage laborers, but housewives—that makes capital accumulation possible.

NOTES

1. The term "exploitation" is used here in the sense that social separation and hierarchization have taken place between producers and consumers. The original situation in an egalitarian community—that in which those who produce something are also its consumers—has been disrupted. Under exploitative conditions, nonproducers appropriate and consume the products and services of actual producers. See Sohn-Rethel 1978.

2. For a further discussion of these questions, see Mies 1979; 1980.

3. Gandhi introduced the term Harijans (Children of God) for the untouchables. But this euphemism has not abolished untouchability. The term Harijan is used today in the same pejorative sense as formerly.

4. Purdah means keeping women away from the eyes of the public, particularly of men, by means of veils, separate rooms or railway compartments, and similar means of segregation.

5. In the cities this has, of course, changed to a certain extent, since more white-collar jobs are available for women of the upper castes. But even there, upper-caste women hardly work in factories or as sweepers, even if their families are poor.

6. It is a great dishonor for a man to go to his wife's brother or mother for support. This shows not only that he is not capable of feeding his wife, but also that he has to be fed by his wife's family, which always has a lower status.

REFERENCES

Engels, Friedrich. 1973. Origin of the Family, Private Property and the State. New York: International Publishers.

Handbook of Statistics West Godavari District. 1977.

Marx, Karl. 1974. Kapital. London: I. Lawrence and Wishart.

Mies, Maria. 1973. Indische Frauen zwischen Patriarchat und Chancengleichheit. Meisenheim/Glan: Anton Hain. Rev. English vers., Indian Women and Patriarchy. New Delhi: Concept Publishers, 1980.

_____. 1978. "Methodische Postulate zur Frauenforschung," Beiträge zur feministischen Theorie und Praxis 1, no. 1. Translated into English as Towards a Methodology of Women's Studies. The Hague: Institute of Social Studies, 1979.

_____. 1979. "Social Origins of the Sexual Division of Labour." Paper presented at the Conference on Underdevelopment and Subsistence Reproduction, University of Bielefeld. Published in German as "Gesellschaftliche Ursprünge der geschlechtlichen Arbeitsteilung," Beiträge zur feministischen Theorie und Praxis 3, no. 3 (1980).

_____. 1980. "Capitalist Development and Subsistence Reproduction: Rural Women in India," Bulletin of Concerned Asian Scholars 12, no. 1.

Sohn-Rethel, Alfred. 1978. "Zur kritischen Liquidierung des Apriorismus," in his Warenform und Denkform. Frankfurt, pp. 49-75.

Thurston, E. 1915. Castes and Tribes of South India. Reprint. New Delhi.

Verghese, S. K. 1979. "Developments in International Competitiveness of India in 1970s," Economic and Political Weekly, October 13, 1979:1718-26.

2

WOMEN WORKERS
AND
THE GREEN REVOLUTION

Gita Sen

INTRODUCTION

Conceptual Issues

The theoretical premise of this chapter is that the subordination of women in the rural areas of the Third World has two aspects. First, women are members of households that differ in their access to land, other means of production, and wage incomes. Thus, the conditions of their work (as agricultural laborers for others or on the family farm, as field laborers or primarily in the home) are dependent on the survival strategies of households in specific relation to land and rural resources. Change in landholding patterns and in methods of agricultural production differentially affects different rural households and the work that women from these households do. Second, rural households are not harmonious, egalitarian social units, but hierarchical structures embodying relations of subordination and domination based on gender and age.

The subordination of women is commonly expressed in the sex-based division of labor (women are usually responsible for the work of food processing, fuel and water collection, and child care, over and above whatever work they may do outside the home), in the control over women's childbearing capacity and nutrition, in the limits placed on women's physical movements (such as purdah), and often in an ideology of female inferiority. The particular forms that subordination takes vary among different classes of rural households.

A complete understanding of the position of rural women from poor peasant and agricultural laborer households, and of the effects on them of agrarian change, would require us to analyze both of the above aspects. It is only thus that we can fully comprehend the contradictory situation of women. Their own survival is bound up with that of the household to which they belong, but they are subject to subordination within the household as well. In this chapter, we concentrate on the first aspect, the effect of agrarian change on women as workers outside the home. This is mainly because recognition of the importance of the second aspect is just dawning among Indian social scientists, and there is little information available on the subject at present.

A study of the effects of agrarian change on the patterns of women's work in agriculture raises several questions. First, what, precisely, are the changes in the distribution of land and other means of production? Second, how does this affect the survival conditions of different rural households and, hence, the participation of women from these households in agricultural work on and off the family farm? Third, does the labor process in agriculture (the social and technical relations of production) change? Fourth, how do these changes alter the sex-based division of labor in agriculture?

While changes in women's participation in agricultural work and in their place in the division of labor can be related to changes in landholding patterns and in the agricultural labor process through questions such as those raised above, our answers can only be partial ones. Fuller answers would require an understanding of the connection between women's work in agriculture and within the domestic sphere, however that is defined in the particular social context. An important motive for examining these connections lies in the need to understand how processes of capital accumulation affect preexisting patriarchal relations within peasant households. The subordination of women in such households is often expressed through restrictions on their physical mobility and their confinement to domestic tasks or work on the family farm. To what extent does the reshaping of social relations consequent on capitalist penetration include a change in such expressions of patriarchy? Specifically, to what extent do women become wage laborers outside the family farm?

There are, obviously, two alternative answers to this question. Either the economic pressures of involvement in commodity production for sale and of proletarianization may force a breakdown (or at least a reshaping) of the proscriptions on women's participation in work outside the home, or patriarchal domination is powerful enough to withstand such forces. I will argue in this chapter that, for the regions studied here, the former hypothesis seems consonant with the evidence.

In regions of India where women have traditionally done little fieldwork, the financial pressures of the Green Revolution seem to have led to greater participation in wage labor by women from small farm households. I do not argue that women experience such wage labor as liberating in and of itself. Indeed, it is far more likely that they view it mainly as a lengthening of their total work time. But participation in wage work creates pressures for "rewiring" the division of domestic tasks within the home. How this is actually accomplished will affect the newly emerging patterns of gender relations in peasant households. This aspect is not explored directly in this chapter. Rather, I focus solely on the external pressures that shape women's participation in wage labor. I hope, however, that even the partial answers that I can provide will provoke further study and discussion of these issues in the context of current processes of rural change in the Third World.

The main argument of this chapter is that powerful forces connected with mechanisms of capital accumulation in agriculture tend to lessen the differences in the rates of women's participation in wage labor across regions with markedly different preexisting gender relations. Second, there is also a tendency toward similarity in the gender-based hierarchies among agricultural wage laborers. These underlying forces may take different regional expressions based upon variations in the prior distribution of land and landlessness, the pace of technical change (especially mechanization), and the size of the unemployed rural labor force.

The specific focus of this chapter is the impact of land reform and the so-called Green Revolution on women workers from poor peasant and landless labor households in two regions of India: Haryana/Punjab and Thanjavur. These two regions differ in a number of respects. At Indian independence in 1947, Haryana/Punjab had a more powerful group of middle-level farmers who mainly grew wheat, while Thanjavur was dominated by large landowners involved in wet rice cultivation, and had a history of landless labor going back to precolonial times. Both regions are showpieces of the Green Revolution, which got off the ground in India in 1965.[1] The basis for capitalist farming had been laid before then by land reform measures that became a part of government policy upon independence.

Changes in the patterns of women's agricultural work in the two regions have both similarities and differences. On the one hand, the pressures for women to do agricultural wage labor and similarities in the agricultural labor process have been translated into similar patterns of labor force participation and similar conditions of work for women in terms of the division of labor, the range of tasks, and wage differentials. On the other hand, differences in the initial conditions of landholding and landlessness in the two regions have meant that land reform and the Green Revolution have had a different impact on the extent of employment of women in agricultural wage labor.

In the rest of this introduction, we shall discuss the general features of land reform and the Green Revolution in India. The sections on Haryana/Punjab and Thanjavur examine the effects of these changes on women's wage labor in those regions through an analysis of changes in landholding patterns and in the agricultural labor process. The conclusion compares the results for the two regions, and raises some questions for further empirical and theoretical analysis.

Land Reform and the Green Revolution

Since 1947 land reform in India has had three major, stated purposes: to provide security of tenure to tenants, to fix "fair" rents, and to impose ceilings on land ownership. The main intents of the legislation were to do away with the problem of absentee ownership and to improve the conditions of small tenants. The private ownership of land was not viewed by the government as a problem in itself. The actual implementation of the legislation was impeded by the fact that rich peasants and large tenants formed the rural base of the Indian National Congress party. The numerous legislative loopholes have meant that land reform has not significantly improved the conditions of the small and poor peasants.[2] However, it has laid the basis for the emergence of capitalist agriculture, since in many areas the rich farmers and large tenants have been able to expand their holdings, to shake off excessive rent payments, and to remove the older, absentee landlords of the colonial period. It became possible for a farmer, in the name of "personal cultivation" (which is defined in the land reform laws to exclude cultivation by tenants, but to include cultivation with wage labor), to produce with hired, free labor and to accumulate capital and land without hindrance.

The Green Revolution in Indian agriculture began with the Intensive Agricultural Development Programme (IADP) in 1960-61. This marked a radical shift in governmental consciousness of rural problems, and a furthering of the movement toward capitalist labor processes in agriculture. While land reform legislation remained on the books, the comprehensive community development approach was abandoned in favor of a program that concentrated exclusively on expansion of agricultural output, especially of food grains[3] (Rudra 1978). On the recommendation of a group of "experts" from the Ford Foundation, a package of high-yield varieties of seeds (HYV), chemical fertilizer, pesticides/herbicides, and irrigation was introduced in a number of districts in 1960-61. The program's large-scale expansion, the so-called Green Revolution, began in 1965, spreading beyond the initial districts that had been carefully chosen for soil, for climate, and, particularly, for assured irrigation.

Under traditional agricultural practices, the typical farm produced a number of inputs for the production process. Thus, seeds were carried over from the previous harvest, fertilizer was gotten from animal manure, pests were removed by hand, and irrigation depended on the monsoons or tanks and canals. The complete transformation of the technology of cultivation in the Green Revolution means that hybrid seed stock must be regularly renewed through purchase; animal manure is inadequate, and must be supplemented by chemical fertilizer; and better water control and pest elimination are necessary because the HYV are sensitive both to the quality of irrigation and to pests that flourish once the ecological hardiness of traditional seed strains is lost. Hence, seeds, fertilizer, pump sets/tubewells, and pesticides all have to be purchased rather than being produced on the farm.

This "finance intensity" of the new technology often necessitates multiple cropping for profitability. This in turn requires rapid seed-bed preparation, creates sharper peaks in labor demand, and generates incentives for tractors and other kinds of farm machinery. On the harvest side, the growth of output increases the demand for harvest labor and leads to possible replacement of human labor by machines for reaping and threshing.

These features of the new technology were incorporated into the government's policy of initially making it available only in regions of assured irrigation to those farmers who could buy the new inputs and obtain credit easily from banks: the rich farmers. Subsequently, the rate of adoption of the new technology has varied by size of farm, since it is more difficult for smaller farmers to adopt it profitably. A corollary has been the growing importance of large tenants, who are essentially capitalist farmers leasing land to take advantage of the profitability of the new technology. Furthermore, tenanted land has increasingly been resumed by landowners in the Green Revolution regions, not so much to evade land reform legislation as to engage in profitable cultivation with hired labor.

While the new technology has had greater success in wheat-growing than in rice-growing areas (a point to which we shall return in our discussion of regional variation), its general impact on the labor process in the two regions of our study has been similar, though with variations of degree. There has been an increasing tendency for the distinction between permanent and casual laborers to be based on the former's working with machines, fertilizer, pump sets, and other high-technology items, and the latter's being employed mainly for harvest labor.

The emergence of capitalist tenant farmers, the resumption of land, and the ascendancy of new types of laborers over older sharecropping and rent-paying tenants have taken different patterns in the two regions. These differences are connected partly to the landholding structures after a decade of land reform, and partly to the differences between HYV wheat and rice.

TABLE 2.1

Agricultural Laborers, by Region, 1971

	Haryana	Punjab	Tamilnadu	India
Agricultural laborers as percentage of agricultural workers	24.85	32.11	49.34	37.79
Agricultural laborers as percentage of total workers	16.24	20.20	30.46	26.33
Agricultural laborers as percentage of rural workers	18.90	24.80	38.10	30.70

Sources: Parthasarathy and Rao 1975; data on Tamilnadu from Sinha 1978.

HARYANA/PUNJAB

Traditional Patterns

We shall first discuss briefly the initial conditions in terms of landholding patterns and women's work in agriculture. Historically this was a region of widespread peasant proprietorship. Situated in northwestern India, it is an area in which irrigation expenditures had been relatively high even under the British. By the early 1970s, 83 percent of net sown area was irrigated in Punjab, and 52 percent in Haryana, compared with 20 percent for the country as a whole (Dantwala 1978). The average size of operational holding has been higher than for India as a whole. [4]

Agricultural laborers have constituted a smaller proportion of rural workers and of agricultural workers than the all-India average (agricultural workers include both agricultural laborers and cultivators). At independence over half the land area was under owner occupancy. The percentage has increased steadily since then, initially because of land reform but increasingly because of the eviction of tenants and resumption of tenanted land for cultivation with hired labor since the coming of the Green Revolution.[5] When the Green Revolution came to Haryana/Punjab, it was a region with a high proportion of owner-cultivators, a relatively low proportion of agricultural labor households, and high irrigation. Indeed, even before the introduction of HYV technology in 1965, mechanization had begun in the region—for example, the number of threshers had increased from none in 1947 to 20,000 in 1964 (Dasgupta 1977a).

As for women's participation in agricultural work, Haryana/Punjab is usually considered a region where women traditionally have done relatively little fieldwork. Although there is usually serious underreporting of women's work on family farms (and despite the large incidence of such farms in this region), the statistical reports of low female participation are borne out by impressionistic evidence gathered by field analysts. The general explanation of this phenomenon has been in terms of the influence of West Asian, Islamic culture, but a great deal more work needs to be done on this question.[6]

In what became the main Green Revolution belt of the Punjab (the districts of Ludhiana, Jullundur, Kapurthala, Gurdaspur, Patiala, and Amritsar), women have traditionally done relatively little fieldwork—the proportion of female workers to total agricultural workers ranged between 1.7 percent and 3.8 percent in 1961 in these districts (Billings and Singh 1970b).[7] Despite the low overall rates, the labor force participation rates for women from rural labor households, and increasingly from small cultivator households, are much higher than the average for all women (Table 2.2).

In addition, in the poorer and more hilly districts of the old state of Punjab, women have typically been known to do more agricultural work, even plowing in some areas when the men were away, working as migrant laborers. In general, however, plowing was almost inevitably done by men: by the owner-cultivator, his family members, or permanent farm servants. Women, despite their low participation rates, performed a fairly wide range of tasks. They leveled the fields in some regions, and loaded, unloaded, and spread the farm manure. In irrigation, while men mainly bunded and made water courses, women actually applied water except in the northern, prosperous region of Punjab. Planting and sowing were done by

women, who followed the plow, dropping seeds, and transplanted
rice seedlings where rice was grown. Women also hoed and weeded
in all regions. The harvesting season involved a large number of
women casual workers—in the more prosperous, northern region
of Punjab, men cut the wheat crop while women were more involved
in picking cotton, plucking corn and millet, harvesting groundnuts,
and stripping sugarcane before it was crushed. Thus, although
women traditionally formed a relatively small fraction of the agricultural labor force, and although there was a fairly rigid sexual
division of labor in fieldwork, they performed quite a variety of
tasks. This has been changed by the new technology.

TABLE 2.2

Female Labor Force Participation Rates (LFPR), 1971
(percent)

	Haryana	Punjab	Tamilnadu
Labor force participation rate for rural women	3.17	1.26	19.88*
LFPR for women of small cultivator households	19.20	26.50	59.70
LFPR for women of rural labor households	17.80	38.90	60.30
Women agricultural laborers as percentage of total women workers	21.91	10.08	46.70
Women agricultural laborers as percentage of total agricultural laborers	7.54	1.36	36.67

Note: Rows 2 and 3 are from round 25 of the National Sample
Survey, 1970-71.
    *From 1972 Census.
    Sources: Gulati 1975a; Parthasarathy and Rao 1975; Sinha
1978.

Small Farms' Viability and Women's Wage Labor Participation

Let us first examine the impact of the new technology on the conditions of survival of small farm households. [8] Between 1961 and 1971—that is, before and after the adoption of the new technology—there was a rise in the concentration of land and assets in Haryana and Punjab. This was reflected in an increase in the percentage of cultivating households with operational holdings less than five acres in size. [9] It is necessary to know whether this represented a tendency toward increasing pauperization and proletarianization in the region, since such a tendency would have serious consequences for the conditions of survival of small farmers.

The classic argument about rural proletarianization can be summarized as follows. The introduction of new technology and mechanization, and increasing dependence on production for the market, tend to increase the minimum size of the economically efficient farm. This in turn causes smaller farmers to lose land through debt, mortgages, forfeitures, or sale, and thus sharply increases the proportion of very small farmers on the brink of ruin, and of landless laborers—a process of increasing pauperization and proletarianization. This pattern would seem to accord well with the experience of the Green Revolution regions, since, as argued in the introduction to this chapter, the new inputs are "finance intensive." The greater use of purchased commodity inputs and the need for credit have meant that larger farmers are able to adopt the new technology with greater ease.

Despite this, it cannot be said unequivocally that the minimum size of the economically efficient farm has increased. This is because, up to certain levels of mechanization, the new inputs can be adopted by smaller farmers. HYV seeds, fertilizer, and water are divisible inputs that can be used by smaller farms, although their yield-improving impact is diminished if they are not applied in fairly rigid combinations. Thus, some of the small farmers have been able to adopt at least some of the new inputs, and this has improved the money value of their assets. [10] This is especially true for the HYV wheat strains, which are fairly hardy, and therefore less risky than the HYV rice adopted in Thanjavur. The adoption of new inputs by small farmers even extends to some farm machinery—for example, small farmers can rent (rather than buy) tractors for plowing and seed-bed preparation.

A decline in minimum viable farm size is perfectly compatible with growing inequality in landholding and asset holding. In fact, it is an interesting case of the simultaneous concentration of landholding in agriculture and the continued existence of small farms. How-

ever, this phenomenon is likely to be overturned by tendencies toward the adoption of newer techniques in the form of additional mechanization. In the light of these counteracting tendencies, S. Bhalla
(1977a) has argued that the downward shift in acreage structure in
Haryana is due mainly to subdivision of land among family members
on larger farms. Although the reasons behind such subdivision are
not clear, one may surmise that it reflects a decline in the minimum
viable farm size. However, even in the most advanced regions of
Haryana, very small farms in the under-five-acre category are not
genuinely viable now, since their annual consumption seems to out-
strip their annual income (see Table 2.3). Over time, therefore,
we would expect a process of genuine pauperization to be set in
motion.

TABLE 2.3

Income, Consumption, and Saving in Haryana, by Region
and Size Class of Operational Holding, 1969-70
(Rs.)

Size Class of Operational Holding (acres)	North		Center		South	
	(1)	(2)	(1)	(2)	(1)	(2)
0.005-5.0	2,603	-358	2,088	-682	1,768	-1,112
5.0-10.0	5,297	972	3,071	-779	3,935	-304
10.0-20.0	10,378	4,764	5,004	-94	5,272	-108
20.0-30.0	16,054	8,372	8,381	-331	8,297	3,077
30.0 and over	22,553	10,534	14,099	2,695	8,755	1,357
Average	7,811	2,830	5,239	-122	4,238	-125

(1) = net household income.
(2) = saving: net household income minus consumption.
Note: In the most advanced region, the North, even households in the 5-10-acre class have positive saving. This is not true
for the other regions. We take this as an indicator of the greater
economic viability of smaller farms in the North, although it is not a
proof thereof.
Source: G. S. Bhalla 1974.

Furthermore, subdivision was not the only reason for the decline in farm size. Although, in the most advanced regions of Haryana, 66-96 percent of the households that were net losers of land in the period lost land due to subdivision, S. Bhalla (1977a) points out that 27-44 percent also lost land to resumption. Resumption implies the return to "personal cultivation" of previously tenanted land by larger farmers having the new technology and hired laborers. Unfortunately, Bhalla's published data do not show us whether this had a differential impact on under-five-acre farms as opposed to larger ones. It would appear, however, that the number of small farms increased as a result of both causes mentioned above, as well as of some renting and/or purchase of small plots by previously landless households. [11] As a result of these three factors, farms in the very small (2.5 acres or less) category grew from 39 to 59 percent of all farms in the under-five-acre category between the early 1960s and the early 1970s.

Another tendency operating toward a greater concentration of land is the shift in tenancy patterns. Larger farmers now account for the bulk of leased-in, tenanted area in Haryana/Punjab. [12] In fact, in the more advanced areas in Haryana, farms in the under-five-acre category gained no land through either purchase or leasing between 1961 and 1971 (S. Bhalla 1977a). Thus, although the tendency toward subdivision of larger farms seems to indicate some reduction in minimum viable farm size, the resumption of land and the increase of large tenants implies that access to land is becoming increasingly difficult for small farmers in the advanced Green Revolution areas. As is seen in Table 2.4, in 1971 the under-five-acre farms had access to only 11 percent of total area in Haryana and 15 percent in Punjab, despite the increase in their numbers. One might argue that concentration of land can be offset by raising the intensive margin of cultivation through multiple cropping. Yet the extent to which this is possible and profitable for small farmers is limited by their capacity to purchase adequate amounts of the new inputs. The typical pattern on small farms is for only part of the annual output to be produced with the HYV technology.

How do the growing "finance intensity" of cultivation, the declining availability of land to small farmers, and the proliferation of small farms affect the wage labor participation by women from small farm households? Some hypotheses can be put forward on the basis of cross-sectional comparisons of three regions of Haryana, although it must be emphasized that these hypotheses are tentative, and need to be corroborated by further field study. Table 2.5 shows that as we move from backward to advanced areas of the state, there are significant differences in both the overall wage labor employment of women and in the employment of women from households whose main income is cultivation.

TABLE 2.4

Distribution by State of Operational Holdings
and Area Operated, 1970-71

Size Class of Operational Holding (acres)	Haryana		Punjab		Tamilnadu*	
	(1)	(2)	(1)	(2)	(1)	(2)
Up to 2.5	27.4	3.5	37.6	5.7	58.8	17.1
2.5-5.0	18.9	7.2	18.9	9.4	20.9	20.5
5.0-10.0	22.5	17.0	20.4	20.0	13.1	24.8
10.0-25.0	23.1	38.1	18.0	38.1	6.1	24.6
25.0 and over	8.1	34.2	5.0	26.9	1.1	13.0

(1) = Percent of holdings.
(2) = Percent of area operated.
*Tamilnadu includes Thanjavur.
Source: All-India Report on Agricultural Census 1970-71.

    Although women form only 8.5 percent of agricultural laborers in the most backward region, they account for 15-16 percent in the two more advanced, high-technology regions. This runs counter to the historical pattern of low female participation in the more prosperous regions of the Punjab. This feature is all the more interesting because Table 2.5 has data only for permanent and regular casual laborers, and does not include the seasonal casual laborers—traditionally women have formed a higher proportion of seasonal casual labor (at harvest time, for example) than of regular casual labor.[13] Thus, a greater proportion of the regular agricultural labor force in the Green Revolution areas consists of women.
    This higher proportion of women laborers in the more advanced regions can probably be explained by the greater overall labor demand and shortage of labor in these regions. If one presumes that male agricultural laborers are more likely to be already employed as permanent laborers (as the data in Table 2.5 seem to indicate), and that they are the first to be employed at the casual labor tasks made available by the new technology, then the pool of female casual labor would be drawn upon as male labor was exhausted. In backward regions where the demand for casual labor is low relative to supply, most of the tasks might be filled by men. In the more advanced regions of high labor demand and a tight labor market, a greater number of women may be employed as male labor

is used up, resulting in a higher proportion of women in the total of labor force in these regions.

This presumes, of course, that some flexibility emerges in the sexual division of casual labor. Such a presumption is not entirely unreasonable, given that the more rigid sexual division is increasingly between permanent and casual laborers in the more advanced areas, and not among casual laborers as such. The higher proportions of women agricultural laborers in the Green Revolution areas of Haryana may be explained by a growing demand for laborers in the face of relatively small proportions of landless laborers available for hire. Under such conditions it is possible for women to obtain wage employment in these areas.

Turning now from the question of the greater availability of casual work for women to the question of women's willingness to work for wages, we again find a significant difference between the more backward and the more advanced regions. This is especially true for women from households whose main income source is cultivation—that is, small farming households. As Table 2.5 shows, in the most backward region over 81 percent of female laborers come from landless labor households and only 18.7 percent from households whose main income source is cultivation. In striking contrast, 38.9 percent of all regular female laborers in the most advanced region, and 49 percent in the next most advanced region, come from households whose main income source is cultivation.

This high proportion of women laborers from cultivating households in the Green Revolution areas has two possible explanations. On the one hand, the use of the new technology may have released women from some traditional tasks on small farms. It is more likely, however, that the increased "finance intensiveness" of the new technology has put such a premium on money incomes in small farm households that women are being sent out from these households as agricultural wage laborers. This is being done not only at seasonal peak times, but also on a more regular basis. Thus, while the men, who have traditionally done most of the actual fieldwork, continue to work on the family farm, the women are being sent out as wage laborers to supplement the money income of the household. Therefore, women's labor force participation results from the need for money incomes to ensure the small farmers' ongoing capacity to use and profit from the new technology, in a situation of growing competition for land and "finance intensity" of cultivation with the new technology. One would expect that this need would become more critical, ceteris paribus, the more the small farm household has adopted the new technology.

TABLE 2.5

Distribution of Permanent and Regular Casual Agricultural Laborers, by Sex: Haryana, 1972–73

	Region A			Region B			Region C		
	(1)	(2)	(3)	(1)	(2)	(3)	(1)	(2)	(3)
Female laborers as percent of									
All agricultural laborers	15.1	27.9	2.0	15.6	20.9	—	8.5	9.3	—
Laborers from landless agricultural households	13.1	31.4	2.6	10.3	15.8	—	17.0	21.2	—
Laborers from agricultural households with land	13.2	22.8	—	14.4	19.6	—	—	—	—
Laborers from households whose main income source is cultivation	23.2	32.2	—	29.2	32.9	—	6.5	6.5	—

Percent of female laborers from

	A (1)	A (2)	A (3)	B (1)	B (2)	B (3)	C (1)	C (2)	C (3)
Landless labor households	51.8	45.3	6.4	32.5	32.5	—	81.3	81.3	—
Agricultural labor households with land	9.4	9.4	—	18.5	18.5	—	—	—	—
Households whose main income source is cultivation	38.9	38.9	—	49.0	49.0	—	18.7	18.7	—
Percent of male agricultural laborers	100.0	43.1	56.9	100.0	70.0	30.0	100.0	91.2	8.8

(1) = Total laborers.
(2) = Regular casual laborers.
(3) = Permanent laborers.

Note: Region A is the most progressive and C the most backward in adoption of the HYV technology.
Source: S. Bhalla 1976; the percentages in rows 1–4 were calculated by the author.

Sexual Division of Agricultural Labor

We now turn to the changes in the agricultural labor process induced by the new technology in order to understand women's position in the changing hierarchy of laborers. The labor process in agriculture has five main subprocesses: seed-bed preparation, irrigation, interculture, harvesting, and sale. Each of these consists of a number of further processes: plowing, planking, leveling of the soil, application of manure/fertilizer; bunding and maintaining water channels, water application to the fields; hoeing, weeding, and pest control; reaping, binding, threshing, and winnowing; and crop storage, transport, and sale. The new technology affects not only the manner in which these subprocesses are carried out, but also the annual labor demand and its peaks. It also affects the composition of the labor force between yearlong, permanent employees and casual workers, and therefore the composition by sex and age.

A number of forces operate simultaneously to affect the composition of the labor force between permanent and casual workers: the extent of mechanization, the composition of the available pool of laborers, the amount of labor shortage, and hence the types of contracts into which farmers enter. S. Bhalla (1976) found that the Green Revolution in Haryana has almost reversed the relative importance of permanent and regular casual laborers.[14] The highest proportion of permanent to regular casual laborers was found in the most advanced Green Revolution areas in 1972-73. (Unfortunately, her published data do not cover seasonal casual laborers.) The increase in the proportion of permanent laborers may be the result of two sets of forces that are influential in the Green Revolution areas. On the one hand there is what we may call the "mechanization effect," which may affect different types of labor unevenly (see Table 2.6). On the other hand there is the "labor shortage effect," which may determine the kinds of contracts that farmers are willing to sign.

The introduction of the new inputs has not reduced the demand for permanent labor, though some of the tasks done by permanent laborers have changed—for example, replacement of plows and animal teams by tractors, of Persian wheels by pump sets, and of farm manure by chemical fertilizer means that permanent laborers and family workers operate more machinery. The demand for casual labor has been affected in two ways. The use of tractors for seed-bed preparation reduces the demand for casual labor for plowing, while the use of threshers reduces harvest demand. This may be called the "mechanization effect." On the other side the overall labor shortage and the need to have trained operators for the new equipment may increase the number of longer-term contracts.

This is the "labor shortage effect." Although we cannot know for certain without further investigation, these two effects working together may account for the decline in the ratio of regular casual laborers to permanent laborers in the more advanced regions.

TABLE 2.6

Labor Required, by Technology Level,
on a Ten-Acre Punjab Farm, 1969

Technology Level	Monthly Demand (man-days per acre)
I	51.0
II	60.1
III	59.2
IV	52.5
V	42.2
VI	37.4
VII	49.4

I = irrigated with Persian wheel, traditional seeds, 150 percent crop intensity.

II = irrigated with Persian wheel, HYV with necessary inputs, 150 percent crop intensity.

III = irrigated with pump set, HYV, 180 percent crop intensity.

IV = level III with wheat thresher, corn sheller, 180 percent crop intensity.

V = level IV with tractor, cane crusher, 180 percent crop intensity.

VI = level V with wheat reaper, 180 percent crop intensity.

VII = level VI with 220 percent crop intensity.

Source: Billings and Singh 1969.

Casual labor is concentrated in harvesting and to some extent in planting, having been displaced from most other aspects of the crop cycle on the larger farms. The large and sharp peak demands for casual labor draw migrants from poorer regions—for instance, eastern Uttar Pradesh. This large demand for casual labor has also created the possibility for an increase in women's employment.

In the hierarchy of the laborers—permanent over regular casual over seasonal casual—women workers are at the lower ends under the new technology. S. Bhalla's (1976) data for Haryana show that except for a very small proportion (1 percent of all women laborers in the most advanced region), all women laborers in all regions are casual laborers, either regular or seasonal.[15] While it is true that even traditionally, women have been only casual laborers, both the causes and the implications of this under the new technology are worth noting.

It is very likely that at least some of the tasks that women traditionally did have now been mechanized. This is especially true of wheat threshing, corn shelling, sugarcane crushing, sowing, and weeding. To the extent that reaping machines have been introduced, they have displaced women laborers from traditional tasks. On the other hand, most of the tasks created by the new technology, especially those having to do with operation of machines, or careful regulation and measurement of doses of water, are done by male laborers. The resultant narrowing of the range of tasks done by women has probably caused a "crowding" of women into a few jobs, a phenomenon that is well known in the labor markets of advanced capitalist countries. Women workers are now increasingly limited to those traditional jobs that have been minimally affected by the new technology, and to seasonal labor at harvest time. This crowding has led to relatively low wages in these jobs even in excess of the traditional disparity between wage rates paid to men and women. Wage rates in general have not kept up with productivity increases in the Punjab. But while the index of real wage rates in all other operations increased, albeit minimally, the index for cotton picking, a female task, fell from 100 in 1961 to 86 in 1977 (S. Bhalla 1979). Table 2.7 shows that in Haryana both the wage rates received for different operations and the number of days of employment are lower for women laborers than for men.

Should we expect that women's low position in the agricultural labor force would be translated into a greater militancy? S. Bhalla (1976) notes that, because of its access to landholding, the "new class" of permanent laborers from cultivating households is the least militant of all laborers in this region. These workers keep their distance socially from the casual and landless agricultural laborers, who tend to be more militant in their demands. For women laborers, however, these are conflicting tendencies. While women are almost uniformly casual laborers, in the more advanced regions a high proportion of them belong to landed households. Another factor counteracting independent female militancy is that, in the most progressive regions, harvest teams of casual labor are hired and work in family groupings. This is an aspect that requires further research.

TABLE 2.7

Wages and Days of Employment of Women Laborers,
by Region in Haryana, 1969-70

	North	Center	South	All Haryana
Female casual wage rates as percentage of male casual wage rates				
Kharif				
Sowing	51.4	79.4	91.2	64.7
Harvesting	79.4	68.2	83.1	82.6
Other	76.3	72.6	74.0	78.2
Rabi				
Sowing	87.6	83.5	74.9	85.6
Harvesting	81.3	81.4	89.3	84.1
Other	84.4	75.9	90.2	85.0
Average	79.2	76.0	84.9	81.8
Female average days employed as percentage of male days employed				
Kharif				
Sowing	30.8	35.4	34.3	32.4
Harvesting	49.9	90.3	51.1	58.5
Other	55.1	40.1	13.1	27.2
Rabi				
Sowing	28.3	22.9	30.1	28.3
Harvesting	47.4	77.0	54.7	57.3
Other	66.8	46.3	19.6	36.8
Average	31.3	35.9	27.5	30.6

Source: G. S. Bhalla 1974.

The effects of the new technology on women workers in
Haryana/Punjab may be summed up as follows. While land reform
led to a temporary increase in the proportion of women cultivators,
this was only on paper, and reflected the widespread tendency to
parcel out land titles among family members in order to get around
legal limits on landholding. The effect of the new technology has
not been so much to push women out of agriculture altogether as to
narrow the range of tasks done by them and to place them at the
lower end of a hierarchy of permanent and casual labor. Both their
wage rates and the amount they earn annually are low. So far as
women's participation in agricultural wage labor is concerned, the

growth in the number of small farms in the region, coupled with the attempts by small farmers to adopt the new, "finance intensive" technology, has led to greater participation in casual wage labor by women of small landholding households. Their contribution to the household's money income, and hence to its ongoing ability to farm land under the new technology, is therefore crucial. As a corollary, the proportion of women laborers from landless labor households is lower in the more advanced regions compared with the more backward regions of Haryana.

THANJAVUR

Traditional Patterns

As in the section of Haryana/Punjab, we will first outline the traditional patterns in landholding and in women's work before examining the impact of the new technology. Landholding in Tamilnadu (which includes the Thanjavur district) has historically been different from the pattern in Haryana/Punjab. Large landlords have coexisted with a high proportion of landless laborers in the rural population and a large number of households operating very small farms. As can be seen in Table 2.4, even in 1970-71, after the rapid growth in the number of small farms in Haryana, Tamilnadu still had a higher percentage of households with farms of less than 2.5 acres. In the district of Thanjavur, the region under study, there are still a large number of family estates of about 100 acres and a few of 1,000-5,000 acres. Furthermore, about a quarter of the land is owned by temples or by four rich monasteries that are exempt from the ceiling on landholding (Gough 1977b). The average size of operational holding is lower than the all-India average, while agricultural laborers are a higher proportion of all agricultural workers and of all rural workers than the all-India average.[16] This contrasts with Haryana/Punjab, for which the reverse is true. Although the proportion of landless laborers in agriculture was below the all-India average in 1963-64, it was higher than the corresponding figure for Haryana/Punjab.

Although land reform has led to some decline in land held by absentee Brahman landowners in Tamilnadu, the main beneficiaries have been those already owning 15-50 acres, while the change for the lowest landholding groups has been statistically insignificant (Kurien 1978). Irrigation has been fairly extensive in the state as a whole, and especially in paddy cultivation in Thanjavur even before the Green Revolution.[17]

In Tamilnadu the new technology came to a region having extremely unequal landholding, a precolonial history of landless labor,
a high proportion of rural households with very small holdings, a
high proportion of agricultural laborer households in the rural population, and a specialization in wet paddy cultivation.

This is a region where women (non-Brahmans and Harijans)
have traditionally worked in the fields, both on family farms and as
agricultural laborers for hire. Women workers in paddy cultivation have performed the whole range of tasks—sowing, transplanting, weeding, applying cow dung and green manure, harvesting,
threshing, and winnowing. Only plowing and bund maintenance have
been exclusively male tasks. Gough (1977c) argues that, in this region of high female participation in the labor force, women and men
have traditionally been paid the same wage rates for harvesting.
However, for tasks where the sexual division of labor was more
rigid, the jobs done by men have traditionally had higher rates of
pay than those done by women.

Small Farms' Viability and Women's
Wage Work Participation

As we have seen, the most significant effect of land reform
was to shift some land from absentee landlords to rich farmers
owning 15-50 acres. Land reform did not substantially alter the
overall landholding patterns. However, despite little change in
acreage structure, there have been changes in the caste basis of
landholding. The Brahman landowners have increasingly become
an insignificant economic force, although they still exercise considerable social authority in the villages through the caste hierarchy.[18] Only about 2-3 percent of Thanjavur's cultivated land has
been bought from landlords by the government under the laws limiting landholdings, and distributed to the landless. The biggest impact of land reform on the Harijan agricultural laborers has been
to provide them with house sites of 0.02 or 0.03 acre each.

Turning to tenancy, we note that Thanjavur traditionally had
the highest proportion of tenant households in Tamilnadu (Sivaraman
1973).[19] However, tenancy as such has been declining in importance—tenant cultivators as a whole constituted 28 percent of the
male agricultural work force in 1952, but only 24 percent in 1976.
While part of this is due to disguised tenancy engendered by land
reform laws, qualitative evidence tells us that old forms of tenancy
in Thanjavur have been declining and are being replaced by cultivation with wage labor. In accord with this, the percentage of agricultural laborers has increased from 52 percent to 65 percent of

the male agricultural work force between 1952 and 1976 in Gough's village (see Table 2.8).

TABLE 2.8

Agricultural Laborers as Percent of Work Force
in Thanjavur, 1951-71

	1951	1961	1971
Agricultural laborers as percent of agricultural work force	37	47	59
Agricultural laborers as percent of total work force	27	33	42

Source: Gough 1977a.

Cultivating tenants who lack documents of tenancy may have to pay 60 percent of the gross produce as rent, whereas documented tenants pay 40 percent on paddy land. Most tenants retain only 7-30 percent of the gross produce after paying rent and cultivation expenses. (Sharecropping tenancy gave way to fixed-rent tenancy in the late nineteenth and early twentieth centuries in this region.) Despite the high rents, small cultivators have adopted the HYV technology to the extent possible. This technology is much less developed for rice than for wheat in India.

There are three main problems with the HYV rice varieties: they are often too short-stemmed to withstand flooding conditions; they mature early, and often have to be harvested in the rain; and they are susceptible to more pests and diseases that flourish in wet conditions. The most tricky problem for Thanjavur is water control. Thanjavur is dependent for its irrigation on the southwest monsoon that feeds the Cauvery River system from June to September. If this rain is delayed, as happens relatively often, then planting of the kuruvai (kharif) paddy crop is delayed. This delays harvesting, which may have to be done during the heavy northeast monsoon in October-November. The delay in the kuruvai crop in turn delays the planting of the thaladi (rabi) crop, which suffers from water shortages in February. Thus, double-cropping is an extremely risky business in the absence of wells to tap the groundwater table. As in Punjab/Haryana, it is not the eagerness of the small cultivators to profit from the new technology that is in question, but their ability to do so. To afford a filter point or tubewell is to control water supply better and to achieve some independence from the monsoons—this is much easier for the large farmers.

Although Gough notes increasing doubts about the HYV in 1976, the district's total rice production increased.[20] Most of this was due to double-cropping and intensification rather than extension of cultivation. There has also been a diversification of production.[21] Further, between 1951 and 1974 the number of tractors in Thanjavur increased at a simple annual growth rate of 212 percent, oil engines by 73 percent, and electric pumps by 178 percent. As would be expected, much of this increase is accounted for by larger farmers.

The riskiness and difficulties of HYV rice cultivation have compounded the basic "finance intensity" of the new technology. Hence it is more difficult for smaller farmers to profit from the new technology in Thanjavur than in Haryana/Punjab. This is partly reflected in the fact that the lower 60 percent of rural households in Tamilnadu actually suffered a decline in the average value of their total assets between 1961-62 and 1971-72.[22] (In Haryana and Punjab, there was an increase in average asset holdings even by the lowest decile of rural households.) Coupled with large-scale tenant evictions, and a big increase in the absolute and relative size of the agricultural laborer population, the difficulties faced by small farmers indicate a more "classic" case of proletarianization than in Haryana. That is, the smaller farmers are unable to adopt the new technology adequately, are being dispossessed of land, and are being reduced to the ranks of agricultural laborers.

As a result, growing numbers of women from non-Brahman families who previously worked only on family farms are being forced to work as coolies after their family land is alienated. This tendency toward the loss of land has shown up in the decline in women cultivators as a proportion of women agriculturists between 1950-51 and 1970-71.[23]

Sexual Division of Agricultural Labor

The greatest changes in relations of production have occurred with respect to agricultural laborers. Rural slavery had turned into bonded labor (pannaiyal) by the late nineteenth and early twentieth centuries (Gough 1977a). This happened as private property in land replaced the prebendal system by which slaves and land were allocated by the kings to members of the nobility and the caste hierarchy. The pannaiyal was generally tied to the landowner by debt

rather than hereditary servitude, though in practice many remained
tied to the same family for generations. They were often given
small plots to till, and were paid a daily quota of paddy (unhusked
rice), plus other food, clothes, and other goods, plus some grain
at harvest time. Usually wife, husband, and children could all be
called to fieldwork, animal care, and domestic chores. They were
generally rehired at the beginning of each year unless the landowner
dismissed them by liquidating their debt.

A group of casual day laborers (coolies) had also emerged by
the end of the nineteenth century. The nineteenth century in Thanjavur saw the district's integration into the British colonial economy
as an exporter of rice and of plantation labor to Ceylon and Malaya.
This had been accompanied by the increasing appropriation of land
as private property, and by the consequent breakdown of the social
structure of mutual rights that guaranteed a subsistence, however
meager, to the rural slaves. The coolies emerged from this process bereft of any systematic guarantee of survival, and dependent
on such work as they could find at daily wages that were increasingly paid in cash. The process was accelerated after 1930, when the
demand for plantation labor declined.

The living conditions of the coolies were so miserable that,
at a time when Thanjavur was exporting rice, they were often reduced to eating field rats and carrion as their only source of protein.
The more steady guarantee of employment and subsistence made the
position of bonded laborer a relatively enviable one, a phenomenon
that persists today. However, the proportion of bonded laborers
has declined over time. Table 2.8 shows the steady process of proletarianization in the rural areas. Not only did the agricultural
labor force grow in absolute and relative terms between 1951 and
1971, but the proportion of casual laborers increased sharply. [24]
This phenomenon must be attributed to the eviction of small tenants
and the increased mechanization that has come with the new technology.

In addition to casual coolies, bonded labor has been giving way
to a small group of regular coolies (who may own bullocks and implements) who are wage workers typically employed by a single employer for the year. This group of permanent farm servants is most
akin to the naukars (permanent laborers) in Haryana. However,
while in the most advanced regions of Haryana naukars tend to predominate, in Thanjavur they form a small proportion of all agricultural laborers.

The relative surplus reserve of casual coolies acts to depress
wage rates despite the successes of the Communists in organizing
labor, especially in eastern Thanjavur. In 1948 militancy among
laborers was evident in struggles with the landowners. Although,

for a number of reasons, including repression by the state government, there was a lull in activity between 1957 and 1967, there was renewed militancy coupled with landowner violence from 1968 on. Perhaps as a result, the incomes of bonded laborers and regular coolies have not declined. Furthermore, some of the old customs by which bonded laborers were subordinated (beatings or forced drinking of cow dung mixed with water as punishment) have almost disappeared. There is greater political awareness and pride among the workers. However, the living conditions of casual coolies have deteriorated, mainly because of the inadequacy of employment. Many of them find work for only one-third of the year, and even at harvest time there is a surplus of laborers, including migrants from surrounding districts. In this case the workers have been known to share work and wages among themselves. Although certain public amenities like street lights and drinking water have been provided by the government, the general consumption standards (especially food) of the casual coolies have declined.

For women members of the agricultural labor class, the existence and growth of a large relative surplus population in agriculture has meant that they tend to be pushed out of work. In fact, Gough suggests that "There is now so much surplus population in agriculture, that male coolies are sometimes hired to do work traditionally done by women." The decline of bonded labor has had a major impact on this. Whereas previously the entire family— woman, man, and children—was engaged to work, nowadays both regular and casual coolies are hired independently. For women the decline in the pannaiyal relation has meant a decline in certain useful perquisites, such as medicine during childbirth and clothing. Further, fuel, wood, and other items that could previously be collected from the waste land now must be purchased or collected from land farther away, involving more labor, time, and effort. In terms of the amount of employment available to women, it would seem that both the narrowing of the range of tasks done by women (as a consequence of mechanization) and the relatively large surplus army of labor work in the same direction. toward a reduction in women's employment. This is different from Haryana, where, as was seen, women's tasks have become more narrow, but the tightness of the labor market works to provide women with employment.

Turning to wage rates, we find that the wage rates for male tasks are generally higher than the wage rates for female tasks. In 1976, on the average, most male agricultural laborers were paid Rs. 6 per day while women were paid between Rs. 3.50 and Rs. 4 (Gough 1977a). [25] It is obvious that higher wage rates have little to do with a higher requirement of skill or effort. It is well known, for instance, that transplanting paddy seedlings requires great skill,

as well as being the most backbreaking and onerous of all tasks in
wet paddy cultivation. It is invariably women's work and is relatively low-paid. Although customarily there has been a wage differential, I would argue that its impact on women laborers is harsh-
er now. Although the woman from the bonded pannaiyal household
was paid less than the man (except at harvest time), she was able
to ensure a steady subsistence for herself and her children through
her connection to the male member of the household. Casual laborers, on the other hand, are hired independently and regardless of
which other household members can obtain work.

Thus, lower wage rates for women at a time when casual
labor has become the order of the day means greater hardship and
a more meager subsistence, especially for widowed or otherwise
single women. That is, lower wage rates paid to women of bonded
laborer households have potentially a less harsh impact (so far as
subsistence consumption is concerned) than lower wage rates paid
to women hired independently as casual laborers. This problem is
exacerbated by the relatively lower number of days worked by women
laborers now than in the past. [26]

Let us sum up the effects of the Green Revolution on women's
labor force participation and conditions of work in Thanjavur. First
of all, the eviction of small tenants and the greater difficulties of
small farmers in adopting the HYV technology have led to more non-
Brahman women working as casual wage laborers to add to household income from labor. Second, the overall surplus of laborers,
exacerbated by the new technology, has meant that women no longer
do some of their traditional tasks. In addition, there appears to
have been a tendency for their employment to decline overall (Gough
1982).

A final but important point has to be made. In Thanjavur,
where militancy among poor tenants and landless laborers has been
fairly high, women workers have been quite articulate in demanding
their rights. In 1968, at a high point of the struggle, women workers were at the forefront. In the village of Puducheri in eastern
Thanjavur, women laborers were very militant in trying to prevent
landowners from using scab labor at harvest time. For this, 42
women were arrested and jailed. In the village of Kilvenmani some
months later, after struggles between landowners and laborers, 44
women, children, and old men were surrounded in a hut and burned
to death by the landowners (Sivaraman 1973). Thus women workers
both suffer and organize against their oppression.

CONCLUSION

We have tried to argue in this chapter that the effects of the
intensification of capitalist agriculture (via the Green Revolution)

on women's work in two regions of India exhibit both similarities and differences. The similarities arise from the fact that the basic forces of change are the same in both cases: the decline in absentee landowners, the consolidation of land by rich farmer cultivators, the growing insecurity of small tenants, and tenant switching* as a result of land reform legislation. These factors altered the patterns of landholding and broke down many of the preexisting ties that simultaneously bound smaller tenants to landowners and gave to the former some guarantee of year-round subsistence. However, land reform did not of itself alter the direct relations of production, since tenants continued to farm land and pay sharecropping rents. In many cases rent was now paid to a rich farmer who supervised or otherwise took an interest in cultivation, or may even have begun some cultivation directly with wage labor, though this was not a major trend.

The introduction of the HYV technology led to changes in the relations of production as wage labor came to replace both sharecropping tenancy and previous forms of bonded labor. In addition, the conditions of economic survival of farmers were altered drastically by the growing "finance intensity" of cultivation, the riskiness of the new crops, and the difficulty in access to land. These factors became especially critical for smaller farmers·in both regions. However, differences in the prior patterns of landholding and landlessness, and the distinctions between the technological constraints imposed by HYV wheat and rice, have been translated into differing patterns of pauperization and proletarianization in the two regions.

In Thanjavur what we might call the "classic" pattern of proletarianization has prevailed. Despite their willingness to be innovative with the new technology, the risks involved in adopting and double-cropping the HYV rice have cast doubt on the economic viability of smaller farmers. In addition, a large number of tenant evictions have occurred. Given the preexisting large numbers of small tenants and landless laborers, there have been very large absolute and relative increases in the ranks of agricultural laborers. While some regular coolies are employed year-round on the large farms, this has not been sufficient to offset the absolute growth in landless labor, resulting in a sharp increase in the proportion of casual to regular laborers.

In Haryana/Punjab the pattern of proletarianization is more complex. Starting from a situation of large numbers of medium-

---

*Switching from one tenant to another on the same plot so that the tenant does not gain long-term rights.

level owner-cultivators, few absentee landlords, and few landless laborers, the new technology in wheat decreased, if only temporarily, the size of the economically viable farm and made possible subdivision of medium and larger holdings.[27] Thus, while some tenants were evicted and lost land, the downward shift in the acreage structure seems to have been substantially due to farm subdivision. Hence, there has not been as rapid a swelling of the ranks of landless laborers as in Thanjavur. Rather, there is a continuous complaint among landowners about labor shortages, especially at harvest time, despite in-migration of labor from other districts. (In contrast, complaints by landowners in Thanjavur are not about labor shortage but about labor militancy.) As a result the ratio of permanent to regular casual laborers is higher in the more advanced regions within Haryana, as has been seen.

These similarities and differences in the patterns of proletarianization and the conditions of small farmers affect the participation of women in wage labor and women's place in the hierarchy of laborers in the two regions. In Haryana the decline in acreage structure and the growth of smaller farms have meant that women of small farm households are working as casual laborers to augment household income from cultivation. In Thanjavur, on the other hand, the eviction of small tenants has led to more non-Brahman women working as casual laborers in order to add to household income from labor. In Haryana the overall shortage of labor, especially at harvest time, has meant that while the range of tasks performed by women has narrowed as a result of the new technology, women have not been pushed entirely out of the ranks of agricultural laborers. Rather, they have settled as casual laborers at the lower end of the hierarchy of permanent and casual laborers. In Thanjavur the overall surplus of laborers has meant that women no longer do some of their traditional tasks, and there has been a tendency for their employment to decline overall.

Thus, despite the traditional differences in women's participation in agricultural work in the two regions, the processes of change engendered by the Green Revolution have had many similar effects, not only in the willingness of women from small farm households to participate in agricultural wage labor, but also in the actual conditions of labor. The differences lie in the kind of contribution that women's wage employment makes to the small farming household, and in the extent to which a reserve of unemployed laborers acts to push women out of employment.

As mentioned at the outset, the analysis needs to go further, to explore the effects of agrarian change on women's position within rural households. Are relations of subordination eased or strengthened by women's participation in wage labor? Do women workers become more or less dependent on male household members? Does this vary by class for different rural households? How is it affected by worker and small peasant organization? by women's militancy? How does women's participation in wage labor affect the sexual division of labor within the home in tasks such as cooking, cleaning, and child care? Such studies are both extremely necessary and only just beginning in India.

NOTES

1. It may seem a little odd to compare two states—Haryana and Punjab—with Thanjavur, which is a district within the state of Tamilnadu. However, work on women in the context of changing land relations is still very rare in India, and so we have had to piece together such information, based on secondary and tertiary sources, as is available. Our major data sources have been the work of Gough in Thanjavur and S. Bhalla in Haryana. Hopefully, some interesting hypotheses regarding the impact of change on women workers will emerge from this. We should also point out that the paucity of relevant time-series data forces us to use cross-sectional variation across regions within Haryana as a proxy for change over time (with all of the well-known problems and cautions). For Thanjavur, Gough's fieldwork in 1951-52 and 1975-76 provides an indication of variation over time.

2. In 1960-61, after approximately a decade of land reform, 72 percent of landowning households, each owning less than five acres, accounted for only 20 percent of total owned area. The average size of owned holding was 4.98 acres (Minhas 1974). Similarly, 73 percent of rural households operating less than five acres each accounted for 19 percent of total operated area (Patnaik 1975).

3. The shift in government policy can be seen as a product of growing concern over the adequacy of food production, and an acknowledgment of the power base of the Congress party in the rural areas.

4. The former state of Punjab was divided into the states of Punjab and Haryana in 1966. The average size of operational holding was 9.5 acres in Haryana, 7.2 acres in Punjab, and 3.6 acres in Tamilnadu, compared with an all-India average of 5.8 acres (All-India Report on Agricultural Census 1970-71).

5. The area under owner occupancy in the Punjab increased from 51.4 percent in 1947 to 66.4 percent in 1957 and to 80.9 percent in 1969-70 (Dasgupta 1977a).

6. One explanation given for the higher sex ratio (defined as the number of women in a population per 1,000 men) in Tamilnadu

is the higher participation by women in the labor force (Bardhan 1974). Although this explanation is quite appealing, in that it suggests that women's importance in agricultural work has a very material impact on their nutritional and mortality standards, it does not quite explain the fact that the sex ratio among small cultivator and agricultural labor households is lower in Tamilnadu than in Haryana, although Punjab is uniformly the lowest of all. (See table below.)

Sex Ratios of the Rural Population, 1970-71
(number of females per 1,000 males)

	Haryana	Punjab	Tamilnadu
Rural areas	870	868	990
Small cultivator households	975	880	956
Rural labor households	924	816	828

Source: Visaria and Visaria 1973.

7. The proportion of females to total agricultural workers (which by census definition includes both cultivators and laborers) is not a reliable estimate for the actual amount of involvement in agricultural work, whether manual or supervisory. One of the effects of land reform legislation has been to increase on paper the number of female cultivators, since women family members were registered as landholders in order to avoid ceilings on landholding. The proportion of women among agricultural laborers does not suffer from this defect, but it excludes work done by women on family farms.

8. Our analysis for poor peasant households in this region is derived from G. S. Bhalla (1974) and from S. Bhalla (1976; 1977a; 1977b; 1979). Haryana is divided in their analyses into three main regions—North, Center, South—in decreasing order of importance of the Green Revolution technology.

9. Between 1961 and 1971, S. Bhalla's (1977a) survey for Haryana showed that the percent of cultivating households in the very small (0.005-2.5 acres) group increased from 6 percent to 27 percent, while the percent in the next size group (2.5-5 acres) increased from 10 percent to 19 percent.

10. Between 1961-62 and 1971-72 the average money value of assets increased for all deciles of rural households in Haryana, and for all but the lowest decile in Punjab; for Tamilnadu the asset position of the lower 60 percent of rural households worsened. In

all three cases, however, the concentration ratios of asset holding increased. Among all Indian states Tamilnadu had the highest inequality in both years. Punjab and Haryana, which ranked fifth in descending order of inequality in 1961-62, ranked second in 1971-72 (Pathak, Ganapathy, and Sarma 1977).

11. The renting/purchase of small plots by previously landless households cannot be attributed to the declining size of the economically viable farm, since all such purchases in the 0-5 acre group occurred in non-Green Revolution backward regions (see S. Bhalla 1977a, Table 15). Resumption of land by bigger farmers for self-cultivation occurred in the more progressive areas.

12. In 1971-72 farms above ten acres (operational holding) accounted for 56.7 percent of leased area in Punjab and 59.4 percent in Haryana (Laxminarayan and Tyagi 1977).

13. The permanent laborer is defined as one who has an annual or longer-term contract. The casual laborer is one who is hired on a daily basis. There are two types of casual agricultural laborers: the regular casual laborers, whose main occupation is agricultural labor, and the seasonal casual laborers, who work some days in the fields, especially during harvest time, but whose main occupation is not agricultural labor.

14. Cross-sectional comparison in Haryana shows that in the most progressive areas, the ratio was 49 percent permanent to 51 percent regular casual (ignoring the seasonal casual laborers) in 1972-73. For male laborers alone, the ratio was 57 percent permanent to 43 percent regular casual. In the next most advanced region the ratios were 25 percent permanent to 75 percent casual for all laborers, and 30 percent permanent to 70 percent casual for males alone. In the most backward region the ratios were only 8 percent permanent to 92 percent regular casual for all laborers, and 9 percent permanent to 91 percent regular casual for males alone (S. Bhalla 1976).

15. In the most advanced Green Revolution area at harvest time, about 72 percent of female laborers are seasonal casual laborers. Of the rest, 27 percent are regular casual laborers and 1 percent are permanent laborers. This must be contrasted with the fact that 57 percent of male laborers (permanent plus regular casual) are permanent in this region (S. Bhalla 1976).

16. See note 6 and Table 2.1.

17. In Thanjavur irrigated area was 79 percent of gross cropped area for all crops and 96 percent for paddy in 1961-62 (Kurien 1978).

18. In an intensive study of a village in Thanjavur, Gough (1977d) found that Brahmans owned only 30 percent of the land in 1976, as opposed to 57 percent in 1952. Non-Brahmans owned 50

percent in 1976, as against 36 percent in 1952, and Harijans increased their ownership of land from 0.2 percent to 3.2 percent.

19. In Gough's village 42 percent of the land was under tenancy. This consisted of 20 percent under noncultivating tenants, 17 percent under cultivating tenants with documents legalizing their tenancy, and 10 percent under cultivating tenants without documents; about 5 percent of the land is being leased twice, first to a noncultivating tenant and then to a cultivating tenant (Gough 1977d). This last category, cultivating tenants who have been unable to obtain documents legalizing their tenure despite reform legislation, constituted 28 percent of the male agricultural work force (cultivators plus laborers) in 1952, but only 15 percent in 1976. On the other hand, documented tenant cultivators, many of whom are doubtless larger tenants, had risen to 10 percent of the male agricultural work force in 1976.

20. Thanjavur's rice production grew by 164 percent between 1950-51 and 1973-74 (Kurien 1978).

21. Paddy accounted for only 70 percent of total cropped area in 1972-73, as against 79 percent in 1961-62 in Thanjavur (Kurien 1978).

22. See note 12.

23. Women cultivators were only 14.7 percent of women agriculturists in 1970-71, as against 47.5 percent in 1950-51.

24. In Gough's village, agricultural laborers grew from 52 percent of the male agricultural work force in 1952 to 65 percent in 1976, while coolies (casual laborers) alone went from 21 percent to 49 percent (Gough 1977d).

25. In 1975-76, in Gough's village, the wage rates for different tasks were as follows: Rs. 8-Rs. 11 per day for plowing and carting with worker's bullocks; Rs. 5 for plowing and carting with the landowner's bullocks; Rs. 4-Rs. 5 for sowing and plucking seedlings (the above, except for sowing, are mainly male tasks); Rs. 3-Rs. 4 for transplanting; Rs. 2-Rs. 3 for weeding; and the paddy equivalent of Rs. 6 for harvesting and threshing (these are female tasks, save for harvesting, which is done by both men and women). Bonded laborers, both male and female, were paid about 15 pounds of paddy as harvest wages, but the wages paid per day for men and women varied for most other agricultural operations—5 pounds per day for men, and 2.5 pounds per day for women (Gough 1977a).

26. Some data for two villages can be found in Gough (1982).

27. Further analysis of the conditions of reproduction of medium farms is necessary if we are to understand precisely why subdivision actually occurred once it became possible.

REFERENCES

All-India Report on Agricultural Census. 1970-71. New Delhi:
Government of India, Department of Agriculture.

Appu, P. S. 1975. "Tenancy Reform in India." Economic and
Political Weekly (EPW), August. (Special number):1339-75.

Bardhan, K. 1977. "Rural Employment, Wages and Labour Markets in India—A Survey of Research." EPW, June 25:A34-48.

Bardhan, P. 1974. "On Life and Death Questions." EPW, August.
(Special number):1293-1304.

_____. 1976. "Variations in Extent and Forms of Agricultural
Tenancy—Analysis of Indian Data Across Regions and over
Time." EPW, September 11 and 18:1505-12, 1541-22.

Beteille, A. 1974. "Agrarian Relations in Tanjore District." In
A. Beteille (ed.), Studies in Agrarian Social Structure. New
Delhi: Oxford University Press, pp. 142-70.

Bhalla, G. S. 1974. Changing Agrarian Structure in India. New
Delhi: Meenakshi Prakashan.

Bhalla, S. 1976. "New Relations of Production in Haryana Agriculture." EPW, March 27:A23-30.

_____. 1977a. "Changes in Acreage and Tenure Structure of Land
Holdings in Haryana, 1962-72." EPW, March 26:A2-15.

_____. 1977b. "Agricultural Growth: Role of Institutional and
Infrastructural Factors." EPW, November 5 and 12:1898-1905.

_____. 1979. "Real Wage Rates of Agricultural Labourers in
Punjab, 1961-77." EPW, June 30:A57-68.

Billings, M. H., and A. Singh. 1969. "Labour and the Green
Revolution—The Experience in Punjab." EPW, December 27:
A221-24.

_____. 1970a. "Mechanization and Rural Employment." EPW,
June 27:A61-72.

_____. 1970b. "Mechanization and the Wheat Revolution—Effects on Female Labour in Punjab." EPW, December 26:A169-74.

Chandan, A. 1979. "Victims of Green Revolution." EPW, June 23:1035.

Committee on the Status of Women in India. 1974. Towards Equality. New Delhi: Government of India.

Dantwala, M. L. 1978. "Future of Institutional Reform and Technological Change in Indian Agricultural Development." EPW, August. (Special number):1299-1306.

Dasgupta, B. 1977a. "India's Green Revolution." EPW, February. (Annual number):241-60.

_____. 1977b. Agrarian Change and the New Technology in India. Geneva: United Nations Research Institute for Social Development.

Frankel, F. 1971. India's Green Revolution—Economic Gains and Political Costs. Princeton: Princeton University Press.

Gough, K. 1977a. "Colonial Economics in Southeast India." EPW, March 26:541-56.

_____. 1977b. "The 'Green Revolution' in South India and North Vietnam." Social Scientist 6, August:pp. 48-64.

_____. 1977c. "Changing Agrarian Relations in Thanjavur, 1952-1976." Essays in Honour of A. Aiyappan, Kerala Sociological Review (special issue).

_____. 1977d. "Agrarian Change in Thanjavur." In K. S. Krishnaswamy et al. , eds. , Society and Change: Essays in Honour of Sachin Chaudhuri. Bombay: Oxford University Press.

_____. 1982. "Agricultural Labour in Thanjavur." In J. Mencher, ed. , The Anthropology of Peasantry. Bombay: Somaiya Publications Ltd. , pp. 275-89.

Gough, K. , and H. Sharma, eds. 1973. Imperialism and Revolution in South Asia. New York: Monthly Review Press:222-45.

Gulati, L. 1975a. "Female Work Participation—A Study of Interstate Differences." EPW, January 11:35-42.

_____. 1975b. "Occupational Distribution of Working Women—An Inter-state Comparison." EPW, October 25:1692-1704.

Joshi, P. C. 1975. Land Reforms in India. New Delhi: Allied Publishers.

Kurien, C. T. 1978. "Dynamics of Rural Transformation—A Study of Tamilnadu, 1950-1975." Madras: Madras Institute of Development Studies. (Mimeographed.)

Laxminarayan, H. 1977. "Changing Conditions of Agricultural Labourers." EPW, October 22:1817-20.

Laxminarayan, H., and S. S. Tyagi. 1977. "Inter-state Variations in Types of Tenancy." EPW, September 24:A77-82.

Manmohan Singh, H. K. 1979. "Population Pressure and Labour Absorbability in Agriculture and Related Activities—Analysis and Suggestions Based on Field Studies Conducted in Punjab." EPW, March 17:593-96.

Mencher, J. 1978. Agriculture and Social Structure in Tamil Nadu. New Delhi: Allied Publishers.

_____. n.d. "Women and Rice Cultivation in India." (Mimeographed.)

Minhas, B. S. 1974. "Rural Poverty, Land Distribution and Development Strategy: Facts and Policy." In P. Bardhan and T. N. Srinivasan, eds., Poverty and Income Distribution in India. Calcutta: Statistical Publishing Society, pp. 252-63.

Mukherjee, P. K. 1970. "Concentration Ratio of Operational Holdings." EPW, September 26:A97-100.

Omvedt, G. 1977. "Women and Rural Revolt in India." Social Scientist 6, nos. 1 and 2, August and September:3-18, 22-41.

Parthasarathy, G., and G. D. R. Rao. 1975. "Minimum Wages Legislation for Agricultural Labour—A Review." EPW, September 27:A76-88.

Pathak, R. P., K. R. Ganapathy, and Y. U. K. Sarma. 1977. "Shifts in Pattern of Asset-holdings of Rural Households, 1961-62 to 1971-72." EPW, March 19:507-17.

Patnaik, U. 1975. "Contribution to the Output and Marketed Surplus of Agricultural Products by Cultivating Groups in India, 1960-61." EPW, December 27:A90-100.

Rudra, A. 1978. "Organisation of Agriculture for Rural Development: The Indian Case." Cambridge Journal of Economics 2, no. 4, December:381-406.

Saini, G. R. 1976. "Green Revolution and the Distribution of Farm Incomes." EPW, March 27:A17-22.

Sen, C. Forthcoming. Essays on the Transformation of India's Agrarian Economy. New York: Garland.

Sinha, J. N. 1978. "Rural Employment Planning—Dimensions and Constraints." EPW, February. (Annual number):295-313.

Sivaraman, M. 1973. "Thanjavur: Rumblings of Class Struggle in Tamilnadu." In K. Gough and H. Sharma, eds., Imperialism and Revolution in South Asia. New York: Monthly Review Press, pp. 246-64.

Visaria, P., and L. Visaria. 1973. "Employment Planning for the Weaker Sections in Rural India." EPW, February. (Annual number):269-76.

3

PEASANT PRODUCTION, PROLETARIANIZATION, AND THE SEXUAL DIVISION OF LABOR IN THE ANDES

Carmen Diana Deere
Magdalena León de Leal

The sexual division of labor has long been considered a key variable in the analysis of women's subordination.[1] Yet the theoretical relationship between women's subordination and the division of labor not only remains a source of contention, but is clouded by considerable ambiguity in its specification. There has been insufficient discussion of the difference between two quite different propositions: the sexual division of labor as the basis of, as opposed to a manifestation of, women's subordinate position in concrete circumstances. Whereas the former implies that women are subordinated because of the sexual division of labor, the latter implies that the sexual division of labor reflects women's subordinated position within society.

The analytical ambiguity is partly due to a failure to specify clearly the aspects of human activity under consideration: the sexual division of labor in productive activities as opposed to the sexual division of labor between productive and reproductive activities. This distinction is of importance because the growing body of empirical work suggests that while the former is quite heterogeneous cross-culturally, the sexual division of labor in reproductive activities is most homogeneous.

In the vast majority of social groupings, women are responsible for the activities associated with human reproduction: the

The authors would like to thank the editor of this volume, Lourdes Benería, and several anonymous reviewers from the ILO for useful comments and support in the preparation of this chapter.

reproduction of labor power on a daily basis (domestic work or daily maintenance activities) and the reproduction of labor over time, or biological reproduction and child rearing (see Benería 1979). The sexual division of labor in productive activities, however, whether in peasant agricultural or artisan production, commerce or wage employment, appears to vary tremendously. In the case of agricultural production, Boserup's (1970) pioneering work illustrates the variation in female agricultural participation across continents and countries. This heterogeneity suggests that women's participation in productive activities can in no way be biologically determined. Moreover, Boserup clearly demonstrates how the sexual division of labor in agricultural production has been modified by changes in such factors as type of cultivation system and forms of property, as well as the introduction of new crops and technology. More recent research shows how women's productive work is affected by changes in the relations of production and how it varies according to the class position of different groups of women.[2] The variation in the sexual division of labor over time and across class groupings suggests that the division of labor by sex in productive activities is not just culturally determined, but is responsive to material conditions of production.

In this chapter we demonstrate the importance of taking into account material conditions in analyzing the sexual division of labor in productive activities by considering the process of development in agriculture in three Andean regions.[3] We analyze the effect of uneven development across these regions and of the process of social differentiation internal to each region on the sexual division of labor in peasant agricultural production and wage employment. We argue that an analysis of economic factors must be taken into account to explain the variation in the sexual division of labor within productive activities and between productive and reproductive activities. While we do not analyze the basis of women's subordination, we illustrate the manner in which the sexual division of labor in production tends to build upon women's subordinated position in the sphere of reproduction.

The three regions of the Andes that we study—Garcia Rovira and El Espinal in Colombia and Cajamarca in Peru—illustrate the uneven development of capitalism in Andean agriculture. Defining this development in terms of the prevalence of capitalist relations of production—the sale and purchase of labor power—we differentiate among the three regions in terms of the participation by peasant households in wage labor. Whereas in Garcia Rovira only 20 percent of the peasant households have at least one labor market participant residing in the household, 55 percent of the households in Cajamarca and 70 percent of the households in El Espinal have labor market participants. On this basis we characterize Garcia Rovira as a region of noncapitalist relations, Cajamarca as a region of predominantly capitalist relations, and El Espinal as a region of advanced capitalist relations of production.

The region of Garcia Rovira, located in the northeastern Colombian highlands in the department of Santander del Sur, is characterized by the predominance of smallholder agriculture. While the majority of peasant households are independent producers, sharecropping is common in the region. Tobacco constitutes the principal cash crop, and most households also raise animals and produce subsistence food crops such as corn and beans. The development of the labor market in the region is incipient; traditional, reciprocal labor exchanges among peasants still constitute the primary form of labor procurement. Nonetheless, since at least the turn of the century, the area has provided both temporary and permanent migrants to other regions of Colombia and, more recently, to Venezuela. We characterize Garcia Rovira as noncapitalist because noncapitalist relations of production predominate in rural social relations. Nonetheless, it must be kept in mind that this area is joined to the national economy as a source of labor.

El Espinal, located in the central lowlands of the Magdalena River in the department of Tolima, is among the regions of Colombia that has experienced the most rapid development since the 1950s. It has a well-developed rural labor market and highly capitalized agricultural enterprises, as well as a medium and rich peasant sector, producing cotton, rice, and sesame for the national market. At the turn of the century, this region was characterized by large cattle haciendas where servile relations of production prevailed. The development of agricultural farms and of a rural proletariat was related to the period of import-substitution industrialization and the growth of the Colombian internal market, which stimulated the entrance of national capital into local agriculture. A rural proletariat was directly created through the expulsion of the peasantry from the haciendas and indirectly through the concentration of the remaining peasantry on the least productive land. We characterize this area as advanced capitalist because wage labor or capitalist relations of production dominate rural relations. This area is integrated into the national economy as a producer of agricultural commodities.

The province of Cajamarca, located in the northern Peruvian highlands in the department of the same name, is characterized by the coexistence of modern dairy enterprises alongside a numerically significant smallholder sector. The hacienda system dominated this region until the 1950s. The entrance of foreign capital into the area, in the form of a milk processing plant, stimulated the conversion from agricultural crop to dairy cattle production on the haciendas, as well as their breakup and transformation into capitalist enterprises. An independent peasant sector was re-created through the land sales resulting from the breakup of many of the haciendas. However, the majority of independent producers had access to insufficient land to produce their subsistence requirements, which compelled them to seek wage employment. Today the local labor market is well developed, and capitalist relations of production are increasingly predominant within the peasantry. We thus characterize this area as predominantly capitalist. Cajamarca features aspects of both forms of integration to the national economy found in the Colombian regions—in this case, integration into the Peruvian social formation through the production of luxury commodities, and the provision of cheap labor. [4]

This chapter draws on sample survey data as well as on data collected through participant observation in each of the three Andean regions. [5] The first section considers the sexual division of labor in peasant agricultural production. The range of agricultural activities in which women participate is first analyzed, and then a more detailed analysis of the sexual composition of the agricultural labor force in fieldwork activities is presented. It is shown that the sexual division of labor in agricultural production varies among regions, but particularly according to the process of social differentiation among peasant households. In the subsequent section, unequal access to the means of production among peasant households is related to the process of proletarianization and differential labor market participation by sex. The insights to be drawn from a comparative analysis of the process of development in agriculture for the sexual division of labor and for women's continued subordination are summarized in the concluding section.

THE SEXUAL DIVISION OF LABOR IN PEASANT AGRICULTURAL PRODUCTION

In this section we first consider the range of agricultural activities in which women in the three Andean regions commonly engage. We then focus on the sexual composition of the labor force in agricultural fieldwork. It is shown that the division of labor by sex varies according to the specific agricultural task, the form of labor procurement, and, most important in the case of the familial agricultural labor force, according to the household's class position.

The Range of Female Participation in Agricultural Activities

Participation in agricultural production is traditionally con-
ceptualized in terms of performance of tasks associated with agricultural fieldwork. While our subsequent analysis of the sexual
division of labor also focuses on this more restricted definition of
what constitutes agricultural work, it is important that we first
draw attention to the myriad activities encompassed in a broader
conceptualization of agricultural production. A broad definition
must include all of the activities connected with both crop and animal
production, irrespective of whether the final products constitute
use values for the family's consumption (subsistence production) or
exchange values sold on the market (commodity production). The
activities associated with crop production include the production of
the means of production (such as making or repairing tools and
infrastructure improvements on the land, as well as the collection
of inputs, such as fertilizer); the tasks associated with fieldwork;
personal services associated with fieldwork, such as cooking for
field hands; agricultural product transformation or processing
tasks; the tasks involved in transporting, storing, and marketing
the harvest; and the myriad tasks associated with organizing agricultural work and decision making (such as procuring labor and
draft animals). Among the activities associated with animal production are feeding and grazing, attention to health care, animal
by-product activities (milking, shearing, gathering eggs), transformation activities (skinning the hides, cleaning wool, butchering,
and marketing).

The importance of taking into account a broad definition of
the activities encompassed within agricultural production among
the peasantry results from the fact that the sexual division of labor
may vary among the component tasks. The extent of the bias in
the measurement effort depends on the degree of specialization
according to gender as well as on the extent to which predominantly
male or female activities are excluded. Table 3.1 presents data
on how common it is for at least one woman within the peasant
household to participate in each of five agriculture-related activities for which comparable data are available for the three regions.
The measure of participation according to the incidence of female
participation in an activity within the peasant household allows us
to demonstrate the variation in women's involvement in different
agricultural tasks and the importance of a broad definition of agricultural work.

TABLE 3.1

Percentage of Households Where at Least One Woman
Participates in Agricultural Activity

Activity	Garcia Rovira (noncapitalist)	El Espinal (advanced capitalist)	Cajamarca (predominantly capitalist)
Agricultural field work[a]	18 (n=123)	25 (n=130)	85 (n=93)
Agricultural processing[b]	53 (n=104)	33 (n=86)	100 (n=105)
Agricultural services[c]	95 (n=138)	33 (n=27)	61 (n=93)
Animal care[d]	88 (n=121)	45 (n=32)	95 (n=92)
Marketing[e]	24 (n=132)	40 (n=139)	88 (n=77)
Weighted average, all activities	40 (n=114)	29 (n=94)	86 (n=92)

n = number of households where the activity is carried out.

[a]Includes field preparation, seedling preparation, planting, transplanting, weeding, cultivating, harvesting, and threshing.

[b]Data for Garcia Rovira and El Espinal are primarily for tobacco processing, although some corn and cotton processing activities are included. Data for Cajamarca include all processing activities, primarily for wheat, barley, and corn.

[c]Agricultural services consist primarily of cooking for field hands, although in Garcia Rovira and El Espinal other personal services may be included.

[d]Data for Garcia Rovira and El Espinal include mainly the care of large farm animals, whereas the Cajamarca data include the care of both large farm animals and the smaller "house" animals, such as chickens, cuyes (guinea pigs), and rabbits.

[e]Includes the marketing of both crops and animals.

Sources: Garcia Rovira and El Espinal: ACEP 1978 survey of municipalities of Enciso, Garcia Rovira and El Espinal, El Espinal. Cajamarca: 1976 Peasant Family Survey.

Table 3.1 shows that in Garcia Rovira, the noncapitalist Colombian region, at least one woman in the vast majority of households participates in animal care activities or in services related to agricultural production (mainly cooking for field hands). In half of the households women take part in agricultural processing activities during the year, principally tobacco processing. But in only 18 percent of all households do they participate in agricultural fieldwork, and in only slightly more do they market the goods produced on the farm.

The Colombian region of advanced capitalist development shows quite a different pattern. First, there is no one activity in El Espinal in which women in over half of all the households participate. But, in contrast with Garcia Rovira, the range of agricultural activities in which women engage in the households where they do participate is more evenly distributed. The most common activity for women is the marketing of agricultural products. In the few households that raise animals, women also commonly participate. Again agricultural fieldwork represents the most infrequent activity for women. This is in contrast with the predominantly capitalist Peruvian region of Cajamarca, where women are involved in all aspects of agricultural production. It is just about as frequent for women to participate in agricultural fieldwork as to be involved in animal care, the processing of agricultural products for sale or home consumption, and the marketing of farm products.

The most striking difference among the three regions concerns agricultural fieldwork. Whereas in Cajamarca almost all households have at least one woman engaged in fieldwork, female participation in the Colombian regions appears to be much more restricted.

Agricultural fieldwork by women is more common in the Colombian area of advanced capitalist development than in the noncapitalist region. Nevertheless, in these regions women are performing tasks related to direct field production in a large number of households. In both regions, for example, it is much more common for women to be involved in processing activities than in fieldwork. In Garcia Rovira the high number of households where women perform services for agricultural workers suggests that women's work by the cooking pots is complementary to men's work in the fields. The importance of taking into account a broad definition of agricultural work in order to measure women's participation in agriculture is certainly evident.

The analysis of the variation in women's participation by type of activity and region gives some insight into the nature of the sexual differentiation of work among the three regions. Garcia Rovira, the noncapitalist region, exhibits a much more rigid demarcation of what are considered male or female activities than do the other two regions. In the two areas that have undergone capitalist development, the sexual division of labor appears to be more flexible. However, these two areas differ considerably in terms of the magnitude of the incidence of women's participation in agricultural work. In the Colombian region of El Espinal, the low female involvement in all agricultural activities suggests that what must be explained is the difference between households where women participate in any agricultural activity and those where they do not. However, the high degree of female participation in all activities in the Peruvian region of Cajamarca suggests that cultural factors that distinguish the regions cannot be disregarded in explaining why women's agricultural involvement is more commonplace there. In order to explore these differences, we now turn to a more detailed analysis of the sexual division of labor in one activity, agricultural fieldwork.

The Sexual Composition of the Agricultural
Labor Force on Peasant Farms

The most accurate measure of the sexual division of labor is the sexual composition of the labor force engaged in an activity. This measure takes into account both participation rates (the proportion of men and women 13 years of age or over in the activity) and the relative amount of time dedicated by each sex to the activity. Table 3.2 shows that women contribute 21 percent of the total labor employed in agricultural fieldwork on peasant farms in the predominantly capitalist region of Cajamarca. The sexual composition of the labor force differs, however, according to the form of labor procurement. While women account for 25 percent of the total family labor employed in agricultural fieldwork, they constitute only 14 percent of the labor procured through reciprocal labor exchanges and 10 percent of the wage labor.

Women's participation is particularly important in harvesting and threshing tasks, where they constitute approximately one-third of total labor. It is for these activities that female wage workers are commonly employed and labor exchanges that include women are common. Nonetheless, the data show that women form an important component of the familial labor force for other agricultural field activities as well.

The Colombian data set distinguishes between permanent and temporary labor employed on the unit of production. As Table 3.3 shows, women provide only 5 percent of the temporary labor utilized on peasant farms in Garcia Rovira, the noncapitalist region,

TABLE 3.2

The Sexual Composition of Agricultural Labor Employed on 93 Peasant Farms, by Form of Labor Procurement, Cajamarca, Peru

(percent)

Tasks	Family Labor			Reciprocal Labor			Wage Labor			Total		
	Female	Male	Total	Female	Male	Total	Female	Male	Total	Female	Male	Total
Field preparation	14	86	100 (n=656)	11	89	100 (n=114)	1	99	100 (n=123)	12	88	100 (n=893)
Planting	25	75	100 (n=487)	8	92	100 (n=72)	2	98	100 (n=97)	20	80	100 (n=656)
Weeding	26	74	100 (n=1,071)	14	86	100 (n=261)	—	100	100 (n=183)	21	79	100 (n=1,515)
Cultivation	16	84	100 (n=294)	11	89	100 (n=71)	1	99	100 (n=65)	13	87	100 (n=430)
Harvest	36	64	100 (n=480)	18	82	100 (n=114)	33	67	100 (n=105)	33	67	100 (n=699)
Threshing	38	62	100 (n=349)	21	79	100 (n=92)	30	70	100 (n=93)	34	66	100 (n=534)
Total	25	75	100	14	86	100	10	90	100	21	79	100
n -	849	2,488	3,337	100	624	724	67	599	666	1,016	3,711	4,727

n = total labor days employed in the task.
Source: 1976 Cajamarca Peasant Family Survey.

73

TABLE 3.3

Sexual Composition of Temporary Labor Employed on Peasant Farms,
Paid and Unpaid, by Activity: Colombia
(percent)

	Paid[a]			Unpaid			Total		
	Women	Men	Total	Women	Men	Total	Women	Men	Total
	Garcia Rovira (noncapitalist)								
Plot preparation	1	99	100 (n=7,246)	3	97	100 (n=1,025)	1	99	100 (n=8,271)
Planting	1	99	100 (n=5,745)	20	80	100 (n=878)	4	96	100 (n=6,623)
Cultivation[b]	—	100	100 (n=10,999)	2	98	100 (n=1,958)	—	—	100 (n=12,957)
Harvest	4	96	100 (n=7,563)	32	68	100 (n=1,367)	8	92	100 (n=8,930)
Processing	14	86	100 (n=4,199)	45	55	100 (n=1,152)	21	79	100 (n=5,351)
Total (163 households)	3 (n=1,025)	97 (n=34,727)	100 (n=35,752)	19 (n=1,196)	81 (n=5,184)	100 (n=6,380)	5 (n=2,221)	95 (n=39,911)	100 (n=42,132)

74

								El Espinal (advanced capitalist)		
Plot preparation	3	97	100 (n=4,911)	14	86	100 (n=480)	4	96	100 (n=5,391)
Planting	4	96	100 (n=3,127)	35	65	100 (n=229)	7	93	100 (n=3,356)
Cultivation[b]	30	70	100 (n=11,711)	22	78	100 (n=3,238)	11	89	100 (n=14,949)
Harvest	29	71	100 (n=15,488)	28	72	100 (n=2,951)	29	71	100 (n=18,439)
Processing	49	51	100 (n=258)	69	31	100 (n=61)	53	47	100 (n=819)
Total (216 households)	16 (n=5,805)	84 (n=29,690)	100 (n=35,495)	25 (n=1,720)	75 (n=5,239)	100 (n=6,959)	18 (n=7,525)	82 (n=34,929)	100 (n=42,454)

n = total labor days employed in the task.

[a] Paid labor includes labor paid in cash or kind, and reciprocal labor exchange.

[b] The category "cultivation" includes weeding.

Sources: ACEP 1978 survey of municipalities of Enciso, Garcia Rovira, and El Espinal.

but 18 percent of the temporary labor in El Espinal. Women's participation in Garcia Rovira appears important only for processing activities, in which they provide 21 percent of the temporary labor requirements. In contrast, in El Espinal women constitute an important component of the labor force for processing as well as harvesting tasks.

In both regions, women's participation is relatively more significant among unpaid family workers than among paid labor, which includes labor remunerated in cash, in kind, or by labor exchange. In Garcia Rovira women constitute at least 20 percent of the familial labor in planting, harvesting, and processing tasks. In El Espinal they constitute at least 20 percent of the familial labor in all tasks associated with fieldwork except for plot preparation. The data point to the much more important role of women within the familial labor force in the region of advanced capitalist development, and once again suggest that the sexual division of labor in agricultural production in the noncapitalist region is more rigid, with women's involvement in crop production quite restricted.

In terms of the paid temporary labor force, the relations of production differ considerably between the two regions. Whereas the majority of temporary workers in Garcia Rovira are contracted through the reciprocal labor exchange, the majority of paid temporary workers in El Espinal are wage laborers.[6] Whereas few women appear among those who exchange labor in the noncapitalist region, relations of production in El Espinal have resulted in the employment of women. Women are an important component of the wage labor force in harvesting, processing, and cultivation, as Table 3.3 shows.

Although as detailed data are not available for the permanent labor employed in agricultural fieldwork on the Colombian farms, the composition of the permanent labor force follows a trend similar to that of temporary labor. Women constitute 15 percent of the permanent workers in Garcia Rovira and 20 percent in El Espinal. In both regions the overwhelming majority of female permanent workers on peasant farms are unpaid family members.[7]

In all three regions the data show that women participate in agricultural production to a much greater extent than implied by census estimates. Preliminary estimates for Colombia based on the 1973 census returns predict that women form only 3.4 percent of the agricultural economically active population. And in the 1972 Peruvian census, women constituted only 9.4 percent of the Peruvian economically active population in agricultural activities (ILO 1978, Table 2A).

Our survey data therefore suggest the degree to which women's participation within the agricultural labor force has been underestimated in the census (for a detailed analysis of the problems of the underenumeration of women in the agricultural labor force in Andean countries, see Deere and León de Leal 1981, ch. 1).

The data also indicate that the sexual division of labor varies by region, and within each region, according to the form of labor procurement. In terms of regional differences, the data show that women constitute a much more important component of the labor force employed in fieldwork in the regions with a higher proportion of wage labor than in the region where noncapitalist relations prevail. The variation in female participation by form of labor procurement indicates that women are much more important within the familial labor force than among the labor recruited from outside the household.

There is an important difference in female participation with respect to the relations of production. In Garcia Rovira, where noncapitalist relations predominate, few women are found among the labor force recruited through reciprocal labor exchanges. In contrast, in the regions where wage labor constitutes an important form of labor procurement, women are a significant component of the wage labor employed on peasant farms. This is particularly the case in the region of advanced capitalist development, lending weight to the proposition that the development of capitalist relations of production leads to a less rigid or delineated sexual division of labor in productive activities.

Thus far we have examined the quantitative aspect of the sexual division of labor without attention to its qualitative dimension. Attention to the labor process within agricultural field activities suggests that the sexual division of labor in many activities is a technical division of labor, taking place within the labor process itself. In Cajamarca, for example, during field preparation and planting, both men and women may participate in the same activity, but each usually performs separate tasks. Men always lead the team of oxen plowing the field, while women follow behind and shake soil free from the roots of weeds that are turned over. During planting, men lead the oxen making the furrow while women place the seed. In Garcia Rovira during the tobacco planting, both men and women may participate, but here again there is a technical division of labor. Men make the hole in the ground for the tobacco seedling with an iron cane, and the women put the plant in place. This complementarity in the labor process is also true in harvest activities. In the corn harvest in Cajamarca, women generally gather the corncobs while the men follow behind, cutting the corn plant with a sickle. In the grain harvest men wield the sickle, cutting the wheat or barley stalk, while either men or women gather the crop. Only men, however, load the burros and transport the crop to the threshing ground. In the threshing operation men manage the horses and thresh the grain, while the women sweep up the threshed grain with the help of the children.

A typical aspect of this technical division of labor is that the tasks carried out by women are considered to be much less important, by both men and women, than the tasks carried out by men. This is reflected in the way that both sexes often refer to women's participation in agricultural production as simply "helping out." But the tasks that women carry out when a technical division of labor is employed are certainly important to the production process. If they weren't carried out by women, they would have to be carried out by men—and often are.

It is important to consider the extent to which the undervaluation of female labor results from the sexual division of labor or merely reflects the general subordination of women. One indication of the sexual division of labor as possibly constituting the basis for women's subordination would be differential access to tools or technology. If women were excluded from participation in the tasks that required the use of implements on the basis of their biology, this would lend support to the argument that the technical division of labor places women in subordinate positions.

In Garcia Rovira it was noted that women rarely use agricultural implements; any tasks requiring tools are male-only activities (ACEP 1977a, p. 90). In contrast, in El Espinal, the region of advanced capitalist development, both women and men use the light hoe for weeding tasks as well as a small implement for harvesting sesame (ACEP 1977b, p. 72). But the heavy tools, such as the pick, shovel, and heavier hoe, are regarded as tools that only men can use, and thus the tasks that require their use are male tasks. In Cajamarca the broad range of female involvement in all agricultural tasks suggests that tools are not an impediment to women's work. Although many tasks are characterized by a technical division of labor based on gender, there are others in which both men and women participate and in which women are required to use tools. For example, both men and women cultivate and harvest potatoes with a short hoe. However, overall, women are less likely to engage in those tasks where tools or implements are utilized. And men and women do not consider themselves to work with equal productivity in the tasks that require implements, men being considered as more productive by both sexes (Deere 1978, ch. 6). However, the fact that women are not generally excluded from tasks that involve implements suggests that the technical division of labor cannot be the basis of women's subordination, although it probably serves to reinforce it. Rather, the undervaluation of female labor more likely reflects the general subordination of women.

Differentiation of the Peasantry and Agricultural
Division of Labor by Sex

If the process of development in these regions is to account
for differences in women's agricultural participation, we must go
beyond aggregate characterizations of the sexual division of labor in
each region. For if this process, as evidenced in changing material conditions of production, is to impact upon sex roles, we would
expect to find heterogeneity in the sexual division of labor among
different groups of direct producers according to their position in
the class structure. The starting point of the wage labor/capital
relation is unequal access to means of production. Insufficient
access to the means of production of subsistence is what compels
direct producers to sell their labor power for a wage. And access
to sufficient means of production beyond what the family labor force
can farm spurs the use of wage labor and allows incipient accumulation. This process of social differentiation among direct producers can thus be characterized in terms of unequal access to
means of production and the extent to which direct producers engage in wage labor.

In the three Andean regions access to land, the most important means of production, is quite unequal, as Table 3.4 shows. [8]
In all three regions the majority of households have access to less
than sufficient land to produce their full subsistence requirements.
In El Espinal, the region of advanced capitalist development, over
one-quarter of rural households are landless. Although landless
households were not included in the Peruvian sample, 13 percent
of Cajamarcan rural households can be considered nearly landless,
with access to less than one-quarter of a hectare of land. It is
important to note that it is particularly in El Espinal and Cajamarca,
the two regions that have witnessed rapid development in the second
half of the twentieth century, that the degree of differentiation is
acute. Here the middle and upper strata of the peasantry represent less than one-quarter of all peasant households. Only in the
noncapitalist Colombian region of Garcia Rovira does the middle
peasantry constitute an important component of rural households.

Table 3.5 shows that the sexual composition of the familial
labor force in agricultural fieldwork is closely related to the household's access to the means of production. In all three regions
women constitute a more important component of the familial agricultural labor force in households with less access to means of
production. The proportion of women declines as the household has
access to more land. The differential gender component of the
familial labor force suggests that women's participation in agricultural fieldwork is directly related to rural poverty. Women

TABLE 3.4

Social Differentiation of the Peasantry—Distribution of Survey Households
According to the Amount of Land Held in Usufruct
(percent)

	Garcia Rovira (noncapitalist)	El Espinal (advanced capitalist)		Cajamarca (predominantly capitalist)
I Landless households	5.5 (n=9)	28.7 (n=62)	I Nearly landless households (0.01–0.25 hectares)	13.3 (n=14)
II Smallholder households (0.01–3.0 hectares)	49.1 (n=80)	52.3 (n=113)	II Smallholder households (0.26–3.5 hectares)	63.8 (n=67)
III Middle peasant households (3.01–10.0 hectares)	38.0 (n=62)	13.0 (n=28)	III Middle peasant households (3.51–11.0 hectares)	18.1 (n=19)
IV Rich peasant households (10.01+ hectares)	7.4 (n=12)	6.0 (n=13)	IV Rich peasant households (11.01–100 hectares)	4.8 (n=5)
Total	100.0 (n=163)	100.0 (n=216)		100.0 (n=105)

Note: Land held in usufruct includes land held as private property as well as land procured through sharecropping or rental arrangements.

Sources: Garcia Rovira and El Espinal: ACEP 1978 survey of municipalities of Enciso, Garcia Rovira, and El Espinal; Cajamarca: 1976 Peasant Family Survey.

TABLE 3.5

The Sexual Composition of Familial Participants in Agricultural Fieldwork, by Size of Landholding (percent)

Land-Size Stratum	Garcia Rovira (noncapitalist)			El Espinal[a] (advanced capitalist)			Cajamarca[b] (predominantly capitalist)		
	Percent Female Participants	Percent Male Participants	Total Participants	Percent Female Participants	Percent Male Participants	Total Participants	Percent Female Participants	Percent Male Participants	Total Participants
Nearly landless households	—	—	—	—	—	—	35	65	100 (n=186)
Smallholder households	21	79	100 (n=1,214)	32	68	100 (n=1,486)	27	73	100 (n=2,093)
Middle peasant households	19	81	100 (n=976)	23	77	100 (n=478)	23	77	100 (n=682)
Rich peasant households	11	89	100 (n=124)	21	79	100 (n=121)	17	83	100 (n=375)
Total	20	80	100 (n=2,314)	29	71	100 (n=2,085)	25	75	100 (n=3,336)

[a]Participation is measured on the basis of those household members who always or sometimes participate in agricultural fieldwork; n = aggregate number of participants over all tasks.

[b]Participation is based on labor time contributed to agricultural fieldwork; n = total familial labor days employed on peasant units of production.

Sources: Garcia Rovira and El Espinal: ACEP 1978 survey of municipalities of Enciso, Garcia Rovira, and El Espinal; Cajamarca: 1976 Peasant Family Survey.

participate relatively more in agricultural fieldwork in those households without access to sufficient land to produce their full subsistence requirements from farm activities alone.

There are also important regional differences in the sexual composition of the agricultural labor force. Women's participation in agricultural fieldwork among the poor peasant strata is greater in El Espinal and Cajamarca than in the noncapitalist region of Garcia Rovira. Moreover, in the regions of capitalist development, the difference in women's participation between smallholders and middle peasants is notable; in Garcia Rovira this difference is attenuated. This suggests that an important effect of the process of capitalist development, as reflected in the differentiation of the peasantry, is to contribute to the breakdown of sex roles. The sexual division of labor in agricultural production becomes more flexible as the household loses access to the means of production of subsistence. We suggest that of utmost importance in this process are the effect of rural poverty, which requires all family members to participate in the productive process, and the effect of rural proletarianization.

RURAL PROLETARIANIZATION

The development of the rural labor market is the strongest indicator of the development of capitalism in agriculture, for capitalist relations of production are based on the sale and purchase of wage labor. In the previous section we noted that differential access to means of production in the rural areas has important repercussions for men's and women's work in agricultural production. In this section we consider how the process of social differentiation is reflected in the differing participation of men and women in wage labor.

The data on individual labor market participation rates for all household members over 13 years of age conform to our previous characterization of the degree of development in each of the three regions. As Table 3.6 demonstrates, El Espinal has the highest proportion of labor market participants of the three regions (35 percent), followed by Cajamarca (27 percent) and Garcia Rovira (8 percent).[9] Wage labor participation rates are, as expected, highly correlated with access to land: men and women of poor peasant households tend to participate more in the labor market than do individuals from middle and rich peasant households.[10]

Female participation rates in wage employment follow these overall trends. As shown in Table 3.6, women show the highest participation rate in wage labor in El Espinal (14 percent), followed

TABLE 3.6

Participation Rates in Wage Labor, by Sex—Household Members
13 Years of Age and over
(percent)

Landholding Size	Female	Male	Total
Garcia Rovira (noncapitalist)			
Landless households	20	27	23
	(n=15)	(n=15)	(n=30)
Smallholder households	7	14	11
	(n=126)	(n=137)	(n=263)
Middle peasant households	4	3	4
	(n=113)	(n=125)	(n=238)
Rich peasant households	—	7	4
	(n=20)	(n=27)	(n=47)
Total	6	10	8
	(n=274)	(n=304)	(n=578)
El Espinal (advanced capitalist)			
Landless households	22	82	52
	(n=99)	(n=96)	(n=195)
Smallholder households	14	56	35
	(n=215)	(n=218)	(n=433)
Middle peasant households	7	36	23
	(n=62)	(n=80)	(n=142)
Rich peasant households	4	19	11
	(n=29)	(n=26)	(n=55)
Total	14	56	35
	(n=465)	(n=420)	(n=825)
Cajamarca (predominantly capitalist)			
Nearly landless households	—	30	15
	(n=26)	(n=27)	(n=53)
Smallholder households	14	51	33
	(n=93)	(n=95)	(n=188)
Middle peasant households	3	33	18
	(n=29)	(n=27)	(n=56)
Rich peasant households	—	50	23
	(n=7)	(n=6)	(n=13)
Total	9	44	27
	(n=155)	(n=155)	(n–310)

Sources: Garcia Rovira and El Espinal: ACEP 1978 survey of municipalities of Enciso, Garcia Rovira, and El Espinal, El Espinal; Cajamarca: 1976 Peasant Family Survey.

Note: Cajamarca data based on household members aged 13-60 in 102 households; excludes 2 labor market participants under 13 years of age.

83

by Cajamarca (9 percent) and Garcia Rovira (6 percent). In all
three regions women from landless and smallholder households exhibit much higher participation rates than women from other strata.
In fact, the involvement of women from middle and rich peasant
households in the labor market is negligible. In all three regions
men's labor market participation rates exceed those for women, and
in El Espinal and Cajamarca, significantly so. The labor market
participation data suggest that the development of capitalism in rural
areas proletarianizes both men and women, but that male participation in wage labor is quantitatively more significant.

While female labor market participation appears to be posi-
tively related to the degree of development of a region, the relative
importance of women in the overall labor market shows the opposite
trend. Women form a more important component of labor market
participants where wage employment is least developed than where
the labor market is well developed. [11] In Garcia Rovira women
represent 51 percent of labor market participants, whereas in El
Espinal they constitute only 17 percent, and in Cajamarca, 18 percent. This implies that as wage employment first develops in the
rural areas, it is often geared to female occupations, such as
domestic or other personal services. However, as capitalist relations of production become more widespread, wage labor opportunities increasingly favor men.

The differential labor market opportunities for men and women
are illustrated in Table 3.7, which shows that only in El Espinal
are the vast majority of rural labor market participants employed
in the agricultural sector. In this region the rapid development of
commercial agricultural production in the 1950s and 1960s provided
increased employment opportunities to both men and women. However, a clear differentiation by sex is evident in the type of work
available, with the permanent employment opportunities in agriculture being filled by men, and women participating in agricultural
wage employment only during the period of greatest demand for
labor, generally the cotton harvest. The majority of women agricultural workers are employed for less than four months a year.
Recently the number of agricultural industries in the region has increased with the installation of cotton processing factories, rice
mills, and, most recently, a textile factory. These industries were
attracted by the proximity to the raw material and the abundant supply of labor. But only the textile industry has absorbed both male
and female labor.

In both Garcia Rovira and Cajamarca the labor market participants are rather evenly divided between the agricultural and nonagricultural sectors. However, there are important differences by
sex. Whereas the majority of women are employed in nonagricultural

TABLE 3.7

Labor Market Participants—Sector of Employment, by Sex
(percent)

	Agricultural Sector	Nonagricultural Sector	Total
Garcia Rovira (noncapitalist)			
Women	21	79	100 (n=14)
Men	77	23	100 (n=13)
Total	48	52	100 (n=27)
El Espinal (advanced capitalist)			
Women	68	32	100 (n=28)
Men	92	8	100 (n=137)
Total	88	12	100 (n=165)
Cajamarca (predominantly capitalist)			
Women	27	73	100 (n=15)
Men	51	49	100 (n=69)
Total	46	54	100 (n=84)

Note: The nonagricultural sector includes manufacturing, construction, and services.

Sources: Garcia Rovira and El Espinal: ACEP 1978 survey of municipalities of Enciso, Garcia Rovira, and El Espinal, El Espinal; Cajamarca: 1976 Peasant Family Survey.

work, the agricultural sector is relatively more important for men. By far the most important occupation for women in both regions is domestic service or employment as cooks or laundry workers.

In Cajamarca the development of dairy enterprises in rural areas has required minimal amounts of labor, although both men and women are among the permanent wage workers in this industry. The expansion of capitalist relations of production among the peasantry, however, has largely involved only males, which tends to explain why women form a relatively small component of rural wage earners. In Garcia Rovira few rural wage employment opportunities exist, and the little wage work available in agriculture is generally geared to men. Women who engage in wage work are generally employed in the service sector, although the few manufacturing industries that have developed in the area have employed women as a low-wage labor force. The main agricultural processing plant in the area, a tobacco selection and packing plant, also hires women during some five months out of the year. Nevertheless, the magnitude of employment offered in Garcia Rovira is minimal, and has been insufficient to stem the tide of male and female temporary or permanent migrants to other parts of Colombia and to Venezuela.

The subordinate position of women is reflected both in the type of employment available to them and in the relative remuneration for work performed. The type of employment open to women, particularly where wage labor is incipient, is that which represents an extension of the work that women do in the home—for example, domestic service. In our case studies the development of rural industries has drawn women into activities that they performed in the home: the tedious, repetitive, and labor-intensive tasks associated with tobacco processing and the textile industry.

The type of employment available to women is closely associated with low wages. To take the case of domestic service in Cajamarca, female wages for full-time work in this occupation are one-sixth of what full-time male unskilled labor earns on average.[12] In industrial employment segregation by sex at the work place allows women to be paid much less than men. This is the case in the tobacco processing industry of Garcia Rovira and in the textile industry in El Espinal, where both men and women are employed but the relegation of women to the labor-intensive, "low productivity" jobs seems to facilitate dual wage scales. In Cajamarca the modern dairy industry has been subject to increased minimum-wage regulation in recent years, a situation requiring that men and women be paid equal wages. Although the difference in the average wage paid to men and women in this industry has been attenuated as compared with other types of employment, the particular characteristics of of the milkmaid job—that milking takes place only four or five hours a day—has resulted in women being unable to earn a full day's wage.

The development of agricultural enterprises in El Espinal has provided new employment for women, but it is clear that they form a low-cost, rural labor reserve. On average, women earn 80 percent of what men earn for similar work. And during the harvest, the activity in which the greatest number of women are employed, remuneration is according to piecework. In order to earn a decent day's wage, a woman must usually take her children into the field, so that among all of them they gather sufficient cotton.

It is clear, therefore, that under capitalist relations of production, women are in a position different from that of men. We suggest that capitalism uses the subordination of women to its own advantage; the fact that women are subordinated is what allows the sex segregation of work and tasks, and a lower remuneration for work performed.

CONCLUSIONS

First, our analysis has demonstrated that the sexual division of labor in productive activities is extremely heterogeneous. The division of labor by sex in peasant agricultural production varies by region and according to the specific task, the form of labor procurement, and the household's class position.

Second, our analysis of the uneven development of capitalism in the three Andean regions suggests that there is no linear or determinate relationship between this process of development and the sexual division of labor in production. But certain tendencies are apparent that are closely associated with the process of social differentiation among direct producers. The greater participation of women in agricultural fieldwork in the two regions that have experienced rapid development, and the tendency for this participation to be concentrated among women from the poorer strata of the peasantry, strongly suggests that an important effect of capitalist development and attendant rural poverty is to contribute to a greater flexibility in the sexual division of labor in productive activities. The lesser degree of differentiation in the noncapitalist region, and the lower participation of women in agricultural fieldwork, suggest that the sex differentiation of tasks is much more rigid in this case. This is supported by the data on the sexual division of labor in all activities related to agricultural production that showed a clear demarcation of work according to sex.

Third, the process of development has different effects on different groups of rural men and women. This is clearly evident from the analysis of rural proletarianization. Decreasing access to the means of production compels both men and women from the poor peasant strata to sell their labor power. In contrast, women from the upper strata of the peasantry rarely engage in wage work.

Fourth, the development of the rural labor market presents quite different opportunities for men and women. We have shown that women are generally concentrated in certain occupations that are often extensions of their domestic work, and that they are relegated to low-wage jobs. We have argued, however, that the subordinated position of women in production is not derived solely from the characteristics of their employment but, rather, that the development of capitalist relations of production takes advantage of and reproduces the continuing subordination of women.

In sum, we have shown that material conditions are key in explaining the sexual division of labor in productive activities. Such factors as the social differentiation within a region, and the uneven process of development among regions, must be taken into account to explain variations in the division of labor in productive activities. We conclude that while women might be uniformly in charge of the activities geared to human reproduction, their participation in productive activities is in no way simply reflective of that role.

NOTES

1. The sexual division of labor has been the focus of both Marxist and non-Marxist analyses of women's position in society. The classic Marxist formulation is Engels 1972; see Sacks 1974 and Deere, Humphries, and León de Leal 1982 for a useful discussion of his work. Extensions of Engels' work to the analysis of capitalism are Benston 1969 and the domestic labor debate (for example, see Gardiner 1975). A current formulation of the problem is Benería 1979. For a review of much of the non-Marxist literature on the sexual division of labor, particularly in terms of women's role in the labor force, see Amsden 1979.

2. See Young 1978 for an excellent analysis of how the sexual division of labor in productive activities has varied with changing relations of production in Mexico. The effect of changing relations of production on the sexual division of labor on haciendas in twentieth-century Peru and Colombia is analyzed in Deere 1977 and León de Leal and Deere 1979. Stoler 1977 has clearly shown that in Indonesia the productive work of women varies according to their class position.

3. This paper draws upon material in the manuscript "Women in Agriculture: Peasant Production and Proletarianization in Three

Andean Regions," prepared as the final report under an external collaboration contract with the Programme on Rural Women, Employment and Development Department, ILO, March 1980. The comparative analysis of three regions of the Andes is based on our earlier work in Colombia and Peru. The Colombian data were gathered under the auspices of the Colombian Rural Women Study conducted by the Colombian Association of Population Studies (ACEP). This three-year, national-level study of rural women and agrarian change was funded by grants from the Ford Foundation and the Rockefeller Foundation, and was carried out under the direction of Magdalena León de Leal. Carmen Diana Deere was affiliated to the project as a collaborative researcher; the other researchers included Ingrid Cáceres, Clara González, Diana Medrano, and Lilian Motta de Correa. The Peruvian data were gathered as part of the dissertation fieldwork of Carmen Diana Deere, and were financed by fellowships from the Social Science Research Council and the Ford Foundation. The fieldwork in Cajamarca was hosted by the Socioeconomic Study Group of the Cajamarca-La Libertad Project, Ministerio de Alimentación, Cajamarca, which was under the direction of Ing. Efraín Franco.

4. For a more complete historical analysis of the two Colombian regions, see León de Leal and Deere 1979; Cáceres 1980; and Motta de Correa 1980. The Cajamarcan process is more fully described in Deere 1977 and 1978.

5. The Colombian survey of rural households was undertaken in the municipalities of Enciso, Garcia Rovira, and El Espinal, El Espinal, during April 1978; the data refer to the 1977 calendar year. The survey was designed as a representative sample survey of the agrarian structure. The municipal property registers served as the population for the selection of a stratified, random sample of land held in property. The methodology employed in the Colombian Rural Women Study is fully described in León de Leal and Deere 1980. The Peruvian sample survey, referenced as the 1976 Cajamarca Peasant Family Survey, was undertaken in the districts of Cajamarca, Jesús, and La Encañada in the province of Cajamarca, during June and July 1976; the data refer to the 1975-76 agricultural year. The Peasant Family Survey was designed as a follow-up survey to the 1973 Cajamarca Income Survey undertaken by the Socioeconomic Study Group of the Cajamarca-La Libertad Project. The Cajamarca Income Survey was a representative survey of peasant households, stratified according to land held in property, in 13 districts of the provinces of Cajamarca and Cajabamba, department of Cajamarca. The follow-up survey utilized the observations from the province of Cajamarca to draw a stratified random sample of peasant house-

holds. The methodology employed is detailed in Deere 1978, appendixes A and B.

6. Unfortunately, the form of labor procurement was not distinguished in the survey questionnaire. Our distinction between the two regions is based on field observation as well as on the data on the primary form of employment for household members who work outside their own farm.

7. The number of persons employed on a permanent basis in agricultural production on peasant farms differs significantly among the two Colombian regions. Whereas an estimated 1.8 permanent workers were reported per peasant farm in Garcia Rovira, only 0.9 was reported in El Espinal.

8. All three sample surveys were stratified random surveys based on rural property registers. In Colombia there was often more than one household residing on the land parcel that belonged to one owner. All households on the property were interviewed, and the stratification was based on the total amount of land held in usufruct by all the households. The 1976 Cajamarca Peasant Family Survey, as a follow-up survey to the 1973 Cajamarca Income Survey, included only property owners in the sample. Stratification was also based on the total amount of land usufructed by these households.

9. In the Colombian survey labor market participation was defined in terms of those household members residing in the household for over three months during the 1977 calendar year who were at least 13 years of age and who considered wage work or work for payment in kind to be their principal activity outside the household. There was no time limit on labor market employment for one to be considered a participant. In the Peruvian survey labor market participation was defined in terms of household members who generally resided in the household, were at least 13 years of age, and participated in wage employment at any point during the year or who worked for payment in kind for over 14 days during the year. A time limit was placed on work for payment in kind because this is a very common form of work in the region during the harvest period, and corresponds to cooperative work arrangements rather than to capitalist relations of production.

10. Data on the composition of household income also show the greater reliance of the lower peasant strata on the labor market for their livelihood. In Cajamarca wage income constitutes 56 percent of the mean net household income of nearly landless households and 49 percent of that of smallholders, whereas it represents only 24 percent of that of middle peasant households and 11 percent of that of rich peasant households (Deere 1978, p. 275).

11. Note that our data base allows us only to estimate the sexual composition of the labor market participants, and not of the rural labor force, since it is representative of peasant households (the supply of labor) and not of rural employers (the demand for labor). Only in the latter case would it be relevant to measure the sexual composition of the rural labor force, taking into account the length of employment. See Table 3.7 for the absolute numbers of men and women engaging in wage labor in each region.

12. See Deere and León de Leal 1981, ch. V, for a more detailed analysis of wages.

REFERENCES

ACEP. 1977a. "Informe de campo sobre la región de Garcia Rovira." Bogotá: ACEP, August. (Mimeographed.)

_____. 1977b. "Informe de campo sobre la región de El Espinal." Bogotá: ACEP, September. (Mimeographed.)

Amsden, Alice. 1979. "Introduction." In Alice Amsden, ed., The Economics of Women and Work. London: Penguin, pp. 11-38.

Benería, Lourdes. 1979. "Reproduction, Production and the Sexual Division of Labor." Cambridge Journal of Economics 3, no. 3 (September):203-25.

Benston, Margaret. 1969. "The Political Economy of Women's Liberation." Monthly Review 21, no. 4:13-37.

Boserup, Ester. 1970. Women's Role in Economic Development. London: George Allen and Unwin.

Bourque, Susan, and Kay Warren. 1978. "Perceiving the Sexual Division of Work: Economics and Subordination in Two Andean Communities." Paper presented to the Northeastern Council on Latin America meetings. Yale University, October.

Cáceres, Ingrid. 1980. "La división del trabajo por sexo en la Unidad Campesina Minifundista." In León de Leal, ed., Mujer y capitalismo agrario. Bogotá: ACEP, pp. 168-224.

Deere, Carmen Diana. 1977. "Changing Social Relations of Production and Peruvian Peasant Women's Work." Latin American Perspectives, nos. 12 and 13 (Winter-Spring):48-69.

_____. 1978. "The Development of Capitalism in Agriculture and the Division of Labor by Sex: A Study of the Northern Peruvian Sierra." Ph.D. dissertation, University of California, Berkeley.

Deere, Carmen Diana, Jane Humphries, and Magdalena León de Leal. 1982. "Class and Historical Analysis for the Study of Women and Economic Change." In R. Anker et al., eds., Women's Roles and Population Trends in the Third World. London: Croom Helm.

Deere, Carmen Diana, and Magdalena León de Leal. 1981. "Women in Agriculture: Peasant Production and Proletarianization in Three Andean Regions." Unpublished ILO study.

Engels, Friedrich. 1972. The Origin of the Family, Private Property and the State. New York: Pathfinder Press. (First published in 1884.)

Gardiner, Jean. 1975. "Women's Domestic Labour." New Left Review no. 89:47-58.

ILO. 1978. Yearbook of Labour Statistics. Geneva: ILO.

León de Leal, Magdalena, and Carmen Diana Deere. 1979. "La mujer rural y el desarrollo del capitalismo en el agro Colombiano." Estudios rurales latinoamericanos 2, no. 1:77-107. Condensed English version, "Rural Women and the Development of Capitalism in Colombian Agriculture." Signs: Journal of Women in Culture and Society 5, no. 1 (1979):60-77.

_____. 1980. "Plantemientos teóricos y metodológicos para el estudio de la mujer rural." In Magdalena León de Leal, ed., Mujer y capitalismo agrario. Bogotá: ACEP, pp. 1-25.

Motta de Correa, Lilian. 1980. "Transformación de la unidad doméstica y el trabajo de la mujer campesina en una zona de avanzado desarrollo capitalista." In Magdalena León de Leal, ed., Mujer y capitalismo agrario. Bogotá: ACEP, pp. 117-67.

Sacks, Karen. 1974. "Engels Revisited: Women, the Organization of Production and Private Property." In M. Rosaldo and L. Lamphere, eds., Women, Culture and Society. Stanford, Calif.: Stanford University Press.

Stoler, Ann. 1977. "Class Structure and Female Autonomy in Rural Java." Signs 3, no. 1 (Autumn):74-89.

Young, Kate. 1978. "Modes of Appropriation and the Sexual Division of Labor: A Case Study from Oaxaca, Mexico." In A. Kuhn and A. Wolpe, eds., Feminism and Materialism. London: Routledge and Kegan Paul, pp. 124-54.

4

RESOURCE ALLOCATION AND THE SEXUAL DIVISION OF LABOR: A CASE STUDY OF A MOSLEM HAUSA VILLAGE IN NORTHERN NIGERIA

Richard Longhurst

This chapter examines the work of women and their access to productive resources, and analyzes the determinants of these in the context of a village of the Moslem Hausa in northern Nigeria. Various hypotheses are examined in the context of the modernization of this particular rural area, and implications are drawn for rural development policy. After a description in "Introduction" of the study location, research methods employed, and general aspects of social structure in the locality, the section "The Development of Seclusion" briefly reviews the literature on women's work in Nigeria's Hausaland, and discusses the nature of female seclusion in this area. The third section, "Women and Their Work in the Local Rural Economy," presents empirical material on the returns

The research on which this chapter is based would not have been possible without the research facilities and fellowship provided by members of the Department of Agricultural Economics and Rural Sociology of Ahmadu Bello University, Zaria, Nigeria. The staff of the Department of Community Medicine of the university and of Malumfashi Hospital also contributed greatly. The cooperation of the district head and other officials of Malumfashi District and of the families and village officials in the area was also essential for the work, and was generously provided. Drafts of the chapter have been reviewed by Diana Forsythe, Sam Jackson, Kate Young, Ingrid Palmer, and Lourdes Benería, and the author is most grateful for their comments. However, the author is solely responsible for the content of the chapter.

to work done by women in the case village, together with a discussion of women's access to productive resources. The occupations
and work of men are also presented briefly in this section. In the
final section of this chapter, "The Role of Women," some specula-
tions are made about how rural modernization might be affecting
the work of women, and some implications are drawn for rural development policy.

INTRODUCTION

With a change in development policy toward a greater effort
to reach large numbers of the rural poor in developing countries,
a parallel research effort is required to examine the economic activities of various groups, of which women are probably the most
important. From the point of view of development policy, it is
essential to understand who decides what is to be done and how resources are to be allocated and appropriated. This inevitably requires a disaggregation of the household into its separate members
as distinct economic units. The factors determining the sexual
division of labor are broadly related to the exchange of economic
power within and between households in that locality; in a wider
sense the portfolio of work is determined by physical resource endowments as well as by differences in historical development.

The Case Study Location

This study is based on research carried out in a village approximately 50 miles west of the city of Kano in northern Nigeria.
The village is located within Malumfashi District, and will be referred to as the Malumfashi village. The nuclear village is situated
on a main tarmacadam road at a crossing with an unpaved road and,
in the early dry season of 1975, had a population of approximately
1,730 people. It was the headquarters of a village area, which is a
unit of local government; the village head lived there, and this village and five hamlets were under his control. All matters under
his jurisdiction in the hamlets were relayed to him by the hamlet
heads, and he in turn reported to a district head. The village had
a dispensary, and was visited twice a week by midwives and nurses
from a local hospital; it had a weekly market (selling clothes, food,
cooking utensils, animals, furniture, cassette tape recorders, and
watches) and a daily grain market. Three machines were installed
in the village for grinding grain. However, the village had no electricity (this would probably arrive in about five years) or piped

water supply. In the dry season water could be obtained only from
deep, muddy pits. In late 1976 a borehole was drilled by a private
company under a contract with the state government, although its
working was sporadic. The village had several well-stocked shops
as well as numerous traders, called masu-tebur, retailing kola
nuts and perfumes from small tables.

In the year of research, the number of new compounds in the
newcomers' quarters (sabon gari) grew by 12 percent; this and the
preceding information indicates that the village is a fast-growing
commercial center with considerable immigration. Some of this
growth has occurred as a result of the 1973 drought and the desire
to be on a roadside, not only for the distribution of emergency food
supplies in the event of future crop failures but also because of the
greater range of occupations. Communications with the outside
world were good. Small buses stopped in the village every 15
minutes, and the city of Kano could be reached within an hour.
Ownership of radios was common (25 percent of compound heads),
especially among the younger men, and villagers heard of and discussed national and international events. In generalizing from this
case, it is important to remember that this village was on a roadside, and it will be shown that this both presented and denied special opportunities for women's work.

A Note on Methodology

A research project on secluded Moslem women carried out
by a male outsider requires a note of explanation on methodology.
The researcher was fully resident in the village, spoke Hausa, and
lived with a family in a compound. He had a great deal of opportunity to talk with the wives in his compound, despite their seclusion
status, and with the women who came at night to visit them. However, systematic interviewing in this way was not possible, and it
was carried out by a female secondary school student who also
lived in the village. After rapport was built up in the village, the
male researcher gained access to women in several compounds;
neither husbands nor wives objected to interviewing, even on sensitive issues. However, a Hausa male research assistant was not
usually allowed to enter the compound.

General Aspects of Social Structure

The following general comments provide a sketch of social
structures in Moslem Hausaland; later sections provide detail

specific to the case location. It should be remembered that a significant proportion of the population in Hausaland is not Moslem. Generally the Moslem population lives in nucleated villages, whereas the non-Moslem Maguzawa population lives in large compounds scattered throughout the bush. Both groups are settled, cultivate land, and speak Hausa. There is a third group—the Fulani—whose members have their own language but also speak Hausa, are pastoralists and cattle herders, but are increasingly settling and cultivating land.

Among the Moslem Hausa, obligations between a man and his wife are clearly defined: he provides food, water, firewood, housekeeping money, and shelter for the family, and gifts of cloth and perfume at festival times; she provides labor for food preparation, child care, and general domestic chores. Therefore, she is not expected to work on farms or fetch water. If he does not provide food from his own farm, he must purchase it for the communal cooking pot. As long as these obligations are met, each can pursue income-earning opportunities. The arrangement is not always as fixed as this, wives providing food for the cooking pot in some cases.

Married women of childbearing age are secluded; they are restricted to the compound during the day but may leave with their husband's permission. Girls are usually married at the age of 12, after having been betrothed a few years previously. Women past childbearing age are not secluded, and may carry out farm tasks as well as petty trading and traditional midwifery. Secluded women work within their own compounds, either fulfilling their domestic obligations or performing cash-remunerated work of food processing, sewing, weaving, or matmaking. The necessary transactions of buying and selling are carried out at night or through use of their children as intermediaries. Obviously, seclusion is a major determinant of the sexual division of labor. (It will be discussed in greater detail in the next section.)

The Hausa rural economy has an extensive cash orientation, even between close kin. Frequently there are cash transactions between husband and wife if there is an exchange of goods or services between them when they are working in their occupations. Hill (1972, p. 29) has pointed out that cash is regarded as a positive good whose exchange should not be inhibited by personal relationships.

The society is polygamous; men may marry up to four wives, although most have only one. Divorce is easily carried out, especially on the initiative of the husband; for this reason women are anxious to maintain some financial independence. Husbands have the right, which they nearly always exercise, to retain all weaned children after divorce, a fact that discourages many women from seeking divorce. Child adoption occurs, usually between kin, especially if a wife is barren.

Complex gift-giving relationships exist between men and between women. There is a contribution system known as biki, in which one person makes a gift of cash to another in the expectation that it will be returned, and even doubled, at a later date. When contributions reach an impossibly high level, they are reduced by mutual consent. Contributions are made in times of need, particularly when extra expenses are incurred for a family festival such as marriage or name ceremony (christening). Women also develop friendships (kawa) with other women, usually from very early childhood, that involve a formal gift-giving relationship. These relationships represent an extremely important source of informal credit.

THE DEVELOPMENT OF SECLUSION

The Development and Maintenance of Seclusion

The seclusion of women in Moslem Hausaland of northern Nigeria appears to be a relatively recent phenomenon: at the beginning of the century, only the wives of priests (malams) were in seclusion in villages. There is no apparent single reason why seclusion developed in the way it did, nor why it is enforced so strictly. Although the practice is associated with Islam, the Koran is not clear on the matter. It has been pointed out by M. G. Smith (1965, p. 50) that although it could have been recognized as a command of the Prophet, an alternative explanation is that it has developed as a way to reduce the opportunities of wives for extramarital affairs and to tighten the control of men over women.[1] M. F. Smith (1954, pp. 22-23) sees a correlation of the growth of seclusion with the abolition of slave labor at the beginning of the century, arguing that the withdrawal of slave labor from the farms and the corresponding increase in each individual's labor led to a refusal by wives to farm or gather firewood, and to their preference to perform craft and trade work in their own compounds.

However, although this may explain preferences of women for particular types of work at that time, the reasons why seclusion has grown stronger have not been explained. If this vital point is ignored, it is possible to move on nimbly and outline a number of socioeconomic factors that allow and reinforce seclusion by not requiring female labor, such as the prevalence of a high water table, which makes it possible to build wells in compounds (Hill 1972, p. 24), the ubiquity of the donkey as beast of burden (Hill

1972, p. 24), and the general ease of access to land and good grain storage methods, so that families can grow sufficient grain with male labor alone.[2]

Nowadays it is easy to see how seclusion is enforced, because women face considerable social pressures and financial burdens if they do not marry and enter seclusion. First, any woman who does not remarry within a suitable period after divorce or bereavement is not highly regarded by the community, although individual cases may vary. Suggestions may be made that she intends to become a prostitute or that she would not make a good wife. Second, without the help of friends and relatives, which might not be forthcoming in these circumstances, a woman finds it difficult to afford food, clothing, and other essentials. Many informants said that seclusion was increasing for two reasons. First, more people, especially the Maguzawa, embraced the Islamic faith, and, second, since seclusion has predominantly been an urban phenomenon, it has increased with urbanization.

Data presented in the section "Women and Their Work in the Local Rural Economy" on returns per day for women's occupations show that they can earn only a quarter of what men earn. With this income alone they cannot survive. But fear of community disapproval makes it very difficult for women to enter occupations that provide a higher financial return than their present possibilities. Since such occupations (such as trading in cloth or tailoring) are male-dominated, a woman attempting to enter them would be heavily reliant on male advice and contacts. The village woman cannot earn a living without relying on men; therefore she has no economic incentive for trying to live independently. On the other hand, men are anxious to seclude their wives; seclusion is considered the "modern," "urban" way of life—and therefore it gives them status.

The difficulty in explaining why seclusion developed in northern Nigeria is further complicated by the fact that it is not seen in surrounding Islamic areas of Niger, Nigeria, or the Gambia. Therefore, any single factor, such as the influence of the Koran or differences in man-land ratio or natural resource endowments, cannot be postulated.

The Nature of Seclusion

Although the degree of seclusion in Hausaland varies to some extent by income class (women in richer households generally are secluded more strictly), the main differences appear to be linked to the type of community; thus, urban women are secluded much more than rural women, and rural women from nucleated villages are secluded more than those from dispersed settlements. The data from the Malumfashi village support this conclusion. In a sample of 101 women of childbearing age, one-fifth had recently migrated to the village from a remote rural area. Nearly all of these women were not secluded by their husbands, thereby maintaining the custom of the more remote area (see Table 4.1).

TABLE 4.1

Incidence of Seclusion in Relation to Recent Immigration
in the Malumfashi Village

	Women of Child-bearing Age Kept Secluded	Women of Child-bearing Age Not Kept Secluded	Total
Husband migrated from more rural area in last five years	4 (4%)	17 (17%)	21 (21%)
Husband established resident (or recent migrant from less remote area)	73 (72%)	7 (7%)	80 (79%)
Total	77 (76%)	24 (24%)	101

Source: Author's data.

Conflicting evidence is available on how much farming, for example, is done by women in dispersed settlements. Hill (1972, p. 279) reports that partially secluded women do little farming, whereas Jackson (personal communication) reports that women in dispersed settlements near the Kano River Irrigation Scheme in Kano state do farm. Most of the recently migrated women in this study reported having farms.

Although wife seclusion is not as strict as casual observers have stated, women are rarely seen outside the compound except when they go to the clinic. The research supported the observation of Hill (1972, p. 22) in her study of a village near Katsina, approximately 40 miles from our village:

Virtually all women of child bearing age in the gari
(village center), but not in the dispersed farm houses
are in full Muslim seclusion, to the degree that during
the course of a normal day they do not emerge from
their compounds. Although some husbands permit their
wives to go visiting after dark, and there is more roam-
ing about than husbands like to suppose, yet as a householder in the center of the gari, the present writer
rarely saw a younger woman in the street unless some
special event, such as the celebration of the Prophet's
name-day, occasioned her release.

A more recent study (Hill 1972) of a village near Kano City also
records wife seclusion as being severely enforced. In the Malumfashi village there was the uncommon presence of a prenatal and
child clinic. All women were able to visit this with their children
after asking permission from their husbands. However, occasionally
a husband refused his pregnant wife permission to go to the prenatal
clinic. If a child had to be referred for further treatment to the
hospital, which was 20 miles away, the wife usually had to return to
her husband to ask permission to make the journey. Women who
wished to visit relatives and attend marriages were usually able to
go away for many days at a time, especially in the dry season, which
is the slack time with regard to farm work (and, therefore, meal
preparation for workers is not so important).

WOMEN AND THEIR WORK IN THE LOCAL RURAL ECONOMY

Women as Farm Workers

Women in the Malumfashi village do not participate widely in
farm tasks, but some secluded women do go out to the fields to help
in planting and picking crops. Women on the family farm contribute
a very small proportion of the total labor input—about 0.6 percent of
total person-days (on the basis of responses by heads of households)
or 0.7 percent (on the basis of responses by adult women). This is
very similar to figures in agroeconomic surveys carried out in the
area: 0.40 percent in three Zaria area villages (Norman 1972,
p. 30). The contribution made by women as hired laborers on farms
other than their family's will be rather higher if it is assumed (quite
reasonably) that all picking of beans, groundnuts, and cotton is carried out by them. In this case the proportion amounts to 11.7 percent of total person-days. Some planting of crops is also carried
out by women.

In a sample of 101 women (secluded and nonsecluded in 3:1 proportion) in the study village, one-quarter (24 percent) said that they had done some farm work during the previous planting season. The women had worked a total of 366 standard five-hour days, although the majority (85 percent) of these days were worked by only nine women. Picking cotton and planting crops represented over 90 percent of the days worked by women. Two interesting findings are that over one-quarter (27 percent) of all women-days worked were by secluded women on farms other than those of their husbands, and that for virtually all of the days (68 out of 71) worked by all women on their husband's farms, they received payment just as if they were hired labor. Table 4.2 provides data on women-days allocated to and wage rates of different farm tasks, analyzed on the basis of the women's seclusion status and place of work (on or off husband's farm).

The average wage for women for a five-hour day was 0.26 naira (N) (approximately U.S. $0.40) for picking cotton and N 0.16 (or U.S. $0.25) for planting crops. These figures include valuations for payment in kind. They compare with a daily wage for men of N 0.50 (U.S. $0.80) for planting crops and N 0.75 (U.S. $1.20) for weeding crops.

This description, based on women's responses, shows that women do not participate extensively in farm tasks except the picking of cotton and groundnuts. However, they do participate in farm work inside the compound. For planting of crops, where their productivity is likely to be equal to that of men, women are paid less. The comments in this chapter about cash transactions between kin are supported by the payment for work done by women on their husband's farms.

Women as Owners and Cultivators of Land

It is difficult to get information from women about the land owned by them, and almost impossible to get such information from their husbands. The relationship of women to land is very complicated; it is probably true that for men the situation cannot be analyzed through simple categories of landholding status, such as land bought, inherited, rented, or pledged, and this is even more the case for women. The mix of obligations and social relations is difficult to clarify; in this section, therefore, after some general comments, three examples of different forms of landholding by women will be described in order to at least indicate the complexity of the matter.

TABLE 4.2

Farm Work of Women: Allocation of Days, by Task and Wage Rates, According to Seclusion Status and Place of Work

| | Secluded Women | | | | Nonsecluded Women | | | | | Wages | |
| | On Husband's Farm | | On Other Farms | | On Husband's Farm | | On Other Farms | | | | |
Task	Prop. Days Worked (percent)	Daily Wage Rate (N)	Prop. Days Worked (percent)	Daily Wage Rate (N)	Prop. Days Worked (percent)	Daily Wage Rate (N)	Prop. Days Worked (percent)	Daily Wage Rate (N)	Total Days	Per Day	Per Hour*
Picking cotton	9	.39	14	.26	6	.27	33	.22	62	.26	.052
Planting crops	2	.15	10	.20	0	na	19	.14	31	.16	.032
Picking beans	2	.30	0	na	0	na	0	na	2	.30	.060
Picking peppers	0	na	0	na	—	.06	1	.07	2	.07	na
Picking groundnuts	0	na	3	(kind)	—	.05	—	(kind)	4	na	na

1 N = approximately U.S. $1.60 or U.K. £0.90.

*Hourly wages assume five-hour day.

—: less than 1 percent.

Na: sample size not large enough to draw sensible conclusion.

(Kind): payments in kind not measured.

Source: Author's data.

In the crop season (April to January) of 1975, only five out of the 101 women in the sample cultivated land. Three of these women rented their farms (one from her husband) and two owned their farms (one had bought hers from a relative, and one had inherited a farm). It was difficult to measure the acreage of these farms because the husband usually denied their existence and the wives could not come to point out the exact boundaries. However, none of them was greater than one-half hectare, which is not a large farm in this locality; our estimates were that the area planted and cultivated by women was less than 1 percent of the total cultivated area of the village. Each farm required only a day or two to weed completely, and the women contributed very little of their own labor to their farms (only two of the women did their own planting); the work was done without payment by husbands or sons, or by hired labor recruited by the husband. All five women were of secludable age, two being from dispersed rural hamlets and two (who were co-wives) having a husband who did not bother very much about secluding his wives. On their own plots the women grew crop mixes similar to those grown by men.

There is little information available in the literature to indicate the extent of women as landowners in other parts of Hausaland. The women of the non-Moslem Maguzawa own and cultivate land. Hill (1972, p. 279) has observed that women can be large-scale operators in Roni, Hausaland; in the Katsina village of Batagarawa studied by her, the proportion of mapped acreage farmed by women was 4.3 percent (Hill 1972, pp. 62, 335).

The proportion of land that is controlled (owned or held in trust) by women is higher than the insignificant acreage cultivated directly by them; the rest is cultivated by a male. The complex means of inheritance of land by women is difficult to disentangle, partly because of variations in custom in Moslem Hausaland, a point emphasized by the informants themselves, and partly because of preconceived Western-oriented notions of landholding on the part of this researcher. A daughter is legally entitled to inherit land from her father, but usually receives only half of what her brothers inherit. A daughter's portion may be supplemented or even entirely substituted by cash payments from her brother(s) at the time of land division. Women do not inherit land from their husbands. Many men and women said that women "did not bother" with land, but the impression is that this is not so, women either receiving the cash remuneration or allowing a husband or brother to cultivate it. Some secluded women do farm under a variety of arrangements, as the three following examples illustrate.

In the first case a farmer died in March 1976, two months before the coming of the wet season and the planting of crops,

leaving his 35-year-old wife with four sons below the age of ten.
Since no adult male was available to take charge of the land, it
passed to the widow to hold in trust (ajia) until her sons were able
to take responsibility for it. She herself did not inherit any land.
A male friend of the family took charge of managing the farms,
renting out most of them and leaving enough land cultivated to provide grain for the family.

The second and third examples concern the farming of land
under the arrangement called jingina. Debtors pledge their land to
a creditor, who is allowed to farm it until the debt is paid. This
arrangement is often the first step in selling a farm outright. Both
cases involve pledging or pawning between husband and wife. In the
second case a man owed his wife N 2 (about $3.30), and agreed that
as collateral she should plant part of his land free. But after hiring
laborers for the planting and first weeding, she was not able to pay
for further work. The husband reclaimed the land, but allowed her
to keep the farm proceeds.

In the third case a young man could not raise the entire bride
price for his new wife. He therefore pledged his newly inherited
farm to his bride's father for the sum (N 50, or U.S. $80) he could
not provide. The farm, about 0.6 hectare of rich, constantly
manured soil on the edge of the village, was worth at least N 100.
The husband managed the farm for his wife; she paid him the usual
farm laborer's daily wage (N 1) and took the proceeds. When he
has paid off the remaining amount of the bride price, the farm will
revert to his use and he will take the proceeds.

These examples indicate how tenuously women hold land;
seclusion per se does not prevent them from owning or cultivating
land, but they must always do so through the patronage of a male.
Since women do not farm on a large scale, agricultural innovations
will not directly help them. Cultivating land is a man's activity,
and returns from land improvement will accrue in the first place to
them.

Women as Processors and Traders of Food

Women prepare food both as a household obligation and as a
means of earning cash. Processing food for sale is their most important remunerative occupation, and it is an important part of the
cash economy of a Hausa village; nearly all midday meals, and a
small proportion of evening and morning meals, are purchased.
Therefore, rural food processing is an important industry in terms
of people and effort involved at the local level. Simmons (1975,
p. 147) has described it as follows:

The "industry" which accomplishes this daily food processing task is characterized by its small scale, simple
technology and orientation towards its customers. In
most cases, the final product is produced from raw
materials by only one person, perhaps with the assistance of a young child, using only ordinary household
equipment, and it is sold at the place where the cus-
tomer finds it most convenient to eat. No formal standards of quality or quantity are observed by the producers; every producer judges production performance
directly by sales or profits. Gainful employment for
thousands of rural people, primarily women, and a substantial amount of locally-oriented income results from
the functioning of this processing industry.

Of the 101 women surveyed in January-February 1976, two-
thirds had prepared foods for sale since the beginning of the previous
wet season (April 1975). Since younger women have less capital
and more household responsibilities than older women, one might
expect them to be less engaged in commercial food processing. But
the survey showed that the participation of younger women in the
industry is equal to that of older women.
   The most important foods prepared by women are fura (millet
porridge), which when consumed is pounded into nono (soured cattle
milk); kosai, which is fried beancake; and kuli, which is fried
groundnut presscake. Fura is prepared in the morning and consumed as the main midday meal; kosai is a breakfast food or a mid-
morning snack food for schoolchildren, prepared by women at about
5 in the morning; and kuli is prepared over a two-day period for
sale at any time. There are numerous other foods that are less
common and will not be mentioned here.
   The returns on investment and returns per labor hour of kuli
and fura processing have been calculated, and are compared with
Simmons' data for the Zaria area, 60 miles from this study location
(see Table 4.3). A woman's profit per hour from making fura is
roughly comparable with what she might get from working in the
fields: N 0.03 per hour for fura processing, compared with N 0.03
for planting crops and N 0.05 per hour for picking cotton. The total
and per-hour returns on investment for both kuli and fura in the
Malumfashi village are similar to those found by Simmons. Kuli
processing requires much higher investment than fura processing
(by a factor of ten), and therefore is carried out by the wealthier
women. The greater profitability but higher initial investment for
kuli was emphasized by women when complaining about the lack of
formal credit available to them.

TABLE 4.3

Costs and Returns to Production of Fura and Kuli

	Fura					Kuli		
	Malumfashi	Hanwa*		Dan Mahawayi*		Malumfashi	Hanwa and Dan Mahawayi*	
	1976	1971	1972	1971	1972	1976	1971-72	1972
Number observations	12	40	32	16	13	6	72	5
Average amount raw product processed daily (kg)	3.9	8.0	8.1	4.1	5.0	9.8	16.1	15.2
Average daily wages/ profit (N)	.15	.30	.29	.08	.15	.94	.48	.11
Estimated hours to produce	5	8	8	5	5	6	6	6
Wages or profit/hour (N)	.03	.037	.036	.017	.031	.157	.096	.022
Return on investment (%)	29.1	40.5	35.1	25.8	35.2	18.4	26.6	5.5
Return on investment per hour (%)	5.8	5.0	4.4	5.2	7.1	3.1	5.3	1.1

*Simmons 1975, p. 150.
Source: Author's data.

There are few quantitative data available on the extent of women's trading activities, except that provided by Hill on the "honey-comb market" in grains at Batagarawa (Hill 1972, pp. 124-40). This form of market was not present in the Malumfashi village, probably because, unlike Hill's village, it had a daily grain market.

In addition to buying new products and selling processed food, about two-thirds of the women in Hill's Katsina village traded from the seclusion of their houses in groundnut oil, condiments, and seasonings. A similar proportion of women did this work in the Malumfashi village. A few women trade in grain, buying after harvest and reselling when the price has risen. The retail selling of grain in the Katsina village was carried out on behalf of male grain traders by their secluded wives, the actual selling being done by children and nonsecluded women. In villages without formal grain markets, this informal market provides a source of grain at the retail level. As for the relationship between the male grain traders and their wives who retail, Hill (1969, pp. 395-96) notes:

> Enquiries made of the wives of eleven prominent
> kwarami (farmer-traders) show that these women
> were not usually regarded as being free to raise or
> lower the price they charge, or to grant credit with-
> out permission. This is the formal position to which
> there are some exceptions and certainly no kwarami
> could trade successfully unless he could trust his
> wife up to a point. But from what some men frankly
> say, it is also clear that the women, who seem usu-
> ally to receive no fixed commission on sale, are often
> selling, as it were, in partial opposition to their hus-
> bands. They enjoy the opportunities which are pro-
> vided by their seclusion of charging whatever price
> they like to friends, making short-term loans and of
> selling grain which is issued to them for consumption
> in their own household—they are altogether much freer
> than the measurers, their market counterparts, whose
> selling may be watched by the waiting farmer. Foresee-
> ing profit for themselves, many women urge their hus-
> bands on as traders, maybe granting loans for the pur-
> pose. Unlike the men they stand opposed to the estab-
> lishment of a market place.

However, in the Malumfashi village, where a daily grain market assembled in the village square, very little grain retailing by women occurred. Only rice, an expensive grain, was not available at the daily market. It was bought by a couple of traders and retailed by their wives.

A Note on Men's Work and Concluding Comments on the Work of Women

The preceding discussion and description of women's work leads us to three conclusions that, in one form or another, have general applicability to other women's situations: seclusion is a barrier, since it is an obstacle to diversifying the range of jobs women are able to do; despite the constraints of seclusion, women remain very active economic entrepreneurs; and the examples given of women holding land and the descriptions of women as traders show that Hausa women cannot be regarded as passive beings unable to grasp any opportunity. A fourth conclusion—that the returns to their work, compared with those to men's work, are very low—will be discussed in the following paragraphs.

It has been shown that the per-hour returns to women's work that have been calculated vary from N 0.03 for fura processing to N 0.05 per hour for picking cotton to N 0.16 for processing kuli. As has been pointed out, the latter occupation is available to only the better-off women. Before these returns are compared, a brief note on men's occupations will provide some essential background information.

The activity that takes the greatest proportion of men's production time is crop cultivation, which involves the grains—mostly sorghum and millet—and cash crops such as groundnuts and cotton. The presence of land that receives moisture year round, such as marshland (fadama), enables some farmers to cultivate throughout the dry season as well. Detailed labor surveys carried out in the Zaria area (Norman 1972) show that farm labor input is spread throughout the year, although there are concentrations. In the May-August period, 14 to 16 days per month are worked by male adults on the family farm, whereas the corresponding figures in the January-April slack season are 4.5 to 10 days per month. The time devoted to occupations other than work on the family farm remains surprisingly constant throughout the year, being 6 to 9 days per month. Of the average number of working days of adult males in the Zaria survey, 40 percent were spent on occupations other than on the family farm. The data show the importance of nonfarm occupations for men in the local rural economy; most men have a secondary, nonfarming income source.

The work that men do is determined by an interaction of a number of factors: the physical attributes of the village, the extent

of its commercialization, and the access men have to resources
through inheritance or location. There is a range of inherited
occupations, which have been described by M. F. Smith (1954,
p. 16) as being ranked according to prestige: "Hence the phenomenon of occupational class, members of a class being differentiated
as a class from other occupational classes in the community, which
are graded in order of girma (prestige). . . ."

The most important of these occupational classes are the
aristocracy and those who hold office (such as district and village
heads, and scribes) within the system. Then in Smith's ranking
come the priests (malams), merchants, craftsmen, and small
traders, followed in order of declining prestige by brokers, farmers with no important secondary occupation, blacksmiths, hunters,
musicians, and butchers. If the occupation is hereditary in terms
of expertise, implements and clientele are passed on from father
to son. Women are disadvantaged regardless of their seclusion
status. They are prevented from entering these occupations because
of differences in inheritance, their seclusion, and their lack of
economic resources.

Data on returns per hour for male off-farm work are available
from an agroeconomic survey carried out in the state of Kano one
year prior to this research (Matlon 1979, pp. 95-96). These returns show men's work to be better-paid than women's: tailoring
(N 0.20); capmaking (N 0.15); selling firewood (N 0.13); trading in
kola nuts (N 0.13), in used clothes (N 0.15), and in cloth (N 0.27).
Therefore, it appears that the segregation of tasks is allied not only
to the physical separation of the sexes but also to differences in the
returns on men's and women's tasks.

This point is reinforced by the differences between men and
women in access to formal credit sources. Women had practically
no access to credit, whereas several of the richer men in the village had access to sources of government credit (farmers' cooperatives). Women had to rely on such informal sources as relatives or their biki and kawa partners, or on money that had been
hoarded. In the village nearly all of the women were members of
savings organizations (adashi), contributing between N 0.10 and
N 1.00 (U.S. $0.15 and U.S. $1.60) per week. In these organizations women received payments on a rotating basis, and used them
to buy cloth, gifts for their children, animals, or grain, according to the time of year. Some used the money to invest further in
their occupation (sana'a) by buying raw materials or oils. However,
the lack of access to formal credit sources placed them at a disadvantage vis-à-vis men.

THE ROLE OF WOMEN: RURAL MODERNIZATION
AND IMPLICATIONS FOR POLICY

This chapter has examined the sexual division of labor from two aspects: that of "who does what," which is descriptive and has been covered in some detail, and that of the underlying social and economic structure that determines the returns to labor, which has been covered less extensively.

In most societies women are dependent on men for their livelihood, and in Hausa society it appears that this dependency is reinforced by seclusion. As a result of seclusion, there is little commensurability of tasks between women and men. In particular it makes women very individualized, with little chance to protect their skills and markets or to join with other women for economic power. The forms of dependence of women on men are very complex, and vary between married and unmarried women and between women in families of different economic status. It is certainly true that married women in this part of Moslem Hausaland do not do large amounts of certain types of work, such as the on-farm cultivation that might be seen in the Gambia (Haswell 1963), Kenya (Hanger and Moris 1973), Ghana (Hill 1978, pp. 220-30), and Bangladesh (Abdullah and Zeidenstein 1981). Women's situation in Malumfashi should be analyzed with this in mind.

There are several questions that are difficult to answer clearly; the judgments given here are, it must be stressed, formulated by an outsider with a different value system. The first is whether (compared, for example, with those parts of the world mentioned above) seclusion puts a secure "floor" under married women by guaranteeing their food and shelter (usually men meet their obligations in this regard) and time to carry out their market occupations. The position of unmarried women is less secure. Second, there is the question of the "ceiling"—the extent to which, and the nature of which, seclusion limits women's access to information and resources that would allow them to respond to economic incentives and rural development programs.

In addition to this important determining effect of seclusion, patterns found in the sexual division of labor in other rural societies can be found in Moslem Hausaland in Nigeria. Benería, for example, has argued that the focal point of women's economic activities is given by their special role in the reproduction of the labor force. As a result:

Women's productive tasks tend to concentrate on activities that are: (a) compatible with reproduction, and, more concretely, the care of children; (b) related

to class; (c) subordinate to men's work and subject also
to age-oriented hierarchical relations; (d) considered
an extension of domestic activities; and (e) concentrated
in the least permanent and least paid activities (1979,
pp. 9-10).

We may ask whether these factors are relevant to the case of
the village under study. First, with regard to women's productive
tasks being compatible with reproduction and child care, a main
determinant of the sexual division of labor is the restriction of
women's mobility by seclusion. Therefore, the work they do is
limited by their being within the compound; they cannot, for example, migrate seasonally in search of work because of the need to
provide for the family and care for the children. In a manner similar to our discussion of the sexual division of labor, seclusion has
been defined here in two forms: first (a description of) the physical
limitation on mobility, and second (an analysis of) its conceptual
aspects as a determinant of social structure. Therefore, we might
ask whether there is "more" to the coincidence of child care, seclusion, women's work, and women's continual location in the compound. In particular, we might ask how women without children
carry out market work if, as we have shown, they are so heavily
dependent on the children as channels to the market. Does the
need to have children thus further increase women's dependence on
becoming married and, hence, secluded? Probably the issue cannot be separated from the general one of the pressure on women
to marry, but it does indicate the problems of women without children, either their own or adopted.

This point can be combined with the point that women's work
is an extension of their domestic chores, since there is much over-
lap. This is clearly seen in Hausaland; women's chief productive
work is food processing of those items consumed locally. Many
women prepare the same food for family consumption and for sale
at the same time; this is especially true of _fura_. Other market work
that they do is similar to this—hair plaiting, sweeping, pounding—
and is carried out for other women. There is, in such work, a
large element of "taking in each other's washing."

With regard to the relationship of women's tasks to class, it
was seen that the wives of the higher-class households—the aristocracy (_sarauta_), _mallams_, and merchants—were able to carry out
income-earning work that had higher returns (trading in grains,
peppers, and kerosene; processing _kuli_ and groundnut oil) than
could wives of ordinary (lower occupational class) families. They
were able to free themselves of tiring and menial domestic tasks
(such as pounding grain and sweeping the compound) by hiring other

women, although we were not able to determine who paid for these household servants. They may have been paid in kind by sharing in the meals of the household. The work of upper-class women is of the same type (using children as intermediaries), but the returns per hour in Malumfashi are higher.

The subordination of women's work to that of men—the clear-cut sexual division of labor—ensures that most men and women do not have the same type of work; there is little commensurability of tasks. Where they do perform the same sort of work—in families where women help with the planting and harvesting of crops—our data indicate that women are paid for on-farm work by their husbands. Such farm work as threshing and winnowing carried on inside the compound is considered part of the domestic obligations, and generally is not paid.

Finally, considering the poorly paid and impermanent nature of women's work, it has been shown that returns to work for women are very low; in addition, there are strong indications that as tastes become oriented toward commercially prepared foodstuffs (bread, tinned meat, soft drinks), such work will diminish in importance. Therefore, with some qualifications, this study provides a good measure of support for Benería's categorizations.

It is this latter aspect, concerning possible changes over time, that will be explored further with respect to implications for policy dealing with rural poverty and, more specifically, with rural women. A major characteristic of the current strategies in rural development planning is that they should accurately reach target groups in a population rather than be an innovation that brings about production increase in an unspecified group. In this context the design of projects that bring production benefits to women is being considered. The evidence presented here shows that in most families the sexual division of labor is clear-cut and that modernizations and increases in market opportunities can be expected to affect men and women differentially; the impact of different programs on each group can be predicted with some accuracy.

For example, our study indicates that agricultural projects that improve the productivity of land (such as those involving fertilizers, pesticides, or ox-drawn plows) will improve returns in male occupations, but men are under no cultural obligation to pass the proceeds along to the women, although some "trickle-down" will occur in families. Women do not anticipate that men will do so. They would benefit from parallel programs directed toward aiding their own activities of food processing, grain speculation, and weaving. Because the work of men and women is separate, providing outside raw products to one and not to the other is likely to upset the economic balance between the sexes. For example, increasing male prosperity leads men to try to improve their standard of living, which may involve a change of diet. In Hausaland male entrepreneurs are moving into the food processing industry— for example, they are buying fish and frying them for sale. These men are invading an occupation that has traditionally belonged to women, and performing a service that secluded women would find very difficult to carry out since they are restricted to locally acquired raw products. With their limited room to maneuver, it is difficult to see how women can extend their range of occupations in response to this.

For the purpose of analysis of policy impact, it is useful to divide women into four cells as determined by "rich" and "poor," married and unmarried, and to examine their seclusion status. In "poor" families married women are for the most part secluded; unmarried women from "poor" backgrounds are not secluded; and those unmarried and rich are only temporarily secluded. Investments in women's programs such as provision of formal credit will affect each group differently. Improvement in the economic well-being of poor married women will probably encourage them to become fully secluded; rich married women will find it difficult to move into new types of work, and will probably invest their returns in various assets, especially to pass on to, and thus improve the welfare of, their daughters when they leave and marry. Unmarried rich women are essentially "in transit" and are soon, if they wish, able to join a family unit. It is the poor unmarried women who form such a vulnerable group—equivalent to the landless in other parts of the world in terms of their lack of access to any type of institution, either formal or informal. Some kind of "trickle-down" from their female relatives might occur, but this is unlikely to have much impact. Therefore, the provision of capital, although a necessary factor for the improvement of women's status, may not be sufficient; it may, however, trigger the institutional change that is also required.

In very poor families the target group should be the family itself rather than the woman, because the sexual division of labor is less clear-cut and there is little separation of tasks between the sexes. In such families, problems of appropriation will be less acute in first-round efforts. Of course, in terms of the practical problems of designing rural development projects, this method of regarding the family as the basic economic unit and ignoring what happens to the product within the family is easier. The difficulty of targeting resources at specific family members is greater because there might be opposition to it at the policy-making level as well as at the recipient level.

There are good reasons for suggesting that the seclusion of women need not be taken as a given over the next 10 to 20 years, particularly when examining the social and economic events in other countries in a similar situation. Factors such as population pressure, universal primary education, and urbanization will all have an impact. The underutilization of women's labor and expertise is a constraint on the country's development, and it is likely that, with the availability of suitable alternatives and economic opportunities, seclusion may become less binding.

Some investments in women's projects are needed if this is to happen, although such projects will be opposed by those men who see this as a threat to their vested interests and traditions. Other specific recommendations can be made, such as a formal credit system for women, institutions to take the place of the male networks (such as cooperatives for women), and the extension of rural health clinics to reduce the time and energy involved in child care.

Changes benefiting women could be self-generating once the opportunities have been identified; if rural development project planning gets away from always serving a small and homogeneous clientele—usually the large, rich, male farmer growing large cash crops—much of the momentum of rural development (serving large areas, reaching specific target groups, institution building, and developing incentives) could be carried out by the beneficiaries themselves.

NOTES

1. Mernissi (1975), writing from the perspective of Islamic Morocco, has suggested that the control of women springs from an effort to control female sexuality. This effort results from a view of women as powerful and potentially dangerous: "The woman is a dangerous distraction which must be used for the specific purpose of providing the Muslim nation with offspring and quenching the tensions of the sexual instinct" (p. 14).

2. In Bangladesh women in landless families appear to be less rigidly secluded than those from landed families (Abdullah and Zeidenstein 1981).

REFERENCES

Abdullah, A., and S. Zeidenstein. 1981. Village Women of Bangladesh: Prospects for Change. Oxford: Pergamon Press.

Benería, L. 1979. "Reproduction, Production and the Sexual Division of Labor." Cambridge Journal of Economics 3, no. 3 (September):203-25.

Hanger, J., and J. Moris. 1973. "Women and the Household Economy." In R. Chambers and J. Moris, eds., Mwea: An Integrated Rice Scheme in Kenya. Munich: Welforum Verlag.

Haswell, M. R. 1963. The Changing Pattern of Economic Activity in a Gambia Village. Overseas Research Publication no. 2. London: U.K. Overseas Development Administration.

Hill, P. 1969. "Hidden Trade in Hausaland." Man 4, no. 3 (September):392-409.

_____. 1972. Rural Hausa: A Village and a Setting. New York: Cambridge University Press.

_____. 1977. Population, Poverty and Prosperity. New York: Cambridge University Press.

_____. 1978. "Food-Farming and Migration from Fante Villages." Africa 48, no. 3:220-30.

Matlon, P. J. 1979. "Income Distribution Among Farmers in Northern Nigeria: Empirical Results and Policy Implications." African Rural Economy Paper 18. East Lansing: African Rural Economic Program, Michigan State University.

Mernissi, F. 1975. Beyond the Veil. New York: John Wiley and Sons.

Norman, D. W. 1972. "An Economic Survey of Three Villages in Zaria Province, 2," Input-Output Study, I, Text. Zaria, Nigeria: Ahmadu Bello University.

Simmons, E. B. 1975. "The Small Scale Rural Food Processing Industry in Northern Nigeria." Food Research Institute Studies 45, no. 2:147-61.

Smith, M. F. 1954. Baba of Karo. London: Faber and Faber.

Smith, M. G. 1965. The Economy of Hausa Communities of Zaria. Colonial Research Study 16. London: Her Majesty's Stationery Office.

5

ACCOUNTING FOR WOMEN'S WORK

Lourdes Benería

> One of the greatest difficulties in assisting women has
> been the absence of any reliable data regarding their
> number, problems and achievements (Jain 1975,
> "Editor's Note").

INTRODUCTION

The growing amount of literature on women's issues that has
appeared during the 1970s has been instrumental in deepening our
understanding of the nature and extent of women's participation in
economic activities. It has also increased our awareness of the
conceptual and empirical problems that exist regarding this subject.
One such problem is the definition and measurement of women's
work. As studies on women's labor force participation have pro-
liferated, the inadequacies of available statistics in capturing the
degree of their participation in economic life have become progressively more obvious.

Survey work, detailed studies of women's activities, and even
mere observation of everyday life have led to a general agreement
about the obscurity of and low value generally attached to women's

---

Many thanks are due to the ILO colleagues who read the initial manuscript and helped improve it with their criticisms and
suggestions, in particular to I. Ahmed, F. Lisk, M. Loutfi, and
G. Standing. My especial appreciation goes to Z. Ahmad and
D. Ghai for their help and encouragement at all stages of the project.

work in most societies. There are two issues that are interrelated along these lines. One is ideological, and has to do with the tendency to regard women's work as secondary and subordinate to men's. An aspect of this tendency is the fact that an important proportion of women's work is unpaid. Both the ideological and the monetary aspects are clearly symbolized by an expression such as "My mother doesn't work," even though she might be working longer hours than any other household member. "Work" in this case means participation in paid production, an income-earning activity. The ideological aspect is reinforced by the pervasive lack of a clear conceptualization of the role played by women at different levels of economic life. For example, while an effort has been made to evaluate the contribution of subsistence agricultural production to national output, similar efforts to evaluate subsistence work carried out by women in the household have been the exception rather than the rule.

This ideological bias, as will be seen below, is deeply embedded in most of the concepts widely used in the social sciences; dealing with it requires an effort to analyze the roots of this bias and to reconstruct these concepts in such a way that the role of women in society can be placed in its proper perspective.

The second issue is a consequence of the first, and is of a less fundamental but more practical nature. It concerns the actual statistical evaluation and accounting of women's work either as participants in the labor force or in terms of GNP estimations. It is well known by now that most labor force and national accounting statistics reflect a gross underestimation of women's participation in economic activity. Concern over this problem has been expressed repeatedly. Boserup, in her analysis of women's role in the development process, put it clearly when she wrote that "the subsistence activities usually omitted in the statistics of production and incomes are largely women's work" (1970, p. 163). Other authors as well as government bodies and international agencies have also expressed this concern (Gulati 1975; Standing 1981a; United Nations 1976). [1] However, subsistence production, as will be seen below, is not the only area of underestimation of women's work.

Although we do not want to fall into the trap of statistical fetishism, it is important to point out shortcomings of available data for an evaluation of women's work, since they are commonly used for research and planning, and can be the source of numerous biases. The purpose of this chapter is to discuss the reasons for those shortcomings that are rooted in the conceptual categories used. Its focal point is the analysis of statistical biases and of the concepts that feed statistical categories. The section "The Biases of Available Statistics" analyzes the conventional definitions of active labor as commonly used, how they affect data collection, and, more specifically, how they bias the evaluation of women as economic agents. The section on "The Concept of Active Labor" deals with the more theoretical aspects of the problem by linking these definitions to a given conceptual framework of purposes discussed in the last part of the chapter.

THE BIASES OF AVAILABLE STATISTICS

Until World War II statistics on the "economically active population" depended primarily on population censuses. The emphasis on problems of unemployment derived from the Great Depression generated an increased interest in the collection of reliable statistics on the subject. In 1938 the Committee of Statistical Experts of the League of Nations recommended a definition of the concepts of "gainfully occupied" and "unemployed" population, and drew up proposals to standardize census data with the purpose of facilitating international comparisons. As a consequence many countries expanded the collection of statistics on what, from then on, would be called the "labor force" (ILO 1976; League of Nations 1938).

The 1938 definition of gainful occupation was an occupation "for which the person engaged therein is remunerated, directly or indirectly, in cash or in kind." The labor force was defined as comprising the economically active population, which included the unemployed; the objective of this definition was not only to measure the employed population but also to provide some measure of labor availability. Updated labor force definitions adopted by the Statistical Commission of the United Nations in 1966 defined the economically active population as comprising "all persons of either sex who furnish the supply of labor for the production of economic goods and services" (ILO, p. 32). The basic difference between the 1938 and 1966 definitions was that while the former responded to the objective of including the unemployed in the labor supply, the latter reflected an increasing concern not only with unemployment but also with underemployment. The objective was to reach an estimate of the potential labor supply in order to form a measure of the underutilization of labor resources; the potential labor supply was to include not only individuals contributing "to the incomes of their families and to the national product" (ILO, p. 36), but also the unemployed and underemployed.

We can see from this definition that there are two focal points in the conventional measurements of the labor force. One reflects the concern over unemployment, the potential labor supply, and the full utilization of labor resources. The other reflects the link between the concepts of labor force and national product—active labor being defined as that which contributes to the national product plus the unemployed. Both lead to questionable measurements of the labor force—as symbolized by the fact that a domestic activity such as cooking will be classified as performed by active labor only when the cooked food is marketed (and as inactive when it is not). And family members might be classified as underemployed when working in agriculture but not when engaged in household production.

This is because the underlying definition of the national product essentially includes only goods and services exchanged in the market. The problem of underestimation of the labor force is therefore more acute in areas where the market has not penetrated many spheres of human activity. While in industrialized societies the only major exception is domestic production—to the extent that it has not been commoditized[2]—nonmarket production is more prevalent in the Third World.

In order to deal with this problem, efforts have been made, by national and international institutions in charge of labor force statistics, to include nonmarket subsistence production in GNP estimations and subsistence workers as active labor.[3] Hence the introduction of the concepts "potential labor supply" and "marketable goods" in order to measure the contribution of some sectors not yet penetrated by the market. But despite the increasing sophistication in data collection and labor force estimations, important problems remain, and the tendency to underestimate the active population—especially among women—is still a major flaw in available data. Let us examine more specifically the significance of these definitions from the point of view of measuring the female labor force.

In the 1938 definition it was specified that "housework done by members of a family in their own homes is not included in that description of the gainfully occupied, but work done by members of a family in helping the head of a family in his occupation is so included, even though only indirectly remunerated" (ILO 1976, pp. 28-29; emphasis added). Under this definition, when members of a household are assumed to help the head of the family (presumably a male)—for example, as agricultural workers—they are classified as "unpaid family workers"; on the other hand, when the same individuals perform domestic work, such as food processing or water carrying, they are not defined as workers—the rationale being that the former are assumed to be engaged in income-earning activities while the latter are not.

Despite the considerable effort made since 1938 to improve labor force statistics, these concepts have remained essentially untouched until the present time; subsequent work has mainly concentrated on techniques of data collection. For example, the concern for estimating the potential labor supply reflected in the 1966 definitions had implications for female labor: "Particular attention should be given to groups which may be especially difficult to classify, such as female unpaid family workers in agriculture . . ." (ILO 1976, p. 32). However, the problem of underestimation of women's participation in the labor force has not disappeared, as a glance at the relevant ILO literature on the subject indicates (see, in particular, Standing 1981a; Standing and Sheehan 1978). Given the above definitions of the labor force, this underestimation is due to several factors.

First is the problem of defining who is an unpaid family worker. In 1954 an ILO resolution recommended that, in order to be defined as such, an unpaid family worker must work in nondomestic activities for at least one-third of the normal hours.[4] The problem of defining normal hours and how long a family member has worked affects both male and female workers. A typical practice in many countries is that, in order to be classified as an active worker, an individual must have worked a minimum of 15 hours during the two weeks before a census takes place. However, given that involvement in home production is not considered as being part of the labor force, and to the extent that women's unpaid family work is highly integrated with domestic activities, the line between the conventional classifications of unpaid family worker and domestic worker becomes very thin and difficult to draw unless some clear-cut conventions are established. The result is a logical underestimation of women's nondomestic work.

Second, when censuses classify workers according to their "main occupation," the tendency to underreport women as workers in agriculture or any other type of nondomestic production is very prevalent. In India, for example, the 1971 census excluded women whose main occupation was classified as housewife but who were also engaged in other work outside the household; it has been estimated that, in this case, the exclusion of "secondary" work implied a fall in the participation rate from almost 23 percent to just over 13 percent (Gulati 1975). The problem of underreporting has been observed across regions, even though Moslem countries are often mentioned as an extreme case, in particular those of North Africa and Southwest Asia: "With few exceptions, where censuses or surveys have been conducted in these countries . . . the female unpaid family workers were, to a large extent, not recorded" (ILO 1977, vol. VI, p. 11). In Algeria the number of women reported as unpaid family workers in the 1956 census was 96,000; after a postcensus reevaluation of data, it was estimated that 1.2 million women working as unpaid family members had not been reported.

There are several reasons for this underreporting; they range from the relative irregularity of women's work outside the household—that is, the greater incidence among women of seasonal and marginal work—to the deeply ingrained view that women's place is in the household. If census and survey workers do not ask about primary and secondary occupations, they are likely to classify a good proportion of women as working only in the household when this is not actually the case. In many countries it is considered prestigious to keep women from participating in nonhousehold production;[5] when asked whether women engage in such production, both men and women tend to reply negatively even if that is not the case. In addition, underreporting might be due to any economic incentive derived from "hiding" women's income-earning activities—such as the loss of paid social benefits and family subsidies tied to the full-time dedication of the housewife to domestic activities (Benería 1977).

Third, some activities are performed by women at home even though they are clearly tied to the market. This is the case when they sell food and drinks in or near their own home. Clothmaking for nonfamily members and selling of handicrafts and other products inside the family compound are other examples. The proximity to and integration of these activities with domestic work makes them highly invisible; they are likely to go unreported as market activities unless census and survey researchers are conscious of the problem.

Consequently, for an evaluation of women's participation in production, conventional labor force statistics must be approached with great skepticism. Women working as wage laborers will tend to be automatically classified in the labor force, but women working in agriculture or in any other activity not clearly connected with the market might not be—depending mostly upon each country's definition of labor force and upon methods followed to estimate it.

Tables 5.1 and 5.2 provide an illustration of available figures on regional and country activity rates. Compiled by the ILO, they are drawn from country surveys and censuses, and are widely used for international comparisons of labor statistics. Table 5.1 shows that activity or labor force participation rates (the proportion of the population classified as economically active) are much higher for men than for women across regions. It also shows that variations in activity rates are among women; while the lowest average regional rate is found in Latin America, the highest rates, for the three years given, are registered for the more industrialized countries of Europe and North America and particularly for the USSR. Given, for example, the high degree of involvement of women in agricultural production and trade in many African countries, the relatively low rates shown for Africa might immediately be questioned. However, the degree of variation is greater among countries than regions; as can be observed in Table 5.2, activity rates for the 25-44 age group in 1970 ranged from 4.2 percent in Saudi Arabia to 67.5 percent in Zaire and 93 percent in the USSR.

TABLE 5.1

Actual and Projected Activity Rates, by Region: 1975-2000
(percent)

	Males			Females		
	1975	1985	2000	1975	1985	2000
Asia	53.8	52.8	54.0	29.2	27.9	28.2
Africa	51.6	49.3	47.8	24.4	22.9	22.0
Europe	58.2	58.6	56.9	31.4	33.0	34.3
Latin America	48.9	48.1	48.5	14.7	15.4	18.3
North America	56.3	57.4	57.4	32.2	34.3	37.2
Oceania	56.9	55.9	56.1	27.9	28.3	30.3
USSR	53.9	55.0	52.8	46.2	45.0	43.9
World	53.8	53.4	53.0	29.1	28.6	28.2

Source: ILO 1977, vol. V.

These figures should be read only as reported estimates of women's labor force participation rates. For example, the very low activity rates reported for the Arab countries cannot be taken at face value. A census taken in Sudan in 1966, which included questions about both primary and secondary occupations, resulted in a female labor force participation rate of almost 40 percent (Standing 1981a, p. 29), in contrast with other official statistics that report rates barely above the 10 percent level (see Table 5.2). In a survey taken by Deere in the Andean region, it was found that the proportion of women participating in agricultural work was 21 percent instead of the 3 percent officially reported (Deere 1977). This type of underestimation is common across countries, and especially in agricultural areas (Anker and Knowles 1978; ILO 1978). To the extent that the amount of agricultural work performed by women is greater in the poorer strata of the peasantry (Deere 1977; Stoler 1976), it implies that this underestimation differs according to class background and affects women from the poorer strata to a higher degree.

TABLE 5.2

Female Labor Force Participation Rates by Age:
Selected Countries, 1970
(percent)

	10-14	15-19	20-24	25-44	45-54	55-64	65+
Niger	5.1	8.9	10.8	11.1	11.0	10.1	5.5
Sudan	5.4	12.7	11.4	10.3	11.5	10.9	5.9
Bangladesh	13.3	17.8	19.1	20.3	21.3	16.9	11.7
Tanzania	26.2	46.7	50.7	53.1	58.2	56.8	33.7
Honduras	3.2	16.3	19.2	18.2	11.8	3.9	4.4
Dominican Republic	1.8	8.7	12.9	12.9	11.7	9.9	3.9
Zaire	25.5	56.1	61.0	67.5	68.4	50.9	24.7
Burma	23.3	53.1	48.1	51.0	41.1	40.7	30.3
Saudi Arabia	1.3	3.6	5.2	4.2	4.8	4.0	1.9
India	24.3	34.6	41.7	48.8	45.8	34.6	15.0
Pakistan	4.5	7.3	9.1	10.7	10.8	8.3	4.5
Egypt	4.9	6.8	8.0	5.8	5.5	4.7	2.0
Brazil	4.1	24.9	38.5	31.9	26.1	14.2	5.2
North Korea	6.5	57.0	74.6	73.7	75.2	63.6	25.5
Yugoslavia	5.4	45.2	60.3	51.8	40.7	29.2	14.6
Jamaica	0.5	28.7	62.8	60.3	54.8	38.6	12.6
Cuba	0.4	16.3	25.1	22.7	17.5	9.7	2.0
Spain	3.5	36.2	39.0	15.4	14.8	13.4	4.2
USSR	0.0	36.2	82.4	93.0	84.2	18.4	4.0
Sweden	0.3	36.2	58.2	52.1	54.7	35.3	4.0
USA	1.1	36.3	57.5	47.7	56.2	42.5	9.2

Source: ILO 1977, vol. VI.

Two conclusions can be drawn from this. One is that studies on women based on conventional labor force statistics must use a great degree of caution in their analysis of and inferences about women's work.[6] The danger of tautological conclusions is obvious: if active labor is defined primarily in relation to the market, and if production and labor not clearly exchanged in the market tend to be grossly underestimated, then the positive relationship often found between women's activity rates and some index of economic development is clearly circular thinking. This is especially the case when comparing predominantly agricultural with predominantly industrial countries and geographical areas or when comparing data through time. Yet numerous studies on women's labor force participation continue to ignore the problem.[7]

In addition, the implication often derived from this positive relationship—that economic development and industrialization have positive effects on women's emancipation—is far from being obvious. This is not only because women's self-reliance and participation in production and control of resources in less economically developed societies might be greater than statistics lead us to believe;[8] it is also because, although participation in the industrial/urban labor force might provide women with a source of earnings, participation per se does not guarantee freedom from subordination to patriarchal structures or from other forms of exploitation.[9]

The second conclusion is that the great disparity in women's participation in the labor force across countries is likely to be exaggerated, and international comparisons are likely to be misleading, as long as a comparable statistical base is not adopted. Although country and regional differences do exist, comparisons based on figures such as those in Table 5.2 must be qualified with a scrutiny of data collection in each country. In addition, it is necessary that the concepts that have nourished statistical definitions be clarified. It is to this subject that I turn now.

THE CONCEPT OF ACTIVE LABOR

The problem of underestimation of women's work becomes even more acute if we question the conventional definitions of active labor. It is at this level that the ideological dimension in the evaluation of women's work comes in. The basic question arises from the need to define who is engaged in the production of goods and services during a given reference period. In the last resort, it amounts to defining what constitutes an "economic activity" and understanding the conceptual and functional boundaries between it and other types of activity.

For orthodox economics the focal point for the analysis of economic activity is the process of capitalist growth and accumulation, with emphasis on quantitative relations in commodity production. The basic mechanism through which these relations are expressed is the market, which becomes, through the process of price formation, the formal expression of economic activity. Market exchange is tied to the division of labor, which, as Adam Smith emphasized, is viewed as the basis for productivity increases and as the source of the wealth of nations. The production of exchange values is viewed as economic activity, whereas production of use values normally is not. Exchange values take their concrete form through the market and, in that sense, the market becomes the basic source of information for a quantitative evaluation of society's output.

This explains why orthodox economics focuses its attention on the market; although the economic system is regarded, as Robbins has put it, "as a series of independent but conceptually discrete relationships between men [sic] and economic goods" (1932, p. 69), these relationships are viewed essentially from a quantitative perspective. In fact, the almost exclusive attention to quantitative relations in neoclassical economics has often led to identifying these relations with the essence of economic analysis.

It follows from this that activities falling outside the market mainstream are considered peripheral to the economic system, and are not defined as "economic." The history of national income accounting and of labor force statistics, as explained in the previous section, has stayed within this basic theoretical framework. Efforts to incorporate "marketable goods" into national income accounts represent an attempt to apply this framework to nonmarket activities. In the same way, when home-based activities produce goods for exchange, they become "income-earning activities" and the labor engaged in them becomes active labor. That is, when work becomes commoditized, in the sense that it produces goods and services for exchange, it is regarded as an economic activity; participation in the labor force is then measured in terms of labor's links with market activity.

Within the nonorthodox tradition these concepts have often been used in a similar way, despite basic differences from the orthodox tradition. Marxists, for example, have argued that economics cannot be confined to the sphere of quantitative relations between people and economic goods, and that social relations underlying commodity exchange are primary even if hidden behind quantitative relations; as Sweezy has pointed out, "The quantitative relation between things, which we call exchange value, is in reality only an outward form of the social relation between the commodity owners" (1942, p. 27). However, and despite the fact that Marx talked about all labor that produces use values as productive labor, [10] the most prevalent position within the Marxist tradition has been in accordance with his contention that "use value as such lies outside the sphere of political economy" (Marx 1911, p. 19). Sweezy explains this exclusion of use-value production from the investigation of political economy on the ground that Marx "enforces a strict requirement that the categories of economics must be social categories, i.e., categories which represent relations between people" (1942, p. 26).

The reason for this exclusion must be sought in Marx's concentration on the analysis of the capitalist mode of production and of the dynamics of accumulation. Thus, despite the broader definition of economic categories within the Marxist framework, a relative neglect of noncommoditized sectors—such as subsistence production and the household economy—has been a common feature until recently.

During the past few years we have witnessed an increasing realization of the importance of understanding the nature and significance of nonmarket production and its role within the economic system. What is argued in this section can be summarized in two points: first, use-value production does embody a social relation, and therefore should not be excluded from the field of political economy; second, exclusion of use-value production renders the analysis of economic activity incomplete, leads to distortions in the measurement of the labor force, and can reinforce ideological biases related to the undervaluation of women's work.

The central argument of this chapter is that any conceptualization of economic activity should include the production of use values as well as of exchange values, and that active labor should be defined in relation to its contribution to the production of goods and services for the satisfaction of human needs. Whether this production is channeled through the market and whether it contributes directly to the accumulation process are questions that can be taken up at a different level of analysis, and should not bias our understanding of what constitutes economic activity. That is, the argument is far from implying that there is no difference between commodity and noncommodity production, as will be argued below, but that the latter is also part of the realm of economics, and must be analyzed and valued accordingly.

The basis for this argument is provided by the literature on domestic work, reproduction, and subsistence production that has been developed during recent years. In what follows, I present a brief summary of the contributions that are relevant for the purpose of this argument.

Domestic Work and Subsistence Production:
The End of Invisibility

The penetration of economic analysis into the household has
increased progressively. Neoclassical analysis pioneered this
effort with theoretical and empirical work on the factors affecting
women's participation in paid production.[11] Further work along
these lines concentrated on subjects such as the quantification of
domestic production through time-allocation studies, the estimation
of the market value of home production, fertility analysis, and the
economic factors affecting marriage and divorce. This work has
centered on the application of utility maximization and cost-benefit
analysis to the domestic economy. That is, it has applied conventional microeconomics to the analysis of the household, with an
emphasis on quantitative relations.

In contrast, feminist and Marxist literature has centered on
the significance of unpaid household production for an understanding
of the economic role of women within both the household and the
larger economy, and of its implications for an understanding of the
reasons behind women's subordination. It has emphasized the role
of women in the reproduction and daily maintenance of the labor
force—a fundamental point being that household production lessens
the costs of maintenance and reproduction. This is so in comparison
with the costs that would be incurred if the goods and services produced domestically with unpaid labor were bought in the market.
Household production therefore reduces labor costs in commodity
production and, in this sense, can be regarded as having, if not a
direct link with it, at least an indirect effect on the accumulation
process (Beechey 1977; Deere 1976; Fee 1976). While this literature has not always emphasized the feminist questions that focus on
gender differentiation and asymmetrical relations between the sexes,
it has signified an important step in that direction.

Two basic differences between the two approaches can be
pointed out. One is that while orthodox economics, in applying the
concepts used in market-oriented microeconomics to the domestic
economy, tends to blur the distinction between use values and exchange values, feminist and Marxist analysis has stressed this distinction. The other has to do with the political significance of the
analysis; while conventional analysis takes the economic system as
given and tends to describe changes taking place within it, the second
approach asks political questions more directly, does not take the
economic system as a given, and focuses on the role of women
within this system. These questions are formulated both from the
point of view of women's subordination to men—a problem that can
apply to any given economic and political system—and from the

point of view of how this subordination is integrated with exploitation in class society.

Yet both approaches share a common result: domestic labor and its connections with the nondomestic economy are no longer invisible. The incorporation of domestic work into the mainstream of analysis reflects the progressive realization of its importance for a full understanding of women's work and of the sexual division of labor within and outside the household.

Similarly, the analysis of the subsistence sector and of the role that it plays within the larger economy has recently received new attention. This analysis has raised several important questions. Several authors have pointed out the permanence of this sector in many countries of the Third World, not only in agricultural areas but also in urban areas in the form of a marginalized population that either is not absorbed by the capitalist sector or is rejected by it as unemployed labor. Yet subsistence production is indirectly related to market production. As Wolpe (1975) has argued in relation to South Africa, the existence of the subsistence sector allows the capitalist sector to pay a wage that covers only the subsistence needs of the wage laborer—normally a male migrant—rather than the family. The role of women in providing unpaid work within this sector, in domestic and agricultural production, and in cheapening the wage has also been pointed out by other authors (Deere 1976; M. Mueller 1976). The subsistence sector therefore constitutes a source of cheap labor from which wage labor can be drawn as capital accumulation proceeds. Far from being two separate sectors, as the dual economy analysis argues, the subsistence and the capitalist sectors are highly interconnected, to the extent that the latter feeds upon the former.

Use-value production outside of market exchange takes place both in the household and in the subsistence sector. Efforts have been made to include it in GNP calculations,[12] even though its market value is difficult to estimate because it is not exchanged at a price. In particular, agricultural production not exchanged in the market is viewed as "marketable output," and labor engaged in it as being part of the labor force—as the concept of "family worker" indicates. Problems of underestimation in this case are due to practical difficulties in data collection, not to conceptual biases.

In contrast, the few attempts to estimate domestic production have for the most part not generated a clear definition of household production as an economic activity, nor, especially, of domestic workers as active labor (unless they are wage workers). In the last resort, housework is linked with consumption rather than with production by most authors. Galbraith, who included a chapter titled "Consumption and the Concept of the Household" in his book

Economics and the Public Purpose, regards housework as "the labor of women to facilitate consumption" (1973, p. 33).

Yet, recent literature on domestic labor contains a clear conceptualization of domestic work as part of production or reproduction. This is the case with time allocation analysis within the neoclassical framework. Within the Marxist tradition several authors have discussed the need to view the concept of mode of production as including "the relations and forces involved in the production of use values but also those involved in the reproduction of the species (reproduction of people)" (Himmelweit and Mohun 1977, p. 21). However, in the last resort housework is also linked with consumption rather than with production, since it has to do with "production of use values for immediate consumption outside of any direct relation to capital" (Himmelweit and Mohun, p. 28). While this point is important for the purposes of differentiating use-value from exchange-value production and of delineating what activities contribute directly to the process of capital accumulation, it does not justify the asymmetry in the conceptual treatment given to the two types of use-value production. Although it is important to differentiate between activities directly related to capital and activities that are not, and between labor that participates in the commodity sector and that does not, this does not justify the exclusion of any type of nonmarket production from our definitions of economic activity and active labor.

In the conventional definitions of national product and labor force, the rationale for this asymmetry seems to be the assumption that subsistence agricultural production consists of goods normally sold in the market, while household production does not. Yet this assumption becomes even more arbitrary when household production is viewed from a historical perspective. The extent and nature of household-related work—overwhelmingly women's work across countries—varies according to the stage of economic transformation of a given society. The gradual penetration of the market into economic life generates a shift of production from the domestic to the market sphere. In industrialized societies, where subsistence depends predominantly on the wage, the function of domestic work is to "transform" family income into consumable goods and services, only a small part of which is produced within the household. The burden of subsistence therefore falls on the wage, parts of production gradually are removed from the household, and domestic labor tends to concentrate on the transformation of market goods for household consumption.

By contrast, domestic labor in predominantly agricultural societies contains a higher degree of production—as symbolized by the fact that all stages of food transformation are often carried out in the household. In addition to strictly domestic activities, women's work around the household consists of a great variety of subsistence activities—such as water carrying, wood gathering, and food transportation—that often require long hours of work. The burden of subsistence in this case falls on these types of activities together with agricultural work, in which women's participation is also high. Agricultural and household-related tasks are highly integrated in time and space, and productive and reproductive activities are highly intertwined.

In such cases the introduction of the notion of "marketable goods" for the purpose of evaluating subsistence production and measuring the labor force constitutes a projection of a concept specific to commodity production for the purpose of differentiating two types of output—marketable and nonmarketable—that in fact serve similar functions and can hardly be separated. The gradual penetration of the market into rural economies introduces different degrees of direct contact with commodity production and capital. Yet it does not change the productive and reproductive nature of these activities; what changes is the degree of their integration into the market.

Social Relations and Use-Value Production

Now that domestic and subsistence production are becoming analytically more visible, and their proper role within the economic system is being reevaluated, it is increasingly difficult to argue that the production of use values does not embody a social relation. The penetration of analysis into the household and subsistence production has been instrumental in bringing into the open the complexity of "social relations" in use-value production. We can talk, for example, about differences in access to and control over the household means of production, and about the unequal distribution of resources among different household members—as some empirical studies have documented (see for example, Chapter 4 in this volume). A closer analysis of differences in household organization also documents the complexity of relations in regard to household hierarchies by sex and age, and of the division of labor even among members of the same sex (Benería 1979).

Similarly, under a wage labor system in which subsistence depends on the male wage, we can identify, as Seccombe (1974) has done, two levels of exchange—between employer and wage laborer, and between wage laborer and domestic worker—that exist in the interaction between the household economy and commodity production. Thus, it is logical to view the two levels of exchange as equally generating a set of social relations. In the same way, social relations are generated in the interaction between domestic and agricultural production in a subsistence setting—as with women cooking and carrying the meals to the fields, to the extent that those activities can be viewed as part of the agricultural production process.

Two different implications spring from these observations. One is that the assumption of the household as the most basic unit of analysis—as is often done in the social sciences—is not appropriate. The household cannot, for example, be assumed to be a harmonious unit of consumption and production/reproduction; it is precisely the conflicting nature of the relations generated by these functions that is being disentangled by feminist analysis. And this implies that it is important to distinguish between the household as a collective unit and the individual members that are part of it. This is especially so if our interest focuses on the analysis of mechanisms and forms of subordination/domination.

The other implication is that the household cannot be viewed as being isolated in the "private" sphere and distinct from the "public" sphere. The two spheres are highly interconnected, and influence each other. Once the role of use-value production and its importance within the larger economy are understood, the separation between the two spheres becomes artificial. It is in fact this separation that is at the root of the asymmetric treatment given to different types of use-value production.

A full understanding of these implications leads to the conclusion that whether we are dealing with agricultural production or domestic work, within a polygamous household or a nuclear family, use-value production generates "social relations between people" and therefore forms part of "the categories of economics." Once this is understood, it is still possible to differentiate between activities that are directly related to capital accumulation and those that are not, or between that part of the labor force that produces exchange values and the part that is engaged in use-value production.

MEASURING WOMEN'S WORK

The purpose of the previous section was to discuss the concepts that underlie economic categories and to present a framework that can move us beyond conventional concepts of the labor force. Practical implications for data collection and statistical evaluation of women's work can follow from these concepts. But first we might question the usefulness and significance of such an exercise. The two main questions here are why we want to expand our concept of active labor to include use-value production and, especially, what difference it can make for women. It is obviously possible that censuses and survey work might be addressed to evaluating all economic activities, as defined above, and yet be totally irrelevant for dealing with the problems facing women.

Having recognized this possibility, I want to argue that such an exercise has three main objectives. The first is to counteract the ideological undervaluation of women's work and to give recognition to the long hours of labor in which women are engaged. I am in fact only arguing that domestic labor should receive the same treatment as other types of labor engaged in use-value production. But, in addition, I am also underlining the crucial function played by women within the larger economy and pointing out the interaction between use-value and commodity production.

The argument presented here should not be taken as a tacit acceptance of the traditional sexual division of labor by which women remain predominantly in unpaid work. The objective is to bring up the economic significance of this work and to point out, for example, that women clearly engage in a "double day" load when they are responsible for household duties in addition to a load, similar to men's, outside of domestic production. This implies that it is essential to understand that it is not enough to emphasize the need to increase women's participation in paid production as a basis for their economic self-reliance; any development scheme, be it a limited employment policy or an ambitious and radical change, must deal with the question of how to organize production so that women are not burdened with a double load.

The second objective is related to the need to have as much information as possible about women's activities and their role in economic life—the need being symbolized by the quotation heading this chapter. Planning, development programs, employment policies, training and educational programs, and introduction of technological change at all levels (including the household) must be based on accurate information on women's work if they are to be fully relevant to about 50 percent of the world's population.

A typical example of the need for more information is the problem of unemployment and underemployment among women. The lack of accurate estimates of these variables in most countries is a natural consequence of the problems described so far; if women either are not classified or are underestimated as workers, it is likely that they will also be underestimated among the unemployed, since, in order to be counted as such, they must first be defined as part of active labor. Some hints of the high underemployment and unemployment of women in the Third World exist,[13] but for the most part systematic information on the subject is not available. In the industrialized countries unemployment rates among women are higher than among men practically across the board. Such information should be a starting point of any development strategy and employment policy, but it cannot be obtained accurately without an estimate of the proportion of women "taking refuge" in domestic and subsistence production because there is no employment available to them elsewhere.

The third objective in expanding our concept of active labor is to define economic activity so as to relate it to human welfare rather than to a given process of growth and accumulation. As pointed out earlier, it is important to focus on commodity production if we are interested, for example, in understanding the processes of growth of a capitalist economy; a different matter is to move beyond commodity production and focus on all activities contributing to the satisfaction of material needs—as implied, for instance, by a basic-needs development strategy. By differentiating between the broader level of economic activity and the narrower level specific to a given process of growth and accumulation, we are differentiating between all activities contributing to human welfare and those linked to a particular economic system. In this way we transcend the conceptual framework that evolved out of the specific categories linked to capitalist production, of labor put to use for accumulation and profit.

We must now ask the more practical questions about the implications for statistical work of the arguments made in this chapter, lest we be charged with impractical, if not meaningless, thinking. The discussion carried out by the ILO on the issue of labor force statistics and by neoclassical economists working on household time-use data comes close to asking some of the questions posed in this chapter. The issues raised include the difficulty of drawing a line between economic and noneconomic activity, and the distinction between economic activity and housework.[14] Some authors have talked about economic activities that are "marginal"—such as hunting, handicrafts, and growing vegetables—and "auxiliary"—repairing tools for one's work and marketing home-produced goods—that are not likely to be included in labor force statistics unless they are clearly performed for the market (E. Mueller 1978).

In one ILO recommendation on household survey statistics of the labor force, it is suggested that data collection should concentrate on "how people earn their living" (ILO 1979). The difficulty, however, appears when we want to be more specific about what "earning a living" means. While some authors have insisted on concentrating on income-earning activities—that is, on following a market-oriented bias—others suggest that the number of hours of work can be used as an indication of working for a living—which implies that work might not produce an income but is implicitly a part of "economic activity." The exact meaning of economic activity is never defined, but what is clear is that there are problems with the conventional definitions and that an understanding exists of the fact that many tasks performed in and around the household are related to "earning a living."

If we use the expression "make" instead of "earn" a living, it is even clearer that very little difference exists between the various types of subsistence and domestic activities in terms of their contribution to making a living. A similar argument can be made for activities such as food processing, cooking, washing, repairing the house, and taking care of the aged. If, further, we include reproductive tasks as an integral part of the overall process of production/reproduction, we are adding activities such as the care of children to the above list. Taken together, they include all use-value production—of tangible goods as well as services. On the other hand, the list would not include nonwork activities such as recreation and leisure.

For statistical purposes an evaluation of use-value production and of the labor force participating in it requires a detailed investigation of the tasks and the work involved. Survey research carried out at the household level and in the subsistence sector has pioneered the type of research that is necessary. However, what is also needed is systematic data collection by countries that can provide a continuous source of information and that can, to the extent possible, be standardized. One of the problems that immediately comes to mind is how to measure work and labor participation. Use of number of hours of work might be misleading since, given the flexibility of scheduling in subsistence and domestic tasks, work can be carried out with different degrees of intensity—alternating it with leisure time or with breaks of different duration, for instance. This represents a problem not only in measuring labor force participation but also in relation to the measurement of underemployment and labor utilization.

One possible way to deal with these questions is to estimate the average number of hours that household members spend in use-value production—the average based on survey work and depending upon the specific characteristics, such as the level of technology and the extent of use-value production in each country. For those who might be skeptical about estimating an average, it should be pointed out that evidence exists that the amount of time spent on domestic work has not changed considerably through time, and has been found to be very similar across countries having very different characteristics;[15] the variations among countries and through time have to do with the composition of housework and the duration of specific tasks. Thus, while shopping is more time-consuming in some countries, less time is spent on other activities, such as caring for children or cleaning. Averages can take into consideration other differences, such as those between rural and urban households and variations by class.

However, the use of averages should be accompanied by detailed information about the composition and duration of specific tasks. In particular, classification of work and activities can respond to a range of questions:

1. Overall, we want to know about the sexual division of labor and the involvement of household members in use-value production. In particular, the objective is to evaluate women's participation in all tasks contributing to production and reproduction.

2. The distinction between commodity and use-value production can be made clear by distinguishing between income-generating tasks and production for the household's own consumption. To the extent that conventional estimates have included subsistence agricultural production in labor force and GNP calculations, they do not totally coincide with the category of commodity production that is directly tied to the market and to capital. These estimates often blur rather than clarify the distinction between commodity and use-value production. The distinction can be made clearer if statistical data are gathered with this purpose in mind.

3. This distinction is also important for measuring unemployment; questions can be drawn up in such a way as to reveal whether a worker, male or female, is "taking refuge" in the subsistence or domestic sector because of a lack of employment opportunities in the commodity sector. This requires a clear distinction between these sectors.

4. Further breakdown of activities in different categories can provide information for a variety of purposes. Thus, tasks related to reproduction will provide information about demographic factors, child care and schooling needs, time spent in shopping and food transformation, the effect of household technology on domestic work, and the need for community services.

This list is not meant to be exhaustive, but to illustrate at the general level the type of data collection that can be made for a full account of women's work (as well as of other household members, such as children and the aged, whose activities are also underestimated). This account per se tells little about the mechanisms of subordination that this work might entail, but it can provide basic information for the analysis of women's position in society.

CONCLUDING COMMENTS

I have argued in this chapter that, within conventional definitions of labor force, women's participation in economic activities
tends to be grossly underestimated, particularly in areas with a
relatively low degree of market penetration into economic life. This
is due mostly to conceptual and ideological biases concerning the
nature of women's work and to difficulties in collecting accurate
statistics on their labor force participation. As a result, available
information on women's work must be used with caution; in particular, international comparisons can be very misleading if statistical
concepts and data collection used by different countries are not
taken into account.

The main thrust of the chapter, however, is to point out the
shortcomings of conventional labor force concepts. These concepts
are geared to measuring labor participation in commodity production—that is, in production for exchange instead of, for example,
for the satisfaction of basic human needs. The reason for this bias
is to be found in the view that economic analysis and economic categories have been defined in relation to the process of growth and
accumulation; only workers engaged in activities directly related to
that process are conventionally defined as being in the labor force.
The main argument of this chapter is that active labor should include all workers engaged in use-value as well as exchange-value
production, which includes activities such as household production
and all types of subsistence production. At a more concrete level,
narrower categories of labor can be distinguished—such as between
labor engaged in commodity production and labor that is not, or
between income-earning activities and unpaid work. This implies
that the concept of active labor should also include workers who
have an indirect connection to the process of growth and accumulation.

From the point of view of women's work, the purpose of this
conceptualization was underlined in the previous section, and can
be summarized under two main objectives. One is ideological, and
has to do with the proper evaluation of women's work and the eradication of gender-related biases. A full understanding of the economic
significance of household production, for example, implies that wom-
en's work is economically productive and essential for the functioning
of the economic system. Society, as well as women themselves,
must recognize this function in order to avoid succumbing to the
view that it is of secondary importance, which is a basic source of
women's subordination. This can remove the paradox, so commonly

found in the Third World, that a local economy survives thanks to women's involvement in subsistence production while men are un-employed, yet official statistics show low labor force participation for women and high participation for men.[16]

The other objective is of a practical nature, and concerns the dynamics of change; a more general definition of labor force im-plies that development strategies and programs of action must be concerned with the whole spectrum of active workers. Thus, the introduction of more sophisticated technology into household pro-duction will free household workers from time-consuming tasks while widening the range of possibilities of choice between domestic and nondomestic work; employment programs must take into con-sideration the degree of unemployment and underemployment "hidden" in use-value production. Under conventional statistics unemployed women who concentrate in household activities because of lack of opportunities to work outside the household are not con-sidered as either "discouraged workers" or as "unemployed." The implications of this chapter indicate that they are part of active labor, and should be a matter of concern for any employment pro-gram.

NOTES

1. The ILO is currently preparing a report and a draft reso-lution on employment and related statistics for submission to the forthcoming Thirteenth International Conference of Labour Statis-ticians, which is supposed to revise the present international rec-ommendations on this topic.

2. Throughout this chapter the concept of commodity is used in its usual meaning of an output produced for the purpose of being exchanged in the market and sold for a price.

3. The ILO has maintained a continuous interest in devising new approaches to dealing with the problem. In addition to the sources already mentioned, see ILO 1978b; United Nations 1976; Richter 1978; Frank 1977; Bienefeld and Godfrey 1975.

4. Resolution adopted at the Eighth International Conference of Labour Statisticians, Geneva, November–December 1954. See Standing 1981a, p. 30, for a discussion of the subject.

5. An extreme case is the observance of purdah or the seclusion of women, which is viewed in many cases as a "luxury" that poor women cannot afford. This attitude is found in societies where seclusion is an old tradition, such as in Bangladesh, as well as in others where it has been introduced recently, as in some regions of Nigeria (Abdullah and Zeidenstein 1981; see also ch. 4 in this volume).

6. There are two major reasons why female labor force participation may be underestimated in standard labor force surveys. One is conceptual, and deals with the way employment and related concepts are defined for measurement purposes. The other is technical, and deals with the nature of the instrument used in measuring the concepts. Some of the problems of labor force surveys are not necessarily connected to the problems of labor force concepts. For example, the use of proxy response in standard labor force surveys in some countries may result in underestimation of female labor force participation, no matter how one defines the labor force concepts.

7. See among others, UN 1976; Tienda 1977; Cordell and McHale 1975; Boulding 1977; Denti 1968; Saffiotti 1977; Youssef 1974. Tienda, for example, elaborates the proposition that "the proportion of female active labor varies according to indices of economic development" (p. 307), and finds that this is the case for Mexico. Yet her conclusion is based on conventional labor force statistics, and provides a good example of a tautological conclusion.

8. The argument that economic development has often had a negative effect on women has been discussed at length in the literature. See Boserup 1970; and Rubbo 1975, among others.

9. An elaboration of these points is in "Special Issue on the Continuing Subordination of Women in the Development Process," IDS Bulletin 10, no. 3 (April 1979).

10. "If we examine the whole process from the point of view of its results, the product, it is plain that both the instruments and the subject of labor are means of production, and that the labor itself is productive labor" (Marx 1967, p. 181).

11. The analysis of domestic work has taken place within the orthodox as well as the Marxist tradition. Typical examples of the first are compiled in Lloyd 1975, while a summary of the Marxist literature on the subject is provided by Himmelweit and Mohun 1977. Subsistence production and its links with commodity production is analyzed, for example, in Bennholdt-Thomsen 1978; Deere 1976; and Wolpe 1975. On the subject of reproduction, see Edholm et al. 1977; and Benería, 1979.

12. This is so even in the much less frequent case of estimation of domestic production. Illustrations can be found in Walker 1969; Scott 1972; and Vanek 1974.

13. In India, for example, it is clear that among the proportion of the population that have lost access to land, women are less likely than men to find wage employment (Mies 1978). As a result, the Committee on the Status of Women in India (1974) estimated that in 1971 women represented 60 percent of rural unemployment and

56 percent of urban unemployment (p. 160). Yet it is highly likely that these figures underrepresent female unemployment because women can always take refuge in the household and move out of the conventionally defined labor force. A second example comes from Latin America, where it has been estimated that in the rural areas underemployment is more than twice the national unemployment rate, and that most of the unemployed are young people and married women (ILO/PREALC 1976).

14. ". . . There is a problem of specifying what is meant by 'work' thus drawing a dividing line between economic and non-economic activity. The problem is an important one with respect to such activities as growing vegetables, repairing a dwelling, collecting firewood, processing food or scaring away birds" (ILO 1979, p. 8). A similar concern is expressed by E. Mueller: ". . . the distinction between economic activities and housework is basic to the traditional measurement of employment. Yet for the self-employed, and specially for people engaged in subsistence agriculture, the distinction is rather artificial. Activities that may occupy much of their time are on the borderline between economic work and housework, with the result that difficult classification and measurement problems arise" (1978, p. 2; emphasis added).

15. Although research on the subject has taken place mostly in the industrialized and more developed countries, they include a variety of countries at different levels of development and economic and political organization. Szalai's studies (1972), for example, refer to 12 countries, including Peru, East European, and Western countries. An analysis of the constancy of time spent on housework in the United States can be found in Hartmann 1974. However, given that these are the countries that have experienced the greatest amount of change, it is reasonable to expect that a similar situation will be found in other countries.

16. I have called this type of situation "the paradox of Chaouen," to describe the conditions that I observed in this northern Moroccan town, where most men are idle because of the unemployment created by the replacement of traditional crafts by modern imported products; women, on the other hand, busily move around town and in the countryside, carrying the main burden of subsistence and family production. Yet, according to 1975 statistics for Morocco, only 15 percent of the labor force were women (ILO 1977).

REFERENCES

Abdullah, A., and S. Zeidenstein. 1981. Village Women of Bangladesh. Prospects for Change. Oxford: Pergamon Press.

Anker, R., and J. Knowles. 1978. "A Micro Analysis of Female Labor Force Participation in Africa." In G. Standing and G. Sheehan, eds., Labor Force Participation in Low Income Countries. Geneva: ILO, pp. 137-63.

Beechey, V. 1977. "Some Notes on Female Wage Labour in Capitalist Production." Capital and Class (Autumn):45-66.

Benería, L. 1977. Mujer, economía y patriarcado durante el período franquista. Barcelona: Anagrama.

_____. 1979. "Reproduction, Production and the Sexual Division of Labor." Cambridge Journal of Economics 3, no. 3 (September):203-25.

Bennholdt-Thomsen, V. 1978. "Subsistence Reproduction and General Reproduction." Paper presented at the Conference on the Subordination of Women and the Development Process, IDS, September.

Bienefeld, M., and M. Godfrey. 1975. "Measuring Unemployment and the Informal Sector: Some Conceptual and Statistical Problems." IDS Bulletin 7, no. 3 (October):4-10.

Boserup, E. 1970. Women's Role in Economic Development. London: George Allen and Unwin.

Boulding, E. 1977. Women in the Twentieth Century World. New York: John Wiley and Sons.

Committee on the Status of Women in India. 1974. Towards Equality. New Delhi: CSWI.

Cordell, M., and J. McHale. 1975. Women in World Trends. Binghamton: Center for Integrative Studies, State University of New York at Binghamton.

Deere, C. D. 1976. "Rural Women's Subsistence Production in the Capitalist Periphery." Review of Radical Political Economics 8, no. 1 (Spring):9-17.

_____. 1977. "The Agricultural Division of Labor by Sex: Myths, Facts and Contradictions in the Northern Peruvian Sierra." Paper presented at the Joint National Meeting of the Latin American Studies Association and the African Studies Association, Houston, Texas.

Denti, E. 1968. "Sex-Age Patterns of Labor Force Participation by Urban and Rural Populations." International Labor Review 98, no. 6 (December):525-50.

Edholm, F., O. Harris, and K. Young. 1977. "Conceptualizing Women." Critique of Anthropology 9/10:101-30.

Fee, T. 1976. "Domestic Labor: An Analysis of Housework and Its Relation to the Production Process." Review of Radical Political Economics 8, no. 1 (Spring):1-17.

Frank, W. 1977. "The Necessity and Possibility of Comprehensive Information Systems for Agriculture." International Association of Agricultural Economists, Members' Bulletin no. 1 (July).

Galbraith, J. K. 1973. Economics and the Public Purpose. Boston: Houghton Mifflin.

Gulati, Leela. 1975. "Occupational Distribution of Working Women: An Inter-State Comparison." Economic and Political Weekly, October 25, pp. 1692-1704.

Hartmann, H. 1974. "Capitalism and Women's Work in the Home, 1900-1930." Ph.D. dissertation, Yale University.

Himmelweit, S., and S. Mohun. 1977. "Domestic Labour and Capital." Cambridge Journal of Economics 1 (March).

Huntington, S. 1975. "Issues in Woman's Role in Economic Development: Critique and Alternatives." Journal of Marriage and the Family 37, no. 4:1001-11.

ILO. 1976. International Recommendations on Labor Statistics. Geneva: ILO.

_____. 1977. Labor Force Estimates and Projections, 1950-2000. Geneva: ILO.

_____. 1978a. "Condiciones de trabajo, formación profesional y empleo de la mujer." Report prepared for the Eleventh Conference of American State Members of the ILO.

_____. 1978b. "Estudio Detallado de las Actividades de la OIT en Materia de Estadistica." Geneva: GB. 208/PFA/8/1.

_____. 1979. "Household and Expenditure Statistics, 1968-1976." Geneva: ILO. (Internal circulation.)

_____. Annual. Year Book of Labour Statistics. Geneva: ILO.

ILO/PREALC. 1976. The Employment Problem of Latin America. Santiago, Chile: ILO/PREALC.

Jain, Devaki. 1975. From Dissociation to Rehabilitation. New Delhi: Allied Publications.

League of Nations. 1938. Statistics of the Gainfully Occupied Population. Definitions and Classifications Recommended by the Committee of Statistical Experts. Studies and Reports on Statistical Methods no. 1. Geneva: League of Nations.

Lloyd, C., ed. 1975. Sex, Discrimination and the Division of Labour. New York: Columbia University Press.

Marx, K. 1911. A Contribution to the Critique of Political Economy. Chicago: Charles Kerr and Co.

_____. 1967. Capital. Vol. I. New York: International Publishers.

Mies, M. 1978. "Consequences of Capitalist Penetration for Women's Subsistence Reproduction." Paper read at the Seminar on Underdevelopment and Subsistence Production in South East Africa, April.

Mueller, E. 1978. "Time Use Data." Ann Arbor: Population Studies Center, University of Michigan.

Mueller, M. 1976. "Women and Men, Power and Powerlessness in Lesotho." In Wellesley Editorial Committee, ed., Women and National Development. Chicago: University of Chicago Press, pp. 154-66.

Reiter, R., ed. 1975. Towards an Anthropology of Women. New York: Monthly Review Press.

Richter, L. 1978. Labour Market Information in Developing Countries. Geneva: ILO.

Robbins, L. 1932. The Nature and Significance of Economic Science. London: Macmillan.

Rubbo, A. 1975. "The Spread of Capitalism in Rural Colombia." In R. Reiter, ed., Towards an Anthropology of Women. New York: Monthly Review Press, pp. 333-57.

Saffiotti, H. 1977. "Women, Mode of Production and Social Formations." Latin American Perspectives 4, nos. 1 and 2 (Winter/Spring):27-37.

Scott, Ann Crittenden. 1972. "The Value of Housework: For Love or Money." Ms. magazine, July:56-59.

Seccombe, W. 1974. "The Housewife and Her Labor Under Capitalism." New Left Review no. 83:3-24.

Smith, A. 1975. The Wealth of Nations. New York: Penguin Books.

Standing, G. 1981a. Labor Force Participation and Development. 2nd ed. Geneva: ILO.

_____. 1981b. Unemployment and Female Labour. A Study of Labour Supply in Kingston, Jamaica. London: Macmillan.

Standing, G., and G. Sheehan, eds. 1978. Labor Force Participation in Low Income Countries. Geneva: ILO.

Stoler, A. 1976. "Class Structure and Female Autonomy in Rural Java." In Wellesley Editorial Committee, ed., Women and National Development, pp. 74-88. Chicago: University of Chicago Press.

Sweezy, P. 1942. The Theory of Capitalist Development. New York: Monthly Review Press.

Szalai, A., et al. 1972. The Use of Time. The Hague: Mouton.

Tienda, M. 1977. "Diferenciación regional y transformación sectoral de la mano de obra feminina en Mexico, 1970." Demografía y Economía 11, no. 3:307-25.

United Nations. 1976. "The Participation of Women in the Development of Latin America." Buenos Aires. February, ESA/SDHA/AC.10/4/Rev. 1.

Vanek, J. 1974. "Time Spent in Housework." Scientific American, November, pp. 116-20.

Walker, K. 1969. "Homemaking Still Takes Time." Journal of Home Economics 61, no. 8 (October):621-26.

Wellesley Editorial Committee, ed. 1976. Women and National Development: The Complexities of Change. Chicago: University of Chicago Press.

Wolpe, H. 1975. "The Theory of Internal Colonialism: The South African Case." In Oxaal et al., eds., Beyond the Sociology of Development. London: Routledge and Kegan Paul.

Yousseff, N. H. 1974. Women and Work in Developing Societies. Westport: Greenwood Press.

6

THE CREATION OF A RELATIVE SURPLUS POPULATION: A CASE STUDY FROM MEXICO

Kate Young

In the text that follows, I am concerned to delineate how a rural surplus population was created in one small area of Mexico, and to show why young girls were particularly "selected out" for migration from this population. The basis for the discussion is a description of the changes that have taken place in the economy of some small agricultural communities in a fairly inaccessible, mountainous area of Oaxaca since the 1940s. These changes led to an out-migration flow that by 1970 had reached such proportions that, despite high birth rates, an absolute decline in population was registered.

I will argue that the creation of a surplus population was not primarily set off by the modernization of agriculture (introduction of machinery, improved seeds, irrigation techniques, use of fertilizers, or consolidation of landholdings) but, rather, by the monetization of the local economy, the introduction of factory-produced consumption goods, and the destruction of much of the nonagricultural domestic manufacturing.

There is considerable evidence from other areas that the form that restructuring of rural economies takes is variable, and that destruction of household manufacturing is a key factor to be taken into account. What I am also arguing, however, is that the relation between the creation of a relative surplus population and population redistribution cannot be understood simply in terms of a growing

My thanks to Jane Winters for her invaluable help in collating all the statistical material in this chapter.

social division of labor. Rather, the population needs to be differentiated according to certain categories of people. I am here taking
up a point Marx makes in his discussion of the forms of relative
surplus population:

> [Capital] wants larger numbers of youthful labourers,
> a smaller number of adults. The contradiction is not
> more glaring than that other one that there is a com-
> plaint of the want of hands while at the same time
> many thousands are out of work, because the division
> of labour chains them to a particular branch of indus-
> try (1970, I, p. 641).

The material presented was collected during two field trips,
one in 1971-72, and one in 1975. All the statistical data on migration were compiled from a household survey undertaken in the village of Copa Bitoo. The survey established the periods that the
adults in the household had been absent from the village for more
than six months, whether they were married or single, whether
they took their children with them, when they left, and when they
returned. At the same time the adults in the household were asked
to give details of their children's and their siblings' migratory history.

In addition, village censuses of 1935, 1944, and 1969 and the
available baptismal records from 1870 on were analyzed to provide
an additional check. Some 50 interviews with migrants in the nearby mining town and in Mexico City provided additional data. The
historical reconstruction is based on the accounts of older people
in a number of villages, including Telana and Copa Bitoo, with the
widow of the Spanish coffee buyer of the 1930s and 1940s, and with
local Oaxacan historians. Ethnographic accounts of other villages
in the area and some local historical accounts were also consulted.

In the text the fieldwork data are presented as follows: first,
the broad pattern of out-migration at the beginning of 1972 is given;
the development of this pattern since the establishment of the migration outflow in the 1940s is then discussed. This is followed by a
discussion of the changes in the economy of the area since 1930 that
led to the creation of a relative surplus population. The reasons
for the particular composition of the migration flow are analyzed in
terms of the sexual division of labor in the rural area and of the demand for female labor in the urban area. Sex-specific direction of
migration is finally touched on in terms of lack of employment for
women in the rural area as well as gender discrimination.

The area referred to is the Highland Zapotec region of Oaxaca.
For convenience I call it the Sierra, although this is not strictly

accurate. The Sierra (comprising the former districts of Ixtlan and Villa Alta) is a very mountainous area throughout which a number of small, compact villages (varying in size from 300 to 2,000 inhabitants) are scattered. Most of the villagers are small-scale agriculturalists producing basic staples (corn, beans, chilies, and squash) for domestic consumption on plots of land that were carved out of the woodland at some time in the past. The land is poor in quality, there is no terracing (despite considerable erosion) nor irrigation, and few plots can be cultivated year after year. In the main they are cultivated for two years running and then left fallow for 5 to 12 years. Few farmers use chemical fertilizers, some have oxen for plowing, and many have a few animals (sheep or cows) that are grazed on plots to try to improve fertility.

Most of the villages have plots of land inside the urban area as well as on the hillsides; these urban plots are privately owned, but all other landholding is nominally communal. Villagers in fact treat most of the cultivable land as if it were privately owned, the only restriction on rights being that plots of land can be sold only to members of the community.

The region divides roughly into two zones: a hotter, humid zone of abundant rainfall where today households grow coffee for export on a small scale, and a drier, more temperate zone where avocados and other fruits (zapote, mango) are grown for the domestic market. Of the two villages referred to, Copa Bitoo lies in the temperate zone and Telana lies in the coffee zone:[1] the former is under the administration of Ixtlan; the latter, that of Villa Alta. In 1972 the population of Copa Bitoo was 1,008, and that of Telana in 1975 was 1,843. Although statistical data on migration refer only to Copa Bitoo (Young 1976), there is no reason to suspect that, in broad outline, migration patterns differ greatly in other villages of the area.

THE SITUATION IN 1972

In Copa Bitoo in 1972, over two-fifths of the adult population had at some time lived for six months or more outside the village. Of the 225 households, just under two-thirds had a member who was living or had lived outside the village for six months or more. At the time there were 496 people living outside the village who had been born there, and 1,008 people still living there.[2]

In the Sierra in general the 1960s was a high out-migration decade, and an absolute decline in population over the previous decade was recorded. The former district of Ixtlan declined by 2.3 percent, and that of Villa Alta by 3.3 percent. In comparison, during the 1960s the population of the state of Oaxaca increased by 16.5 percent, that of the city of Oaxaca by 39.2 percent, and that of Mexico City by 43.8 percent (Dirección General de Estadística 1970). While the 1950-59 out-migration rate for the Sierra as a whole was calculated by one Mexican scholar (Cabrera 1975) as 246 per 1,000, for Copa Bitoo I calculated a rate of 292 per 1,000. The comparative figure of 66 per 1,000 for the state of Oaxaca (Cabrera 1975) gives further indication of the magnitude of the population out-flow from the Sierra.

The majority of serrano (people of the Sierra) out-migrants headed for Mexico City, the mecca of migrants from all over Mexico. For most serranos getting to Mexico City, or DF (Distrito Federal), as most people call it, involves a day's journey to the city of Oaxaca and then another day's bus to truck trip. Copa Bitoo migrants also showed a preference for the capital: in 1972, 60 percent of them were resident there. If we look at migrants by sex, however, a significant difference in the preference for the capital is evident: while some 59 percent of all female migrants lived there, only 44 percent of all males did so. This conforms to the national pattern of urban areas attracting more female migrants than males. A national study shows that in the 1950s the ratio of females to males migrating to urban areas was 100 to 83—for Mexico City the ratio was 110 females to 82 males (CEED 1970).

If migration to urban areas "favors" women, migration in general favors young people. In Mexico as a whole in 1950-59, 68 percent of all female migrants were between 10 and 29 years of age, while 66 percent of male migrants were in that age cohort. Although the Mexican population is a young one, only 57 percent of males fall into this same age cohort (CEED 1970, p. 9). Of the migrants from Copa Bitoo in 1972, just under 50 percent were between 10 and 29, and 75 percent were between 10 and 39. The percentage under 29 might seem rather low in comparison with the national figures, but it in fact confirms the trend to older migrants in successive decades (a point to which I will return shortly).

More notable, however, is the sex differences in age cohorts: in 1972, of all migrants from Copa Bitoo between 10 and 19, 62 percent were female; of those between 20 and 29, only 41 percent were. In the 1960s the distinction is even more apparent: of all the first-time female migrants who left during the decade, 43 percent were under 20 years of age; in contrast, only 18 percent of first-time male migrants were. For the subsequent cohort, those 20 to 29 years old, the situation is reversed: only 38 percent of females versus 54 percent of males. This preponderance of female migrants in the 10-19 cohort is found throughout Mexico (CEED 1970, p. 94).

MIGRATION SINCE 1940

Migration from Copa Bitoo really became established in the 1940s. Prior to this few people left the village permanently for employment elsewhere, and in neither the 1920s nor the 1930s did the total for the decade reach 20 (the total village population in 1930 was 860). In the 1940s, however, a significant number of people left (80 in all). From 1940 on, the absolute numbers of people leaving increased almost every year. Of the total migration from Copa Bitoo, 11 percent took place in the 1940s, 32 percent in the 1950s, and 57 percent in the 1960s.[3] Although the numbers of migrants increased each decade, the rate of increase was not constant; it declined by 40 percent between 1950 and 1960, and by 37 percent in the following decade. If migration in the 1970s continued at the very high rate of the first two years of the decade, the decline in the rate of increase might be reversed.

The study of Mexican population trends makes it clear that while migration was still sex- and age-specific in the 1950s, the trend over the period 1930-60 was to increasing equalization of the sexes and increasing diversification in the age structure of migration flows (CEED 1970, pp. 92-100). An analysis of the data from Copa Bitoo confirms this finding. If we look at the age at which migrants leave, it can be seen that over the period 1940-70 a trend to older first migration is evident. (See Table 6.1.)

TABLE 6.1

Age of Combined Migrants at First Migration, 1940-69
(percent)

	10-19	20-29	30-39	Other
1940-49	44	44	6	6
1950-59	33	47	13	7
1960-69	27	42	21	10

Note: Combined migrants include both those absent from the village in 1972 (migrants) and those resident in the village in 1972 who had once been migrants (return migrants).
Source: Young 1976, p. 85.

An analysis by sex shows that although 10-19 is the age at which most female migrants left (except in the 1960s, when it was 20-29), and 20-29 the age at which most male migrants left, there have been some interesting changes. (See Table 6.2.)

TABLE 6.2

Age at First Migration: Combined Female and
Combined Male Migrants, 1940-69
(percent)

	10-29	20-29	30-39	NN*
Age at First Migration of Combined Female Migrants				
1940-49	54	34	3	35
1950-59	38	42	15	95
1960-69	43	38	19	111
Age at First Migration of Combined Male Migrants				
1940-49	36	53	11	45
1950-59	29	59	12	68
1960-69	18	54	28	113

Notes: Female migrants include 9 percent under age 10 in 1940-49 and 5 percent under age 10 in 1950-59.

Male migrants in 1940-49 include braceros.

Combined migrants include both those absent from the village (migrants) and those resident in the village who had once been migrants (return migrants).

*NN = Total numbers of those who migrated in that decade. Percents do not add up to 100 percent because only 10-39 year olds are included here.

Source: Young 1976, pp. 85-86.

Throughout the period women predominated in the migration flow: in the 1940s (excluding braceros[4]) 78 men left for every 100 women; in the 1950s, only 76; in the 1960s, however, the ratios evened out at 100:101. Over the whole period, taking only first-time migrants between 10 and 29, regardless of where they are now living, for every 100 women who migrated, 93 men did (see CEED

1970, p. 99, for national figures). At the same time a return migrant was also more likely to be a woman than a man.

With migration of older cohorts there has been, as one could expect, a change in the status of migrants. Migrants in the 1970s were more likely to be married and to be parents than they were in the 1940s. In fact, of all migrants in the first years of the 1970s, 47 percent were married and 39 percent unmarried (as against 6 percent and 74 percent in the 1940s). The proportion of first-time out-migrants with children increased from 3 percent in the 1940s to 18 percent in the 1960s.

The pattern of change in marital status over the period is seen in Table 6.3.

TABLE 6.3

Marital Status of Combined Migrants,
Male and Female, 1940–71
(percent)

	Single	Married	Married + Children	Other
1940–49	74	3	3	20
1950–59	62	14	10	14
1960–69	49	17	18	16
1970–71	39	25	22	14

Note: "Other" includes widowed, divorced, and abandoned men or women.
Source: Young 1976.

The statistical data have highlighted some of the sex- and age-specific characteristics of migration from Copa Bitoo, and shown that, very broadly, these correspond to the national pattern. The questions then to be answered are, first, why young people are "selected out" for migration, and why young women in particular should migrate at younger ages than their male counterparts. Second, what factors are at work that make the migration pattern over time take on a more diversified character—in other words, what is going on at the national and the local levels that encourages people of all ages to leave the rural area? Last, what factors direct women to the capital? To answer these questions, it is necessary to look at the economic changes in the serrano economy from 1930 to 1970 within the very general context of the major trends in the national economy. We need to see, first, how the surplus population was created; second, what factors worked to select out certain categories of migrants; and, last, what effect migration had upon the rural area and the capacity of the individual households to survive.

ECONOMIC CHANGE SINCE 1930

The economy of the Sierra can be briefly characterized as largely directed to self-provisioning in the early 1930s. That is, most villages were to a considerable degree self-sufficient in basic foodstuffs; households made clothing and other household necessities for domestic consumption. At the same time there was interzonal exchange through barter of surplus foodstuffs at the small weekly markets, in particular those products that, because of climatic differences, could be produced only in certain villages (for example, wheat and potatoes in the cooler zone, beans and sugar in the hotter zone). There was also village specialization in nonagricultural products: some villages produced textile fiber goods (ropes, bags, tumplines); others, pottery; still others, leather goods (notably sandals), wooden saddles, or metal tools.

It is therefore more accurate to talk of zonal self-provisioning rather than self-sufficient households or villages. Although there was some production of goods for sale outside the zone—some of the ixtle fiber products, particular types of chilies and coffee produced on a very limited scale—these goods were bartered by the producers for a restricted range of manufactured items brought to the zone by petty traders (usually funded by the coffee wholesaler) or for local produce. The local economy was at this period largely unmonetized: coffee, ocote (pitch pine), and (to some extent) salt served as mediums of exchange. Most households took their produce to one or more of the area's six weekly markets (the seventh took place in the city of Oaxaca). There were no full-time traders; even those who specialized in coffee buying did so on a very small scale, and were also peasant producers.

Around the mid-1930s the situation changed very rapidly. A new wholesale coffee buyer (a Spaniard) offered cash, and found many producers eager to trade. At the same time he was generous in giving credit to a few of the small coffee buyers so that from his store they could buy manufactured goods for resale in the serrano markets: kerosene lamps, battery flashlights, hand grinding mills, ready-made clothes, soap, knives. With the increased volume of trade, local families who had kept mules or donkeys and had supplemented the household income through muleteering were encouraged to invest in larger numbers of animals. They also got loans from the coffee merchant, who employed them to take the raw coffee beans to his warehouses in the Valley of Oaxaca (about a week's journey there and back).

This infusion of cash and manufactured goods coincided with an expansion of both federal and state government activity in the zone. The federal government program to increase the provision of primary school education in the rural areas led to a number of schools being opened in the Sierra, or communally financed village schools being recognized and their teachers receiving a government salary. The state officials also began to collect taxes and to draw up modernization programs for the area (which were not implemented until the 1950s because of lack of financing).[5]

Between 1938 and 1954 the price of coffee rose steadily (the world market price rose twenty-two fold), which encouraged more householders in the hot zone to take up coffee growing or to dedicate more land to coffee; at the village level this meant that less land was available for growing the staples (or, in land-rich villages, less good land was available); it also meant the increasing privatization of so-called communal land. Many families without access to land suitable for coffee growing took up wage labor so as to acquire cash; families with coffee plots decreased their production of corn and bought supplies from the temperate villages. In the temperate zone a number of corn producers increased their production for sale to coffee producers, and many of the latter began to pay for labor instead of using the more traditional means of acquiring labor.

Although these changes were not particularly dramatic, they carried within them the seeds of much more revolutionary changes: the privatization of land, wage labor, and the cash nexus. Bartering declined (but did not entirely disappear) as coffee producers no longer exchanged coffee for local produce. Removing one of the main mediums of exchange and replacing it with the more efficient (because more widely exchangeable) cash led to the disappearance of ocote and salt as money equivalents.

During the 1940s another, less structurally but nonetheless significant, event took place. The involvement of the U.S. economy in the war effort had led to a shortage of labor, particularly in the agricultural sector. The U.S. government therefore persuaded the Mexican government to provide this needed labor through the bracero program. In 1944 a recruiting office opened in Oaxaca. Many men from families who had little access to cash, being neither producers of coffee nor surplus maize, nor traders or muleteers, seized the opportunity to work on short-term contracts (six months) for what appeared to them as munificent wages. They returned to the Sierra with tales of the strange ways of North American farmers and consumers, and suitcases full of religious tracts provided by fundamentalist sects (including the Jehovah's Witnesses), watches, battery radios, and savings. A number of men from the temperate zone actively looked for a new cash crop; many of them invested in land and planted avocado trees; in the coffee zone, commerce appeared equally attractive.

The involvement of the United States in the war also gave the nascent Mexican industrial sector a boost, both because of import substitution and production for the U.S. market of certain consumer goods, and because of the lifting of competitive pressure. With the coming of peace—and, for U.S. industry, resumption of consumer production—there was an aggressive expansion of commercial capital into the subsistence hinterlands of Mexico; it was searching for new markets in which to sell goods produced by the growing Mexican industrial sector. Despite its remoteness the Sierra was an obvious area for such expansion, since its population was already involved in producing a cash crop. This was especially true when coffee prices rose rapidly after 1946, providing the means to acquire consumer goods. Tools, domestic utensils (pails, tin bathtubs, hand mills), ready-made clothes, and textiles were in great demand, as were many types of basic foodstuffs—biscuits, pasta, rice, corn—and luxury consumption goods—beer, Coca Cola. Many of these goods were cheaper than local equivalents, and all were more prestigious.

The increased volume of trade made mule trains, the archaic means of transport, quite inadequate. So the local merchants and their allies, particularly the schoolteachers, whose numbers were growing as government investment in primary education expanded, used their political power to secure roads to the principal coffee marketing villages. The first truck reached the chief coffee entrepôt village in 1952; by the end of the 1950s Telana was accessible by road, and became the premier entrepot village (its ousted rival rapidly declined in size and importance because of bitter political strife and a high rate of out-migration). By the mid-1960s Copa Bitoo had its own connecting branch road.

Once the roads were completed, a handful of local traders and coffee brokers invested in trucks in order to expand their activities. In most cases their trucks were bought on time, with the down payment in some cases being loaned by the coffee wholesaler—now a buyer who had no connection with supplying merchandise—against the promise of privileged carriage rights. The trucker-merchants in turn formed a cooperative and divided the area among themselves so as to limit competition—and to keep out what they described as intruders (trucker-merchants from outside the area).

With the more modern transport system and the influx of merchandise, two things happened. Production of locally made goods for exchange declined: raincapes of tule reed were replaced by plastic sheets, leather sandals by plastic shoes, local pottery by much cheaper factory-made goods. The production of locally marketable food surpluses also was affected: the truckers brought in cheaper staples, notably corn and beans, produced elsewhere under more highly capitalized conditions or subsidized by the government. At the same time, with the availability of more rapid transport, the cultivation of certain products for the urban markets (such as avocados, sapodilla, mangos, and certain vegetables) was made possible. Equally, in almost every village small front-room stores began to open, stocking basic staples, cloth, thread, kerosene, soft drinks, beer, and alcoholic beverages; most of these stores sold goods on credit.

The effects of the changes were thus uneven. On the positive side, villagers could be said to have benefited from the expansion of the market, and consequent specialization. At the same time, while more labor was required in some sectors (but often labor of a specific type), it was made redundant in others. In general, redundancy prevailed. This is perhaps best illustrated by the redundancy brought about by the complete disappearance of muleteering and its associated support activities—production of fodder; making of rope halters, riatas, and other gear; breeding mules/donkeys. Some of the old muleteers were employed by the truckers as loaders, or even got jobs in their shops, but the vast majority lost their livelihood. A single truck replaced 33 mules or 80 donkeys and from 8 to 18 men, and cut the round trip time from 7 to 3 days, using only 3 or 4 men. There was also a sharp decline in demand for laborers to produce surplus corn, and a decline in ixtle cultivation and processing because the merchant-truckers imported ready-to-weave cheap fibers from Yucatan.

THE CREATION OF A RELATIVE SURPLUS POPULATION

The overall effects of all these changes were twofold: the restructuring of the economy away from interzonal exchanges and self-provisioning was accelerated—the zone was more firmly integrated into the national economy—and the zonal population became clearly differentiated both economically and socially. Very crudely, the population could be divided into a small number of households primarily involved in commerce (either as producers on a commercial scale or as traders or transporters) that hired labor; a small number without land (or with access only to poor land), who primarily worked as laborers; and the majority of households, which produced both subsistence items and a market commodity of some sort on a small scale, and neither hired labor nor worked regularly for wages. Both land and labor became increasingly commoditized, with much of what was ostensibly communal land becoming increasingly privatized (particularly in the coffee zone) and the price of land suitable for cash crops rising rapidly.

The economic boom largely depended on the maintenance of high coffee prices, but in the mid-1950s they fell sharply. As people sought to maintain income levels, a number of strategies were adopted. Some of the coffee producers attempted to grow more coffee, more cheaply. They were able to buy up the plots of less successful producers, but their ability to expand was somewhat limited by their having to revert to use of unpaid family labor. The avocado growers had less room to maneuver, given the time lag between planting young trees and beginning of production, but some coffee buyers began to speculate in avocados to compensate for lost coffee income. With the growing urban middle class, avocado consumption increased, as did the price, which rose tenfold in as many years. Others, finding it difficult to get work locally, sold their labor outside the zone in the slack season. In general, people felt the pinch of hardship; families found it increasingly difficult to produce or acquire the complex of consumption and production goods that they needed to ensure their survival over the annual cycle, and at the same time lack of local income-generating opportunities began to be felt. In other words, part of the population had become surplus (was no longer guaranteed its conditions of existence), and was in the process of being "freed" for industrial capital.

Prior to the mid-1950s there had been, as already noted, some out-migration from Copa Bitoo. In the 1940s a number of the men who had gone to the United States as braceros out-migrated permanently after their return (either returning to the United States or going to DF). A number of girls between 7 and 19 also left the village, initially going to the city of Oaxaca to work as domestics and to learn Spanish. In the main these girls came from the families of part-time traders who had been encouraged by the coffee merchant to expand their trading activities and by the schoolteachers to invest in the education of their children: schooling for boys and domestic service for girls. A few girls fled to Oaxaca to escape a disagreeable potential (or actual) husband chosen for them by their fathers. These women were often helped to find jobs in Oaxaca by their young female relatives already in service. Some young men left either to train to become schoolteachers or to avoid an unwanted marriage and the responsibilities of early family formation.

After the slump in coffee prices, the increasing need to have cash—to pay taxes and to pay for recently introduced services, such as electricity, running water, medical and postal services—coinciding with a period when local opportunities for earning cash were declining for the majority of the population, led to the buildup of out-migration from the area.

Both temporary/seasonal and permanent migration increased markedly (of total migration from Copa Bitoo, 57 percent left in the 1960s).[6] The seasonal migrants, after preparing their corn plots, generally left for areas within the state (or even further afield) where there was a demand for agricultural labor or for construction workers, and returned for the harvest (some three or four months later). The bulk of all migrants (80 percent) were still under 29, and although young men were leaving in increasing numbers, the typical permanent out-migrant was still a young unmarried woman under 20 years of age (see Table 6.1). The typical seasonal migrant was a married male with several children.

EFFECT OF MIGRATION ON THE VILLAGE ECONOMY

This age-specific migration pattern had considerable repercussions on the rural area. With individual households throwing off "surplus" labor, at the community level this meant that a large proportion of the young adult population from 15 to 29 was absent (for example, in 1971 almost 70 percent of the members of this age group were living outside Copa Bitoo). This, as Table 6.4 shows, had the effect of increasing the proportion of dependent to working-age population between 1950 and 1970. It also meant an acute shortage of labor at critical times of the year.

The change in the relative proportion of these populations meant that in 1970, for every person of working age there was .82 person of dependent age, while in 1950 there had only been .67.[7] If the number of male agricultural producers (women in this area do not cultivate, although they do harvest and process crops) is related to the total population, it appears that while in 1950 one male had to produce foodstuffs sufficient for three persons (actual ratio 1:3.1), in 1972 he had to produce enough for four (actual ratio 1:4.2). The implication of such a change is either that productivity in agriculture would have to rise if customary consumption levels were to be maintained, or that the agricultural producers would have to have

some other means of access to provisions. For agricultural productivity to rise, the peasants of Copa Bitoo would have had to
change their production pattern: using better seeds or fertilizer,
or changing to a different crop. While the richer households in fact
did so (but only from 1969 on, when they began to use chemical fertilizers), the others did not. [8] By 1971 most families in the village
produced insufficient quantities of corn for the year; averaged out,
only five months' worth of corn for the whole village was produced.
(See Berg 1968 for similar figures calculated for the Sierra as a
whole.)

TABLE 6.4

Proportion of Working-Age to Dependent Population,
Copa Bitoo, 1950 and 1970
(percent)

Category	1950	1970
Dependent (0–14, 65+)	40	45
Working age (15–64)	60	55

Source: Dirección General de Estadística 1950 and 1970
censuses.

Age-specific out-migration, then, produced a change in the
proportion of producers to consumers in the community as a whole;
at the level of individual households, I have already suggested a
crisis in access to labor at peak periods of demand.

THE EFFECT OF SEX- AND AGE-SPECIFIC
MIGRATION ON THE HOUSEHOLD ECONOMY

It has been argued thus far that, at a time when the social division of labor within Mexico was changing, the Sierra became an
area in which domestic manufacturing came into competition with
the products of industry and, as a result, declined. At the level of
the household, this contraction was expressed in the freeing of certain quantities of labor time. At the same time, households were
obliged to produce for the market in order to get cash. They had to

invest household labor time in activities producing cash. While some households were able to acquire cash either through producing marketable goods or through their involvement in trade, others were unable to do so, and had only their labor to sell. If a household was unable to adapt to the new conditions, it had to slough off members who were unable to acquire a means of livelihood, or a partial livelihood, locally. In other words, labor not only had been freed but also had been made redundant.

Also at this time (the 1940s) labor was being freed from its communal and kinship matrix through the development of the cash nexus. Prior to the 1940s households had depended upon their own labor supply during most of the year, but at peak periods of need (clearing, planting, weeding, and harvesting) additional supplies of labor could be obtained through two forms of reciprocal labor arrangements. First there was the festive labor party (gozona), to which as many of a household's neighbors, kinsmen, and affines who were free and willing would come. They were given food, alcohol, and cigarettes, and worked on the party giver's plot for the number of days there was food (generally not more than one or two). People could be recruited not only for agricultural work but also for clearing land or building a house. A much smaller number of people could be recruited through exchange labor (mano vuelta)— for example, a man who needed help clearing his land might ask two men to work with him for a number of days. He would repay these days to each helper when they were clearing their land. Fathers could repay with their son's labor.

Typically, reciprocal labor partners were kinsmen (not usually brothers but often father's or mother's brothers' sons) or affines (very commonly sister's or wife's husband). Although agricultural reciprocities had to be repaid within the period of the loan (clearing for clearing, weeding for weeding), many of the other labor loans (such as house building) were long-term. The older the man, the more debts and credits he had accumulated, the denser a history of shared endeavors he had with certain of his kinsmen and affines, and often his neighbors. Thus, the more certain he could be of getting help when it was needed. Younger men, in turn, had many fewer.

With the advent of cash, these labor arrangements rapidly broke down: the ability to hire labor made reciprocal arrangements unnecessary. Hired labor was more efficient both in output and in the control the hirer could exercise over it. In the previous form of command over labor, a householder often had to accept more workers than were really necessary (and feed them as well); or, unless he had sons he could substitute, he had to reduce the number of subsidiary activities he could undertake. Many householders enthusiastically seized upon the new form of commanding labor; families that had little access to cash willingly sold their labor, at least initially, so as to have a source of cash income. With the restriction on the economy in the late 1950s, however, there was a scarcity of cash; many families tried to go back to exchanging labor, particularly mano vuelta (the days of the large-scale festive parties were over, food for such parties now being too expensive).

But many people had become unwilling to do so; even close kinsmen or affines who previously would have exchanged labor often refused, because they could not afford to "work for nothing"; now they either cultivated little and concentrated on selling their labor, or they were relatively wealthy and wanted to invest their time in more remunerative activities than subsistence production. For example, a coffee buyer could, with the help of hired labor, spend only 24 days of his own time preparing and sowing enough corn to ensure him, in a normal season, a year's supply for a family of four. If he did not hire this labor, he would have to invest a total of 130 days in producing the same amount of corn. [9] The return to his labor was much lower than, say, buying coffee from growers, reselling the beans to the wholesale buyer, and investing the profits in ends of cloth to sell locally, or even servicing his political connections in the urban area.

There was also another problem: the number of young men available for mano vuelta exchange was limited; in the 1950s, and more so in the 1960s, many of those between 20 and 29 were migrating out of the area. This problem of availability of exchange labor was most severe for young householders who had separated from their family of origin and whose own family was beginning to grow, but it also affected older families whose eldest son was still not able to work full-time in agriculture. In other words, out-migration may have seemed a sensible solution to the particular problem of the individual family, but at the community level it contributed to an ever-growing scarcity of certain types of labor.

The general effect of the inability of many householders to get the labor they needed was that the bulk of the households lessened the amount of corn grown in order to conform to the "free" labor resources they could count upon—a son or perhaps a single reciprocal labor exchange partner. This in turn led to the household's greater need for cash income to buy the staples it now did not produce. The families' expanded requirements for cash income led to greater reliance on selling labor. But in-village opportunities for employment were limited. With a poor harvest or a sudden need for cash in the family because of illness or death—or an overall need for more cash because of inflation and rising taxes—many households found they had to allocate ever more of their time to selling labor and ever less to producing subsistence.

Many of the households expelled their young adult children (particularly daughters) to the cities as soon as they could, so as to limit the amount of subsistence needed. Often such households became trapped in a downward spiral of poverty from which it was almost impossible to escape, and that usually ended with the out-migration of the whole family. This not only affected young couples with high consumer:producer ratios (see Chayanov 1966), but also older couples all of whose adult children had out-migrated or become independent.

As for nonagricultural work, particularly house building, older men could call upon their long-term labor credits and get the work done for a small cash outlay. Younger men were in a disadvantaged position, having no or few credits, yet being precisely the people who most needed to build a new house for their growing family. Without savings to pay for building a house, young married men could not become residentially independent—a critical life cycle rite of passage. A man (married or not) living in his father's or father-in-law's household was considered to be a preadult and had to defer to the older man's authority. To acquire the needed savings, many young men out-migrated at first temporarily, and then often permanently.

The result, then, of both the constraints on the poor and the opportunities for the wealthier families was the diversification of the migration pattern for the zone as a whole. By the 1970s people of all ages were leaving; couples with or without children, elderly widows/widowers going to join their children, teen-agers, unhappily married men/women. This in turn led to an absolute population decline. In what follows, I will analyze the sexual division of labor that led to gender-related differences in that process.

THE SEXUAL DIVISION OF LABOR

The combined effects of the weakening of kinship and affinity as means of access to labor, and the release of labor time as a result of the area's being drawn into the national economy, produced the paradox of an economy that had both too little and too much labor available. The main reason for this lies in the nature of the sexual division of labor and the constraints it imposes on the free allocation of people to the range of household or community tasks that have to be performed to ensure household reproduction.

The differential effect of the destruction of much of the local nonagricultural household production on the two genders has been noted, as has the release of labor time through the use of more efficient tools. Here the prime example must be the hand mill, which released quantities of female labor formerly invested in grinding corn daily—villagers estimated that it roughly halved the number of hours needed to crush corn on a <u>metate</u> (this was further decreased when the diesel-powered corn mill was installed). Light plastic buckets allowed more water to be brought to the house from the neighborhood springs (women's work); a diversification in diet to include rice or pasta (available in the newly opened local stores) lessened cooking and preparation time; the decline in festive labor arrangements in favor of hired labor lessened the amount of time women spent in cooking for the field hands; soft drinks substituted for <u>atole</u> (a fine corn gruel flavored with cinnamon—the nonalcoholic drink prior to the 1940s); wheat bread for tortillas; factory-made jeans and heavy-duty shirts for homemade clothes and hand-woven fabrics. At the same time social (state) investment in such things as electrification and provision of running water cut the labor investment in domestic activities, mainly the responsibility of women.

When women's labor was freed, it was reinvested, often in tasks that children had carried out before; this was both because the children were either in school most of the year or had migrated out, and because women and children performed some of the same tasks. Women did not take up agricultural work, nor did they take over any of the administrative posts in the village government. There are two probable reasons for this. First, these activities are defining features of maleness, in particular the authority and power of the father as the head of the household. Second, women were not skilled or knowledgeable farmers; they had no practical training, and their training as domestic beings did not give them the necessary muscle development needed, particularly for breaking ground. Some women did begin to weed (particularly when their male kinsmen were absent from the village), and others to work on the in-village plots with the lighter soils. But in the main families in the 1970s appeared to prefer the option of female out-migration to female substitution.

To the extent that the demand for labor in the local area did not conform to the type of labor available, the restructuring of the economy and of the organization of production and the relations derived from it, led to particular categories of people becoming especially "at risk" of migration.

I have argued that the expulsion of young daughters rather than sons was based on a number of factors: the sexual division of labor, which places the burden of subsistence production on men; the fact that many of the activities that women and their daughters carried out were being undermined by more efficient, industrially produced products or were made more productive; the declining importance of affinity as a mechanism to ensure privileged access to labor (daughters were no longer useful as bringers of sons-in-law, since these men were now unwilling to provide labor to their in-laws).

Although a mother might protest her daughter's being sent away on the ground that she needed her help in the house and with child care, her arguments could easily be overruled by those of her husband as manager of the household entérprise. The daughter might also wish to go, in order to "help out" or to "lighten the burden of so many mouths to feed."[10] Many girls in fact said that in the village they "did nothing," while as migrants they could be useful to their families by saving their wages and sending back regular payments—or, if this was not possible, at least being in a position to send money, clothing, or medicine in cases of family crisis. They could also help members of the family who needed medical attention in town, or could place their siblings in jobs when they arrived in the city. Daughters of larger families were probably more vulnerable to pressures to leave home—in 1972, 13 percent of the young female migrants (under 30), as against 7 percent of the males, had more than four siblings in the village—and possibly were expected to contribute to the household budget in a more regular fashion than other migrant girls, but the information is rather scanty on this.

In sharp contrast with the encouragement of daughters to leave, sons were discouraged, if not prevented, from migrating. Often a father would refuse to give one son permission to go until the next was of an age to help in the fields. However, once a young man entered the local village government system (at 18), or if he had a number of close kinsmen prepared to help him in the urban area, he had more opportunity to override his father's objections. If he was already married, he might be greatly encouraged in his resolve by his wife, particularly if she was a return migrant.

URBAN EMPLOYMENT

With girls being encouraged to leave the village when quite young, it follows that many of them leave before completing their primary school education. In fact, having to repeat a year at school was one of the commonest excuses given by the girl or her family for her going to the city; it is better to be usefully employed in Mexico City than doing lessons for a second time. As a result, female migrants' level of education is lower than that of males (see Table 6.5).

TABLE 6.5

Educational Levels of the 496 Migrants, by Sex: 1972
(percent)

F	M	Years of Schooling
29	5	None
41	48	1-4
30	47	5 or more

For girls these low educational levels are no particular barrier to getting a job, as long as they are prepared to work as a
domestic servant. Nowadays, however, many girls are unwilling
to work for long as servants, since this generally involves living
in and being on call 24 hours a day, often without holidays or social
benefits. But even those with some years of experience in domestic
work find that their lack of primary school certificate is a real hindrance in getting other types of work in the industrial and service
sector. In addition, the rate of female unemployment in these sectors is high (and higher than male unemployment) (Arizpe 1977).
The situation is even worse for married women or mothers: regular and full-time employment for women with small children is difficult to find, whether as domestics or in other service work. Many
married women are forced to accept part-time work, home work
(sewing garments or assembling radios or calculators), or various
forms of self-employment (street trading, taking in laundry).

For young men the urban employment situation is more complex. In the expansive phase of Mexican industrial growth (roughly
the 1940s and 1950s), it was relatively easy for young men and boys
without particular skills to get a job in construction or services
(such as porterage jobs in the market). In the early 1950s several
male migrants from Copa Bitoo were able to set up their own small
retail businesses after a short period of wage laboring. Nowadays
it is increasingly difficult for young males to find employment even
with patronage of kinsmen and former villagers (or paisanos, fellow
Oaxaqueños), unless they have some skills in addition to a primary
school certificate, a certificate of completion of military service
or exemption from it, and a letter of good conduct (issued by the
village government). [11] Employers even demand these certificates
from adult men applying for such jobs as night watchman or auxiliary
policeman (see Balan 1969 on credencialismo). Many employers (or

their personnel officers) also demand money for giving the applicant a job. For these reasons young men from poorer families, after finishing their primary education in the 1970s, often went to the local mines for a spell of wage work so as to have a fund to tide them over during their first few months in Mexico City. Over a third of the miners interviewed in 1971 were waiting to move on to the capital as soon as they got word from their relatives of a job opening.

GENDER DISCRIMINATION

There is, therefore, a double pressure on young men that serves to keep them at home: their usefulness to their families as agricultural workers on the household plot, and the nature of demand for labor in the urban area (such demand varies; for example, in the late 1960s young rural men were in demand as bodyguards, private police, or night watchmen). At the same time some young men, particularly those who had spent a few years as head of their household in the village, talked about the advantages of rural life: aqui soy jefe, nadie me manda (here I'm the boss, no one orders me around). The sense of personal worth as a family head—a patriarch—compensated some men for a relentless schedule of work throughout the year, trying to make ends meet. Despite their best efforts, many found it impossible, and ultimately out-migrated. If his wife had been a migrant, she would often encourage him to leave. Most married women also noted how much easier life in town is for them: no carrying of water, no cooking on wood fires or cutting of wood, no washing clothes in icy streams. Furthermore, when children fall sick, there are doctors and health clinics available.

For young girls the situation is the reverse; with decreased domestic manufacturing, and diminishing importance of sons-in-law as sources of labor, girls have become doubly redundant in village households; at the same time parents and daughters know that gainful employment as servants in the city is readily available. For older women the effect of women's lesser social and economic roles in most villages particularly penalizes them if they are unmarried, abandoned, or widowed. With their exclusion from agriculture, women do not have any strong claim to land. [12] Even if a woman should decide to take up farming, she would probably be unable to wrest control over a piece of land from her male kinsmen, since women hold no position of power in the village government. Also, although women do have the right to cultivate communal land, this land is at present in short supply and is generally of poor quality or requires high labor inputs. Only women who have a son old enough to take over the household's agricultural responsibilities, or a son-in-law, or who have a stable source of income that permits them to hire labor can survive in the village on their own.

Even in the villages in the coffee-growing area, where single women can get seasonal employment as coffee pickers, they can earn enough during the harvest to eke out a miserable existence for themselves and their children for the rest of the year only if they work with an intense degree of self-exploitation.[13] There are some further possibilities for such women to get sporadic domestic employment in Telana (washing clothes, embroidering blouses, looking after the bachelor schoolteachers) throughout the rest of the year, but they are very uncertain sources of income. Women's social position as dependents of males—whether father, husband, or son—is still so firmly entrenched that for a woman on her own the rural area is hardly a viable alternative to migration.

Single women are expelled not only from the villages but also from the rural sector as a whole. For men there are still a number of rural employment possibilities—in agriculture, construction, or mining—as well as service sector employment in nearby towns. Few of these occupations require either literacy or facility in Spanish, and many of them can be performed by men of almost any age, since physical strength is often not the main criterion (mining and construction are obvious exceptions). Although many of these jobs are seasonal or temporary, there are some full-time opportunities (for example, some migrants have worked over 15 years in the mines, while others have settled in Oaxaca as shopkeepers or tailors).

For girls or single women the rural employment possibilities are virtually nil—most of them have already been mentioned. They can get jobs in the city of Oaxaca as domestic servants (or prostitutes), but rates of pay are poor in comparison with those offered in Mexico City. One of the few reasonably paid local jobs in the past was that of schoolteacher, but few girls from the zone had sufficient education to aspire to this; nowadays most girls are aware that a rural teacher's pay is lower than that of a clerical assistant in Mexico City. For married women too there is a far wider range of income-earning possibilities in Mexico City than the city of Oaxaca. The lack of employment in the rural area explains in part the tendency for single women migrants to head for urban areas, and differences in wages between Oaxaca and Mexico City helps explain their preference for the latter. The difficulties men experience in getting jobs in Mexico City, and their greater opportunities for employment in the rural area, may account in part for the more diversified migration pattern of male migrants.

CONCLUSIONS

The brief overview of the economic change affecting the Sierra since the 1940s presents a familiar picture: the dramatic restructuring of a zonal economy away from self-provisioning and toward integration into the wider national economy. Production became more directed to the national market, and consumption radically changed with the inflow of manufactured goods. The restructuring of both production and consumption involved the freeing of labor, particularly through the destruction of much domestic manufacturing but also of other activities. Much of this freed labor found no alternative occupations in the area, and thus became both free and redundant: a relative surplus population.

These changes were accompanied by rapid social differentiation and redistribution of wealth. This took the form of the development of a class of small-scale landowners also involved in trade employing labor, and a class of landless (or virtually landless) laborers. In addition to these two classes, there is a stratum of small-scale farmers aiming at simple reproduction—producing just enough for self-provisioning and the market to maintain the household year by year. Although this stratum constantly loses member households (to either of the two polar classes, or through outmigration), it shows no signs, as yet, of disappearing completely. It is replenished through the high fertility rates of its constituent households and by returning migrants with some savings who count on successful trading to survive; it is maintained over difficult periods by the help of its migrant members.

In the case presented, the driving force behind the creation of the surplus population was not, I would argue, the sustained need of industrial capital for labor in the form of dispossessed peasants. Rather, commercial capital's intervention in this rural self-provisioning economy, by opening up a market for industrial products, restructured it in such a way that simple reproduction was no longer possible. Young people were, in consequence, sloughed off. Initially the demand in the urban and industrializing areas for young, strong, and single men and—thanks to the rapid growth of the middle and petty bourgeois classes—for young, healthy, single girls was met by the outflow of young people from rural areas such as the Sierra. But the close correspondence between demand and supply did not continue throughout the various phases of Mexican economic development. The disjunction between the setting free of the rural population and the industrial sector's ability to absorb it is one of the key indicators of the unevenness of capitalist development.

The people freed by the intervention of commercial capital in the rural economy and flooding the urban areas may eventually find employment in the industrial or service sector, but the vast majority eke out a livelihood through part-time employment or self-employment. This in-migration has helped to exacerbate existing urban problems, so the government has tried to stem the migratory flow by investing in the rural areas. But one of the contradictory features of modernization strategies is that with greater public investment in infrastructure (roads, health services, electricity), with greater access to credit, and with encouragement (and often training) to produce more efficiently, productive relations are established in the countryside that merely increase the population outflow. Redistribution of land and wealth again puts part of the population "at risk" for migration.

To illustrate this briefly: in Telana the government set up a coffee producers' cooperative to prevent the exploitation of the producers by unscrupulous buyers, and their consequent impoverishment and out-migration. Producers were guaranteed a price for their coffee (fixed annually by the government), and were allowed to borrow cash against the crop in order to get through cash-flow problems at the time of year when the household's food stocks were generally lowest. In an attempt to encourage production of better-quality coffee, an agronomist lived in the area for part of the year and taught producers how to improve their smallholdings (with terracing, use of fertilizer, pruning); they were also instructed on how to dry the beans so as to avoid blemishes. Most of these improvement techniques, however, required considerably greater inputs of labor at times of the year when household labor (assumed by the government's program to be utilizable) was not available (the women were busy building up stocks of firewood, men were cultivating or were absent on seasonal wage laboring). The loans available were not sufficient to cover the cost of hiring labor, so only those families who could afford to hire labor could become more efficient (and in so doing, produce more). The government as a buyer began to penalize people who brought in stained or badly dried, low-grade beans, by refusing to buy "until later," by offering a lower price, or by refusing credit. Slowly the smaller and poorer producers were being edged out of coffee growing; this in turn undermined their ability to survive in the rural area.

What I have concentrated on in this chapter is the differential migration pattern by gender: although over time the age of first migration for girls has risen slightly (many girls stay long enough now to get 5 years of schooling, those who do leave doing so when about 11 or 12 rather than 8 or 9, as in the 1940s). Nonetheless, they still tend to leave at an age five or more years younger than their brothers. Again, although the proportion of girls remaining to complete primary school has risen over the period, it is still the case that a higher percentage of girls than boys who out-migrate do not have their primary certificate.

The bulk of these young female migrants are both poor and immature, lacking formal and informal training in any skill other than household work and child care; they are also brought up to consider themselves of less importance and worth than their brothers. In the city they find that their employment possibilities are limited, with domestic service being by far the most readily available. For this employment they have had some training, in terms of their role in their own family and of their predisposition to accept a social position of inferiority. As part of the naturally constituted order of things, they also accept that women must serve their naturally ordained superiors. The only change is in what constitutes a superior: in the village it is the male kinsmen in particular and the male gender in general; in the urban area, the members of the employing class, whether young or old, male or female.

Domestic service for these girls is, I would argue, a waste of human resources. It permits little awakening of their latent capacities, and provides no possibility for them to learn a wide range of skills, to value their own work, or to develop an independent and enquiring personality. Rather, it reinforces dependence, and often motherhood is seen as the only escape, even though this may be little more than an institutionalized form of unpaid domestic labor for a single master.

There are a number of steps that could be taken to ensure that young migrant women need not follow in the footsteps of their elder sisters or aunts. These would involve both government intervention, in the form of legislation, and allowing active pressure groups to enforce the provisions of such legislation. For example, young migrant women lack a place where they can stay, and thus are often forced into live-in domestic work that allows their employer to require them to work far longer hours than is accepted in any industry, or even a sweatshop. The government could intervene here by recognizing domestic service as a form of employment like any other, and ensuring the existence of legislation that regulates hours and conditions of work, minimum pay rates, provision of social benefits, and so on. Simultaneously the government could encourage the setting up of a means of monitoring the implementation of the legislation. Here one could suggest that the government should fund (at least initially) a network of inexpensive boarding-houses for domestic workers run by the women themselves or by existing women's groups. These houses could also double as centers where the domestic workers and other women could keep a check on employers' compliance with the law.

Suggestions such as these can end up as mere palliatives, but if women are to be able to take the first steps in organizing themselves, learning by practice how to bring about change, then some formal means are necessary and bear within them the potential for more profound change. Domestic service, in reinforcing dependence, does not encourage the questioning of a system in which wealth permits certain categories of people to condemn others to a life of servicing them. Nor does it encourage them to question a system of relations between the genders in which women are essentially seen either as playthings to entertain men or as drudges to service them. It also deprives them of the self-respect that should come of being able to support oneself and to help one's family. Without such self-respect it is unlikely that they will be prepared to make the sacrifices necessary to change a social system that constantly discriminates against them—not only as women but also as members of the poorest stratum of society.

NOTES

1. The real names of the villages have not been used at the request of the villagers.

2. Throughout this chapter the definition of a migrant is someone who was living, and had lived for more than six months, out of the village when the survey was taken in December 1971, and who was over 15. People resident at that time in the village, but who had at one time been migrants, are called return migrants, but only where it is necessary to distinguish return migrants from villagers (people who have never migrated out). When the term total migrants (or total migration) is used, it refers to migrants and return migrants together. It should be noted that children under 15 are not counted as migrants unless they left the village without their family; in the figures of total numbers of people living outside the village, only actual migrants are included; their children are not included, regardless of whether they were born in Copa Bitoo or in the present place of residence.

3. Although I used an elaborate system of cross checking, it is possible that there was some "wastage" in the figures recorded for the 1940s—that is, that some people who left then could not be picked up from the household surveys or the censuses and baptismal records.

4. In 1944 the American government recruited Mexican males on short-term labor contracts. These recruits were known as braceros. From this area a number of men went for a period of six months or more in 1944 and 1945.

5. The Oaxaca state administrative apparatus had virtually collapsed during the 1910 revolution and its aftermath. This was followed by a virtual civil war that raged in the early 1920s, by the end of which the state was bankrupt. The opening of a national banking system in the 1930s permitted access to credit to start the state machinery working, and for modernization plans to be contemplated.

6. It is customary to make a distinction between temporary or seasonal migration, which generally involves a regular yearly absence of a few months, and permanent migration. The word "permanent" is perhaps misleading, because migrants often return. Perhaps "long-term" or "noncyclical" migration would be a better expression. Nonetheless, I have followed customary usage.

7. These figures are based on the simplifying assumption that none of the under-15s or the over-65s are engaged in productive activities. Although this is not fully justified, nonetheless it is true to say that neither of these categories of people are fulltime producers, nor do they produce anything like the amount that the adult males do.

8. In an agricultural survey made in the village, which was checked by the village authorities, it appeared that only five families used chemical fertilizer. Some of these men were dissatisfied with the results, in part because they had little knowledge of the correct proportions of fertilizer to use or whether the fertilizer supplied by the merchant was the most suitable for local soil conditions.

9. These figures come from the survey mentioned in note 8.

10. It is worth speculating about the effect of this change in the sexual division of labor on women's patterns of fertility. Does fertility decline when women have to substitute for children? The evidence from Europe and the United States would suggest that it might. See Tilly and Scott 1978.

11. It is here that fathers can most directly exert control over their sons who wish to leave. Most young men know that getting jobs without these certificates is hard, and that their urban kinsmen's ability to maintain them while looking for work is limited.

12. Although inheritance is bilateral and partible, since the 1930s men have tended to inherit rights to land, animals, and work tools, while women get house sites and domestic goods.

13. Self-exploitation is a concept used by Chayanov (1966) to describe the mechanism by which members of the peasant household increase their labor input at the periods of peak labor needs. His use of the term is problematic, because it is not clear that the mechanism for increasing the labor input of any individual member of the household is self-engendered. In this case I use it because

the women I am referring to are household heads. Nonetheless, it is still arguable that the term "self-exploitation" hides the structural factors that oblige these single women to work such punishingly long hours for so little reward.

REFERENCES

Arizpe, L. 1977. "Women in the Informal Labour Sector: The Case of Mexico City." In The Wellesley Editorial Committee, ed., Women and National Economic Development. Chicago: The University of Chicago Press, pp. 25-37.

Balan, J. 1969. "Migrant and Native Socioeconomic Differences in Latin American Cities." Latin American Research Review (Spring).

Berg, R. L. 1968. "The Impact of Modern Economy on the Traditional Economy." Ph.D. dissertation, University of California at Los Angeles.

Cabrera, G. 1975. "Población, migración y fuerza de trabajo." Paper presented at Population Symposium, Mexico City. (Mimeographed.)

CEED. 1970. La dinámica de la población. Mexico: Colegio de Mexico, Estudios Economicos y Demográficos.

Chayanov, A. V. 1966. The Theory of Peasant Economy. Urbana: University of Illinois Press.

Dirección General de Estadística. 1940, 1950, 1960, 1970. Population census. Mexico City.

de la Fuente, J. 1947. "Los Zapotecos de Choapan, Oaxaca." Anales de INAH 2 (1944-47).

_____. 1949a. "Documentos para la etnografia e historia de los Zapotecos." Anales del INAH 3 (1947-48).

_____. 1949b. Yalalag, una villa zapoteca serrana. Mexico City: INI.

Germani, G. 1964. "Migration and Acculturation." In P. Hauser, ed., Handbook for Social Research in Urban Areas.

_____. 1965. "Emigración del campo a la ciudad y sus causas." In H. Gilberti, ed., Sociedad, economía y reforma agraria. Buenos Aires.

Iturribarria, J. F. 1955. Oaxaca en la historia. Mexico City.

Kay, G. 1970. Development and Underdevelopment. London: Faber.

Marx, K. 1970. Capital. Vols. I–III. London: Lawrence and Wishart.

Meillassoux, C. 1975. Femmes, greniers et capitaux. Paris: Maspero.

Oliviera, O., H. Munoz, and C. Stern. 1977. Migración y desigualdad social. Mexico City: Colegio de Mexico.

Perez Garcia, F. 1956. La sierra de Juarez. Mexico City.

Tilly, L., and J. Scott. 1978. Women, Work and the Family. New York: Holt, Rinehart and Winston.

Wolpe, H. 1975. "The Theory of Internal Colonialism: The South African Case." In J. Oxaal, T. Barnett, and D. Booth, eds., Beyond the Sociology of Development. London: Routledge and Kegan Paul, pp. 229–52.

Young, K. 1975. "La participación de la mujer en la economía campesina." (Mimeographed.)

_____. 1976. "The Social Setting of Migration." Ph.D. dissertation, London University.

_____. 1978. "Modes of Appropriation and the Sexual Division of Labour." In A. Kuhn and A. M. Wolpe, eds., Feminism and Materialism. London: Routledge and Kegan Paul.

7

FROM RURAL SUBSISTENCE TO AN INDUSTRIAL PERIPHERAL WORK FORCE: AN EXAMINATION OF FEMALE MALAYSIAN MIGRANTS AND CAPITAL ACCUMULATION IN SINGAPORE

Noeleen Heyzer

Development literature dealing with the employment of rural women has tended to concentrate on women in agricultural work. Of equal importance, however, are rural women drawn into urban commodity production. I take up this issue by focusing on rural female migration from the kampongs (villages) and the New Villages of West Malaysia to the labor-intensive industries of Singapore.

This chapter aims to show how migration is a mechanism linking the rural subsistence sector with the urban industrial sector, and makes possible the transition from rural to urban life for certain groups of migrants. I begin by giving a brief account of the background from which the rural workers migrate, and in so doing show some of the existing links between capital accumulation in the urban areas and subsistence production in the rural sector. The chapter then focuses on the types of industries that employ the rural female migrants, and examines the impact of industrial employment on the migrant workers' income-earning opportunities and their differences in response to urban life.

Various frameworks of analysis have been developed to handle the above problems. Theories of modernization maintain that rural migration is the consequence of the breakdown in the precapitalist mode of production. This decay creates a labor surplus for the "modern" factories, paving the way for the conversion of the traditional villager into the "modern town person." These theories fail to grasp that migration is rooted in the dynamics of capital accumulation and is an integral part of uneven development. The analytical framework of the present study begins with the relationship between the process of capital accumulation and female migration. By focusing on the relevant components of this process—the expansion of

investment, the changes in the organization of production and fragmentation of the labor process, and the development of wage labor—
the framework allows a realistic capture of the factors affecting
female migration from the Malaysian kampongs and New Villages to
Singapore's labor-intensive industries (for a discussion of the fragmentation of the labor process and migration, see Santa Cruz Collective 1978 and Brighton Labour Process Group 1977).

THE BACKGROUND

The recruitment of foreign labor and young female labor by
the industries of Singapore must be seen within the context of investment decisions by various multinationals to set up their subsidiaries in Singapore as a result of the expansion of international
business. With the economic boom of the late 1960s and early 1970s,
the economy of Singapore expanded considerably. There was full
employment in the country, and the manufacturing industries formed
the most dynamic sector of the Singapore economy (see Government
of Singapore, Economic Development Board 1974). The manufacturing base was said to have "been solidly established" (Government of Singapore, Economic Development Board 1974, p. 56).
The electronic and electrical products industry became one of Singapore's largest in terms of employment, output, and value added.
Of the total manufacturing investment commitments in 1972, 50. 8
percent was in this industry. Singapore became one of the major
suppliers of electronic products, exporting 96 percent of total output to the United States, Europe, and other parts of the world (Government of Singapore, Economic Development Board 1974, p. 59).
In 1972, when the United States imposed quotas on imports of syn-
thetic and woolen textiles from a number of Asian countries, many
of the textile companies set up subsidiaries in Singapore. There
was an urgent need for a labor force content to work for low wages
in industries offering semiskilled and unskilled jobs.
Recruiting agents were sent to the New Villages and kampongs
of West Malaysia to lure the young females engaged in subsistence
production with promise of wage work, urban living quarters, and
the bright lights of Singapore. Substantial female labor reserves
existed particularly in the New Villages of West Malaysia. In what
follows, I present a brief historical background of this rural population in order to provide some insight into the background of the recruited workers.
The New Villages were created by the British Military Administration in the early 1950s to deny the Communist guerrillas an important mass base and source of supplies and intelligence. (Accounts

of the creation of New Villages are in Short 1975; Clutterback 1973.)
The "Briggs Plan" (named after Sir Harold Briggs, the director of
operations at the time) involved the shifting of a scattered rural
population into controlled resettlement areas, fenced with barbed
wire and controlled by curfews, regular police checks, and guarded
by detachments of special constables. About 650,000 people, mainly of Chinese ethnic origin, were rounded up and resettled into about
600 "New Villages." The only areas available for the creation of
these sites were part of the Malay reservation land. There was opposition to the Briggs Plan from the Malay sultans and state gov-
ernments. However, when persuaded by the British government
that the war against the guerrillas would be lost unless the plan was
put into operation, the sultans made the resettlement of the rural
Chinese conditional on the offer of temporary occupation licenses
(TOLs). This meant that once the guerrilla problem was solved,
the resettled Chinese had to move out of these areas. But the New
Villages and the TOLs have remained to this day.

Although some New Villagers have succeeded in converting
their TOLs into leases, a substantial number have to renew their
license every year for a fee. The land office reserves the right to
cancel the TOL without having to give a reason.[1] This means that
people could very easily find themselves converted into illegal
squatters involved in illegal farming, and faced with the possibility
of having their homes and farms bulldozed by the land office. This
threat of land seizure, the continuing reduction of landholding size
due to a growing population, and increasing rural poverty led the
young, able-bodied men from the New Villages to migrate in search
of wage labor in tin mines and in the main towns of Kuala Lumpur,
Ipoh, Seremban, and Johore Bharu. Several thousand migrate to
the timber industries of Kalimantan and Sumatra, Indonesia, and to
the construction sites and shipbuilding industries of Singapore.

Those who remain behind are mainly the elders, the young
women, and children. They are smallholders, and subsist by growing tapioca, melons, and market vegetables. Several work as artisans. The young women are often unpaid home workers engaged in
household chores and helping in the family workshops and plots in
order to maintain their minimum standard of living. In other words,
they form a latent reserve of labor power that could be used by
entrepreneurs in the urban sector.

A similar picture of impoverishment may be constructed for
the kampongs of West Malaysia. If the poverty line is put at Malaysian $200 per month for a five-person household, 58.5 percent of
all households in Malaysia are under this line. Of these, 82.6 percent are from the kampong areas (Ghani 1977, p. 220).

However, the migration picture is more complex for the kampongs than for the Chinese New Villages, since poverty alone may not result in population movement. The land tenure system and the nature of rent payment under the feudal and semifeudal systems have major influences on whether migration is chosen as a solution to rural poverty. Various studies have shown that while different social classes of peasants exist at the village level, the majority subsist far below the poverty line, caught in various forms of debt bondage to the landlord and local moneylenders (see Ali 1964; Swift 1965; Dahlan 1976a). The possibility of migration for heads of house holds and male family members needed to work on the land is limited. At the same time, there are pressures for certain family members to seek opportunities to acquire cash income elsewhere because of the declining ability of the peasant economy to meet rural subsistence. These family members are often the young women—people who could be spared from the land without the loss of that land. This is reinforced by the existing demand in the urban centers for cheap female labor willing to work in the labor-intensive industries of foreign subsidiaries.

For both the New Villages and the kampongs, migration may be seen as the spontaneous reaction to rural stagnation in which unemployment, underemployment, and subemployment rates are extremely high. This impoverishment creates labor reserves in the form of the migrant proletariat, people who need to migrate in searc of work in order to survive. This migrant proletariat is easily integrated into the capital accumulation process during a period of expansion of business investment, when capital seeks out labor reserves in the rural peripheries and recruits them to the urban centers for commodity production. In the next section, I examine the nature of the female migrant's integration into an urban high-growth economy.

THE FRAGMENTATION OF LABOR AND FEMALE MIGRATION

The nature of the integration of women migrants into urban commodity production may best be understood in terms of changes in the organization of production and the fragmentation of the labor process in the industrial sector. This process refers to "the separation of the two productive forces which at one time were combined in the labor power of the direct producers—namely production knowledge and the physical capacity to manipulate objects and symbols" (Santa Cruz Collective 1978, p. 104). This division between those who produce or apply scientific and technological knowledge in designing and operating the production system, and those whose relationship with the production system is standardized and routinized, is crucial for the understanding of international investment and the relocation of production by international capital.

Elson and Pearson (1980) discuss how in the present phase of the internationalization of capital, the production process is fragmented so that only certain parts are relocated in the Third World—the parts that offer the most advantage in terms of the exploitation of cheap labor. This type of relocation is based on product specialization, which separates the labor-intensive processes from the design, engineering, and marketing processes. Components or subcomponents may be transported to various parts of the world, where they undergo a range of labor-intensive processing. In short, what takes place is a kind of international subcontracting in which skills and knowledge are retained in the developed countries while standardized activities are exported to peripheral countries.

For the above process of relocation to be highly profitable, it is essential that unit costs of production be as cheap as possible, and that the nature of the work force inspire confidence in the safety of the resultant operation. Young women in the peripheral countries are mobilized for this kind of employment because they are considered docile and insecure enough to be hired into the lowest ranks of the industrial hierarchy.

The analysis of the fragmentation of the labor process is extremely useful in articulating the differences between male and female workers in various industries in Singapore. The multinational activities may be grouped into three categories based on differences in their technological character and wage structure. The first group consists of the capital-intensive, high-technology industries paying good wages. These are mainly multinational corporations involved in petroleum and petrochemical products. The industrial workers employed here are usually high-salaried technicians. The second group consists of large, skill-intensive industries involved in the manufacture of transportation equipment, such as the shipbuilding and repairing industry and the automobile industry. In these industries skilled workers outnumber semiskilled operators and unskilled laborers. Heavy physical demands are made on the workers, who are required to work in the sun and rain. There is also great anxiety over industrial accidents, particularly in the shipbuilding industry, which has one of the worst records of fatal accidents among the manufacturing industries. Male migrant workers are commonly employed in this sector because few Singaporeans, in spite of the high wages offered, would do what they classify as "dirty jobs." In fact, in the construction industry 50 percent of the workers are foreigners.[2]

The third important type of foreign subsidiaries is the labor-intensive industries. By 1974, 45.2 percent of the work force in the manufacturing sector were employed in the three major labor-intensive industries: electronic and electrical products, textiles, and wood and wood products (see Table 7.1). It is into these factories that the female migrant workers from the New Villages and kampongs of West Malaysia are integrated.

TABLE 7.1

Persons Employed, by Industry: Singapore, 1974

Industry	Total	Percent-age of MI	Male	Female	Female as Percent of Total
All manufac-turing indus-tries (MI)	234,231	100.0	129,281	104,950	44.8
Textile industry	39,433	16.1	12,676	26,760	67.9
				39,436	
Manufacture of wood and wood products	25,443	10.9	20,058	5,391	21.2
				25,449	
Electronic and elec-trical products industry	48,876	23.7	10,104	28,772	79.3
				38,876	

Sources: Government of Singapore, Ministry of Labour 1974, Table 33, p. 56; Government of Singapore, Ministry of Labour and National Statistical Commission 1974. For electronics industry, Government of Singapore, Department of Statistics 1974.

The characteristic features of these labor-intensive industries are their low skill and wage levels, and their high susceptibility to the business cycle. The jobs found in these industries are actually unskilled, although they are officially classified as semiskilled. They require little knowledge, training, and experience. The basic tasks are learned in a few weeks, although a considerably longer period of practice may be required to reach the necessary level of speed and dexterity.

Even in an expanding economy there are industrial sectors that are more susceptible than others to the business cycle. The problem in these sectors is the creation of a mobile work force that is more or less fully employed during the upward business swing and that can be removed from production during business contraction. Young women workers with marginal income needs, and who can easily be reabsorbed into the family structure, are regarded as ideal for a floating work force. Women workers employed in these sectors have little control over the conditions of their employment. Even a senior worker suffers from considerable insecurity because she possesses no real skill in special demand that would give her bargaining power during a downward business swing. Because of the low wage levels in these industries (the majority of these workers earned between Singapore $3.00 and $6.00 a day as a basic wage in 1974), it is difficult to save money for periods of unemployment.

Besides the high susceptibility to the business cycle and the low wages and low skills offered by these industries, another negative feature is their high level of industrial accidents. A Ministry of Labour report for March 1974 said that one in seven textile workers suffered from hearing impairment (Straits Times 1974a). In a plywood factory surveyed by the Ministry of Labour, 80 percent of the work force was found to suffer from skin diseases attributed to the glues used (Straits Times 1974b). In 1973, out of the 415 accidents in the woodworking industry employing 10,000 workers, 33 resulted in amputation of a limb or finger (Straits Times 1974b). Workers in the electronics factories complain of constant eye strain and fatigue. (For an account of the electronics industry in Singapore, see Pang 1977.) Factories that are not permitted to function in the metropolitan centers because of the harm they cause to human beings are transferred to the periphery, where protest is suppressed. In 1975 a survey by the Industrial Health Unit in Singapore showed that 85 percent of the surveyed factories "set up with financial support and technical advice from the government or international agencies" were "unsafe and unhealthy to workers" (Phoon and Tan 1975, reported in Straits Times, November 17, 1975).

In addition, with the variation in technological levels and conditions of work offered by different industries, sharp social inequalities have emerged. Like all stratified societies, Singapore is faced with the problem of potential instability derived from this experience of social inequality. One mechanism commonly used by ruling elites is the development of a peripheral or marginal work force within the industrial sector, separated from the more affluent sectors. Young women and migrant workers are relegated to this periphery. They form a category of workers that can expand or contract without affecting the "stability" needed for business operation, and that allows a certain profit level to be maintained during a business slump.

These two groups of workers share certain common features that make them attractive to employers as a peripheral work force: they are generally known to be docile, difficult to arouse to militant activity, easily cowed by the threats of employers; they tend to see themselves as temporary workers (see Ward 1975; Castles and Kosack 1973). The young women workers frequently stop working after marriage, and the migrant workers see their purpose in Singapore as getting jobs and earning as much money as possible before returning home. The two groups are not exclusive because of the considerable proportion of women migrant workers from the New Villages and kampongs of Malaysia.

The migrant workers provide the industrial system with all the advantages of a marginal work force of cheap labor without any of the usual political and social cost. While it is in the prosperity phase of a business cycle, the industrial system can easily absorb this marginal group, and during a business depression these workers are the first to be let go and sent back to their home countries. The migrant laborers' expendability was well illustrated during the retrenchment period of 1974-75, when an estimated half of the migrant workers engaged in production work were sent home.[3] There is, of course, always the danger that the migrant workers will eventually settle in the host country as an urban reserve work force and become a threat to political and economic stability.

In Singapore there are two major mechanisms to prevent the above from happening: all holders of work permits must obtain approval from the Ministry of Labour if they wish to marry a Singaporean, and, in exchange for a marriage license, are required to sign a bond that both parties will be sterilized after the birth of the second child. Failure to sign means the loss of certain rights, including refusal of the marriage license; withdrawal of the work permit; failure to renew the migrant's stay in Singapore; and loss of medical, educational, and housing benefits by the Singaporean partner.[4]

In 1978 a new scheme was put into force. It requires employers to furnish reports on the semiannual pregnancy tests administered to female migrant workers. Those who are pregnant and those

who are found to have contracted contagious diseases are to be re-
patriated at the expense of their employers (Straits Times 1978).

The strictness of these regulations for migrant workers is
clear when we understand that the value of the migrant workers to
the economy lies precisely in their mobile labor potential, as well
as their docility. Their function as a reserve of expendable labor
in the overall economic system would change if they were allowed
to be easily assimilated into the host country's population.

There are at present an estimated 120,000 migrant workers
in the industries of Singapore,[5] 51 percent of the total manufacturing work force. While there is little reliable overall statistical information on women migrant workers, some precise data are available on female workers in Singapore. Table 7.2 shows that in 1974,
45 percent of the 234,251 workers in the manufacturing sector are
female workers. By 1977, the female labor force participation in
Singapore for the 20-24 age group reached a peak of 72.1 percent,
but dropped steadily for every successive five-year age group (Lim
1978, p. 42).

TABLE 7.2

Workers Employed in Singapore, by Given
Characteristics and Sex, 1970 and 1974
(thousands)

	1970			1974		
	Total	Male	Female	Total	Male	Female
Manufacturing industry (MI)	143.1	95.0	48.1	234.2	129.3	105.3
Production and related workers (PRW)	255.0	207.6	47.4	320.0	222.0	98.0
		Total		Male		Female
Percentage increase in MI (1970-74)		63.7		36.1		118.3
Percentage increase in PRW (1970-74)		25.5		6.9		106.8

Source: Government of Singapore, Ministry of Labour 1974.

Table 7.3 shows that 81 percent of the female workers in manufacturing industry earn below $200 a month, compared with 32 percent of the male workers.

TABLE 7.3

Workers Earning Under Singapore $200 per Month, 1974

	Total	Number Under $200	Percent
All industries (AI)	824,349	334,567	41
Manufacturing industries (MI)	234,231	126,416	54
Male workers, AI	562,193	175,224	31
Male workers, MI	129,281	41,815	32
Female workers, AI	262,156	159,343	61
Female workers, MI	104,950	84,601	81
Chinese female workers, AI	212,668	123,453	58
Malay female workers, AI	34,821	27,342	79
Indian female workers, AI	11,704	7,382	63

Source: Government of Singapore, Ministry of Labour 1974.

If we classify all female workers by their ethnic group, 58 percent of Chinese female workers earn under $200; 79 percent of Malay female workers and 63 percent of Indian female workers fall into this category. These figures indicate that, compared with the Chinese female workers as a group, a larger proportion of all females in the two minority groups in Singapore—the Malays and the Indians—are in the low-income group. The sharpness of income inequality for female production workers is clearly seen when we examine female earnings in the context of overall income distribution for Singapore (see Table 7.4). These data do not show income distribution by sex and although not as refined as one could desire, do show evidence of a skewed income distribution, with the majority of the female production workers (81 percent) at the bottom of the wage hierarchy (see Table 7.3). At the other extreme, there is a small group of people whose income is approximately that in the developed countries. While more than 50 percent of all the production workers earn under $200 a month, 59 percent of workers with tertiary education are concentrated in the $1,000 and over income group.

TABLE 7.4

Income Distribution in Singapore, 1974
(percent)

	Total Number of Workers	Monthly Income							
		Under $200	200–399	400–599	600–799	800–999	1,000–1,499	1,500 and over	Total
Industry									
Manufacturing industry	234,231	54	32	8	3	1	1	1	100
All industries	824,349	41	37	12	4	2	3	1	100
Occupation									
Professional, technical, and related workers	90,526	13	30	26	11	6	9	5	100
Production and related workers	319,949	50	40	7	1	1	1	0	100
Ethnic group									
Chinese	639,655	38	38	13	5	2	3	1	100
Malay	119,568	54	36	7	1	1	1	0	100
Indian	49,828	44	35	11	3	3	3	1	100
Others (including foreigners)	15,298	17	20	9	9	7	22	16	100
Highest education level									
Not applicable	332,042	50	39	8	2	0	1	0	100
Primary	220,633	46	36	11	3	2	1	1	100
Secondary	162,451	26	41	18	7	3	4	1	100
Postsecondary	50,799	13	29	30	11	7	8	2	100
Tertiary	19,426	3	5	9	13	11	30	29	100

Source: Government of Singapore, Ministry of Labour, Report on the Labor Force Survey, 1974.

THE FEMALE MIGRANTS IN
INDUSTRIAL PRODUCTION

In order to obtain detailed knowledge of the effects of industrial production on women migrants, and the variations in their response to the urban work situation, I worked in an industry that makes extensive use of such workers.

The factory where I worked as "a semiskilled" trainee is owned by Hong Kong investors, and manufactures textiles for overseas markets, particularly the United States.[6] It employs 800 industrial workers, 600 of whom are females. Eighty percent of the female workers are migrants from Malaysian New Villages and kampongs. At the time of my investigation, the composition of the female labor force in the factory was as shown in Table 7.5.

TABLE 7.5

Work Force in a Textile Factory, by Length of Service

Length of Service	Female Singaporeans	Female Migrants	Total
Under 1 year	16	212	228
1-3 years	32	166	198
3-5 years	34	48	82
5 years and over	38	54	92
Total	120	480	600

The table shows that more than half of the Singaporeans had been in the factory for three years or more, while only about one-fifth of the female migrants fell into this category. In interviews with the workers, the main reason given for this marked difference seemed to be that, independent of levels of education and skill, the Singaporean, as a citizen, stands a better chance of promotion than does a migrant.

There is a tendency for the migrant workers to "job-hop" during the first two years of employment. They see greater chances of mobility across industries than within the work place, since they hope to be skilled workers in factories that are short of help. This trend is changing because the government has passed legislation to prevent work-permit holders, who are largely Malaysians, from leaving a particular work place for at least three years.

For most of the female migrants, the abrupt separation of family life from working life is the biggest change that has come about as the result of their moving to Singapore. Prior to migration most of them were engaged in subsistence farming or a small family business. The rhythm of work was, in the main, organized around the household, with responsibilities divided according to age and sex, and clearly articulated with other life activities. In the industrial work place the rhythm of work is generated by the specific organization of the factory's labor process and by the technology and division of labor.

For the migrants from the New Villages, the household unit of production is typically male-dominated, and the roles of women in it are essentially family ones: daughter, wife, mother, widow. The father is usually the head of the family plot or business. Sons usually inherit their father's trade. The females are involved in the plot or business as "helpers," and are solely responsible for household chores like cleaning and cooking. The woman's role in the family is governed by the three rules of obedience developed by Confucian writers: "An unmarried girl should obey her father and elder brother; a married woman, her husband; a widow, her son." Obedience, timidity, and adaptability are regarded as the main virtues of young women.

As women leave the household to seek factory employment, changes accompany this migration; direct control of the elders over the young weakens. An aspect of this loss of control is the growth of personal choice and of romance as the foundation of courtship and marriage. Economically, the young women are less dependent. In fact, 34 percent of the migrant women in the textile factory I studied stated that their fathers provided less than half of the family income, and that daughters contributed as much as one-fifth of their income. The daughter's contribution to the village household is part of the "pooling of income" practice, and the ability to earn a wage has improved the status of young women within the household.

Within the context of the division of labor, however, women are concentrated in the lowest ranks of the industrial hierarchy. In the textile factory the technology and division of labor reduce the worker's control over her work process to a minimum. The work is simple, repetitious, and completely tied to the speed of the machines. She is unable to control the pace and rhythm of her labor; she lacks the choice of techniques; and with the constant pressure, there is little freedom of physical movement. Each operator has a large number of machines to tend, and she must adapt her activities and movements to the technical process. When breaks occur in the yarn, stopping a machine or causing waste of material, the worker must respond immediately or fall behind in her production quota.

There is constant strain and necessity to keep on the move within her work area. (Similar findings are in Morland 1958, p. 30; Smith 1939, p. 18; Blauner 1964, pp. 66-70.)

The majority of jobs in machine-tending industries, like textiles, are semiskilled and unskilled. Workers tend to be interchangeable parts in a machine process, since there is little judgment and initiative required in most cases. Work techniques are incorporated into the machine process, and all decisions are relegated to the supervisor. Within a week it is possible to master the basic skills of the job. After this, skill means the ability to master the fastest technique of doing definite routine tasks and repairing yarn breakages. Jobs in the textile factory that require some initiative and skill are done by male workers, such as the maintenance machinists. Workers receive training on the job. But, for the majority, there really is little skill to be learned. Economically, it is cheap and unskilled workers that these factories want. The kinds of skills that are picked up are determined by the nature of the technology.

Taken in the context of the industrial division of labor, the work tasks found in factories like the one studied are simple and mindless. These "skills" can readily be taught to workers who have never before stood on a production line. In other words, the majority of the female workers are taught little in the way of practical skills and knowledge that would help them make meaningful lives for themselves. However, despite the low level of skills required, hierarchical job categories are created; those at the bottom are remunerated at a lower wage and filled by new women workers, on the ground that the women are less skilled and have fewer years of seniority.

There are six different "skill levels," with different wage rates for each: the semiskilled trainee earns $3.90 a day, with a 20 cent increment every six months until she is promoted to skilled worker—this may take a few years, depending on the management; the skilled worker earns $5.00 a day, with a 25 cent increment every six months; the assistant overseer has the same basic pay as the skilled worker, but receives a 30 cent increment every six months; the overseer has the same basic pay as the skilled worker, but her increment rate is 35 cents every six months; the supervisor is paid between $500 and $600 a month, depending on educational qualifications; there is an extra 80 cents allowance for the night shift. On the basis of the National Wages Council recommendation, all workers are given $25 a month extra.

ECONOMIC INCENTIVES AND THE
MIGRANT WORKER'S RESPONSE

Management frequently uses economic incentives to manipulate work behavior, assuming that the motives of workers in the factory are broadly similar. It ignores the basic characteristic of the labor force: that it is composed of both migrants and Singaporeans, and that even among the migrants there are great differences due to the diversity of areas from which they have come. In the factory under study, efforts were made to reduce absenteeism by paying a monthly bonus for regular attendance, and to increase production output by encouraging long hours of overtime. A bonus was also given to workers willing to forgo their leave. These had very different responses from the Singaporeans and the migrants. Variations in response also occurred in the migrant group, and it became useful to separate the migrants into two different groups: the oscillating migrant (the person who is involved in back-and-forth migration from a relatively nearby region, such as the Malaysian migrants from Johore), and the long-distance and long-term migrant. Of the group under study, 38 percent may be said to be oscillating migrants.

It was found that absenteeism was more marked among Singaporeans than among migrants. According to factory records for a six-month period, 60 percent of Singaporeans had been absent for four or more days each, while only 24 percent of the migrants came under this category. This result appeared surprising at first, for the Singaporeans were comparatively the better-off of the two groups in terms of promotional prospects. Since absenteeism tends to be associated with illness, I had expected it to be more common among migrant women because of overcrowded living conditions, poor food, and the problem of adjustment to a new environment. From interviews with the workers, however, I found that absenteeism was related to the female workers' household obligations. Women needed to take the occasional day off to attend to household chores. Absence for this reason was most common among Singaporeans whose homes were nearby. This form of absenteeism was more widespread among women in unskilled/semiskilled employment than among skilled workers earning higher wages, because the latter tended to lose more financially by missing a day's work.

In periods when there was a demand for increased industrial output, workers were encouraged to work two shifts, particularly on weekends. Both the oscillating migrant and the long-term migrant were willing to work overtime on weekdays. The oscillating migrant who returned to her village on the weekends was unwilling to work two shifts on Sundays, even though it meant getting four days' pay. The long-term migrant very frequently worked the Sunday shifts. The Singaporeans, however, required very high rates of overtime to induce them to work longer hours. Many of them maximized their household income by dividing the day between regular wage employment and some form of family employment at night. A number of Singaporeans in this particular factory helped one or both parents to run hawker stalls or to attend to the family street stall at the <u>pasir malam</u> ("night market").

The bonus that accompanied forgoing the annual leave was a failure as an incentive as far as the long-term migrants were concerned. For these people the annual leave played a major role in maintaining their ties with their village. From personal interviews it seemed that the purpose of seeking urban employment was not to enjoy an immediate increase in their standard of living in the urban area, but to save as much money as possible. This saving was used to meet the needs of the household in the village—for example, to improve the parental house, to buy bicycles for carrying the crops to the market, and to provide cash for gifts and food during religious festivals. What the migrants saved appeared out of proportion to their incomes. They often did not have an adequate diet in order to be able to save and to return to their village during the annual leave with gifts and money as demonstration of their success.

THE FRIENDSHIP GROUPS

In spite of the powerful alienating factors that came from the process of production and work organization in the factory, the young women workers did not seem to be alienated socially. During working hours the workers are arranged into different groups to facilitate the allocation of shift duty. There are three shifts a day (morning, afternoon, and night). Workers in each group move as a unit, doing a different shift each week. In each group the workers are subdivided into groups of between 10 and 15, and placed under the charge of an overseer; the overseers are, in turn, responsible to the supervisor. [7]

People in the same work group are in face-to-face contact, and are motivated to behave in ways consistent with the goals and values of the group in order to obtain recognition, support, security, and favorable reactions. The work groups are an antidote to boredom, monotony, the harsh physical surroundings (noise, heat, and dirt), and the authoritarian and hierarchical relationships with supervisors and management.

Social cohesion results chiefly from group relationships that are most conspicuous during lunch breaks and after working hours. During working hours there are few opportunities for socializing. In the weaving section workers work individually, and the noise level is too high to carry on any conversation. In the roving section opportunities for social interaction are lessened by the heavy work load and by supervisors openly frowning on workers' conversation. Behavior during free time is in complete contrast with that during work. There is plenty of teasing and inquiring into each other's affairs in a loud and noisy manner. Rumors are spread readily; photos, song books, and tidbits are passed around. There is, in short, a complete reaction against the restrictive atmosphere of the factory. The cliques formed at the factory are limited by the similarity of shifts, the ability to speak the same language or dialect, and the length of time at the factory. These close friendship ties give the workers emotional security that sustains them under difficult conditions of existence and compensates for the rigidity and lack of humaneness in the factory.

There is little respect for formal rules and written procedures. My investigations indicate that the breaking of minor rules by workers is a means of showing that they are still in charge of themselves, even in an atmosphere of compulsion. (For a detailed account of the industrial environment in which these workers operate, see Heyzer forthcoming.) This phenomenon is seen in the choice of clothing, in maintaining rules on industrial safety, and in absenteeism. The workers are supposed to wear black and white uniforms and rubber shoes, but they nevertheless come in colored blouses and slacks, and wear slippers. They are supposed to tie up their hair and wear a mask to protect themselves from the dust. They refuse to do this. The rules say that they will be fired if they are absent without leave for three consecutive days. However, on festive occasions like the Chinese Bak Chang festival, they go home to the New Villages, absenting themselves for more than three days without leave. They said, "It is useless to apply for leave. You will not get it." They feel quite safe in their behavior because "a large group of us are doing it together . . . we are experienced workers. The management would not sack us because they are short-handed."

In fact, during this festival the management had to shut down a few machines, and the workers who stayed behind had to do extra work. The workers do not mind doing this because there is an agreement among them that they will take turns going on such leave.

CYCLICAL MIGRATION AND LIMITS
OF SOCIAL CHANGE

None of the migrants see their stay in Singapore as permanent. They speak of returning at least for crisis situations associated with life-cycle events (many women interviewed preferred to have their babies at the parental home) and for social and religious festivals in the village. The frequency of return visits varies from once weekly to once biennially. Only in one case did a migrant stay away from the village as long as six years.

This cyclical or return migration has meant that there are feedbacks to the village from the urban setting. In turn, this makes the urban alternative a reality for others still in the village. Exposure to urban work, however, does not necessarily lead to a transition to urban life. For certain groups the oscillation between rural and urban entails little change in basic values and attitudes, as exemplified by women workers of rural origins who are classified as "the Chinese-educated" by the workers in the textile factory.

In the factory under study, a distinct group of workers was differentiated from the majority, who were Chinese Malaysian workers. This group was labeled by the workers as "the English-educated" (as opposed to "the Chinese-educated"). This classification is actually a shorthand method of differentiating urban behavior patterns from the more traditional ones. Seldom do the terms act as reliable indicators of whether persons have gone to an English or a Chinese school. The English-educated are seen as those who "chitchat a lot," "enjoy life" (that is, they dress up after work and try to speak English, even if it is just "broken English"), and "mix and laugh with people freely." These workers see themselves as people who know "how to work and how to have fun." They regard themselves as "modern" people who are less shy of the world. Factory work is accepted as a necessary evil that has to be done so that they may have the freedom to behave "like modern people": to "go dancing," "stay out late at night," and "dress up." For this group work has been compartmentalized as an aspect of life, a means to an end.

There is a cleavage between the "Chinese-educated" and the "English-educated" workers. The "Chinese-educated" see workers in the other group as "people who waste money." The "English-educated" workers go to the city center more often, visit shopping centers outside Jurong, have visited sophisticated coffeehouses, mix freely with male workers, and emphasize dressing up "like the modern girl." The "nonmodern" workers are hostile on principle to the behavior of the "modern" workers. They believe that these "ought not" to be the "correct" ways of acting. A "good person" does not become easily affected by the bad influences of city life but, rather, keeps to the traditional ways of behavior developed in the family system, and in the New Villages and small towns of Malaysia. It means they "must not be the going-out type," "must not spend too much money," "must send money home regularly." Very seldom do they make trips to town, and generally they are shy of the world. They explain this as being due to their having little money to experiment with, since they have to send money home. Their shyness is also seen as "not knowing how to speak English" and "not knowing how to make conversation." They feel safer with people who behave in ways they understand and who are not "bad company." For this group work is integrated with the extended family system in Malaysia. In other words, industrial work in the city is integrated with the non-work concerns of a less urban community.

Besides keeping to rural values, there is evidence to suggest that only a minority of the female workers become incorporated as long-term industrial workers with opportunities for skilled jobs. The majority remain docile migrant labor employed at the lowest rank of the industrial hierarchy.

In 1974-75 there was a retrenchment of 20,000 workers. Two-thirds of the jobless were migrants who were sent back to their villages in West Malaysia. There is no reliable figure on how many migrants obtained other factory jobs in Singapore. A rough estimate by a Jurong Town Corporation official puts the number at less than 10 percent of the laid-off migrants. The workers in the textile firm studied were laid off indefinitely. However, laid-off electronics workers in Singapore were offered reemployment by factories that were established in West Malaysia and Indonesia. For example, a multinational electronics firm, after laying off 850 workers in Singapore, offered to reemploy them in its new plants in Malacca and Penang, at a lower basic pay. Under this crisis situation a substantial number of migrant workers dropped out of industrial employment and sought reintegration into the rural household. The rest migrated to the new factory sites where their labor was in demand.

The whole layoff program took place with no grass-roots militancy from the displaced women. This general docility seemed to result from the belief that they may be put on the blacklist which was said to circulate among employers in Singapore and Malaysia, and hence increased their difficulty in getting another job. The rumor of the existence of the blacklist circulated among women industrial workers during an incident, commonly referred to in Singapore as "The Gulf Plastic incident," when one of the Malaysian workers remained jobless for a while following her return to Malaysia after being fired for involvement in a protest against a speedup.

Besides the element of fear, there are other reasons why few attempts have been made by women migrants to change the terms on which their labor is used. Various factors operate simultaneously to create a docile work force. First, there is the penetration of certain religious values into the work place. Being ancestor worshippers and coming from a close extended family—characteristics of many Chinese—the majority of the female migrants in the factory are taught the importance of obedience to authority. This reinforces their submissiveness and resignation to the conditions of work.

Second, peripheral industries offering low wages and alienating work conditions employ a very high concentration of young women and migrant workers. This type of employment is not damaging to the female worker's sense of worth and identity, since successful work is not a woman's central life interest. In the case of the migrant workers, the argument is that their home countries cannot provide them with alternative jobs that are more self-realizing.

Third, the authoritarian attitudes of management and superiors discourage the responsibility of the workers. The constant supervision and work pressure develop a dependent attitude. With the suppression of an effective trade union to provide a sense of protection and dignity to the workers, this dependency is further reinforced, especially in an industry where few jobs involve any challenge or demand judgment.

Fourth, because of the workers' relative lack of education, management thinks it is legitimate to concentrate young women workers in jobs that offer little initiative and few possibilities for personal growth and skill development. Workers with low educational levels are said to have low aspirations and are less likely to find the repetitive, noninvolving jobs monotonous. In fact, the submissiveness of the textile workers is an expression of the deep sense of insecurity that comes with being in one of the lowest ranks of the industrial hierarchy.

CONCLUSION: FOREVER MIGRANTS?

It is fairly widely believed that an important element in achieving equality for women is their integration into wage labor. This integration is assumed to bring about opportunities for economic freedom and to provide an important channel for realizing some of their potential by active participation in a growing modern industrial sector. For the rural women in particular, this integration is frequently seen as a form of liberation from the domestic and traditional sectors. The underlying assumption is that once women are integrated into modern wage labor, a dual process is generated for their emancipation. First, they are removed from feudal exploitation and second, technological access creates opportunities that prepare women for skilled jobs. Also, there would be a basis for women to organize collectively for their rights within their work place, alongside male workers.

This chapter, however, captures a different reality. Instead of the emergence of a stable female work force integrated into a system that allows the improvement of women's position, we witness what seems to be a not-too-stable migrant sector that lives within a limiting framework of compulsion. There is the rural world to which the migrants are tied in a variety of ways. There is the economic compulsion of having to earn in the cities in order to supplement rural subsistence. There is the administrative compulsion that prevents migrants from being assimilated and making permanent homes in their host country. There is also an occupational compulsion: not only must the migrants be employed while in the host country (on pain of being expelled), but they are limited to certain kinds of employment. Women migrants are used as a semiskilled urban work force concentrated in low-skill industries: industries with high accident rates, industries that pay very low or urban subsistence wages, and industries that are highly susceptible to the fluctuations of the international market economy. In fact, the formation of this semiskilled work force appears to be an essential part in the maintenance of the overall stability; the inequality generated by the system is borne by a labor force generally known to be docile, difficult to arouse to militant action, and relatively cowed by threats.

NOTES

1. Information obtained in conversation with Fan Yew Teng, former member of the Malaysian Parliament.

2. Minister of Labour, Ong Bang Boon, speech given at the annual dinner of the Singapore Employers' Federation, October 18, 1975.

3. Interviews with officials of the Jurong Town Corporation.

4. See "open letter," dated March 4, 1976, to the prime minister of Singapore from a group of concerned priests; New Nation 1976; and Sunday Times 1976 had carried news of the proposed government measures. See also Straits Times 1977.

5. Officials of the Jurong Town Corporation estimated the number of migrant workers as over 100,000. Selangor Graduates Society 1978 estimates the number as 120,000.

6. I was employed as a semiskilled trainee at the factory for two months. During this time I lived in the workers' quarters and was able to carry out in-depth interviews, obtained access to factory records, and engaged in participation-observational research on the factory floors. After my employment at the factory had ceased, interviews with the workers continued for a period of six months through visits to their living quarters. The study lasted from June 1974 until April 1975, during which period I also visited kampongs and New Villages in West Malaysia from which some of the workers had come.

7. For example, in the roving department the arrangement is as follows: blowing and combing section—1 overseer and 10 workers; drawing and roving section—1 overseer and 11 workers; spinning section—2 overseers and 28 workers; winding section—1 overseer and 12 workers. In each section the workers are again divided according to the nature of their work. In the drawing and roving section, for instance, there are machine tenders, drawers, rovers, and doffers.

REFERENCES

Ali, S. Hussin. 1964. Social Stratification in Kampong Bagan. Singapore: Anthlone Press.

Blaumer, Robert. 1964. Alienation and Freedom. Chicago: University of Chicago Press.

Brighton Labour Process Group. 1977. "The Capitalist Labour Process." Capital and Class no. 1 (Spring).

Castles, Stephen, and Codula Kosack. 1973. Immigrant Workers and Class Structure in Western Europe. London: Oxford University Press.

Clutterbuck, Richard. 1973. Riot and Revolution in Singapore and Malaya, 1945-1963. London: Faber and Faber.

Dahlan, H. M. 1976a. "Micro Analyses of Village Communities in Peninsular Malaysia." In H. M. Dahlan, ed., The Nascent Malaysian Society. Kuala Lumpur: University Kelungsaan Malaysia.

Dahlan, H. M., ed. 1976b. The Nascent Malaysian Society. Kuala Lumpur: University Kelungsaan Malaysia.

Elson, Diane, and Ruth Pearson. 1980. The Latest Phase of the Internationalisation of Capital and Its Implications for Women in the Third World. Discussion Paper DP 150. Institute for Development Studies, University of Sussex.

Ghani, M. N. A. 1977. "Dimensions of Poverty and Poverty Eradication." In B. A. R. Mokhzani and Koo Siew Mun, eds., Poverty in Malaysia. Kuala Lumpur: Persatuan Ekonomik Malaysia.

Government of Singapore, Department of Statistics. 1974. Census of Industrial Production 1974. Singapore: the Department.

Government of Singapore, Economic Development Board. 1974. Annual Reports 1971-74. Singapore: the Board.

Government of Singapore, Ministry of Labour. 1974. Report on the Labour Force Survey of Singapore 1974. Singapore: the Ministry.

Heyzer, Noeleen. Forthcoming. "The Relocation of International Production and Low-Pay Female Employment: The Case of Singapore." In Kate Young et al., eds., Women in the Development Process. Cambridge University Press. First published as IDS mimeograph. University of Sussex, 1980.

Lim, Linda Y. C. 1978. Women Workers in Multi-national Corporations in Developing Countries: The Case of the Electronics Industry in Malaysia and Singapore. Occasional Papers Series no. 9. Ann Arbor: Women's Studies Program, University of Michigan.

Mokhzani, B., and Koo Siew Mun, eds. 1977. Poverty in Malaysia. Kuala Lumpur: Persatuan Ekonomik Malaysia.

Morland, J. K. 1958. Millways of Kent. Chapel Hill: University of North Carolina Press.

New Nation (Singapore). 1976. January 24.

Pang Eng Pong. 1977. The Electronics Industry in Singapore. Monograph no. 7. Singapore: Economic Research Centre, University of Singapore.

Phoon Wai On and S. B. Tan. 1975. "The Industrial Health Unit Survey in Singapore, 1975." Singapore Medical Journal (November).

Santa Cruz Collective on Labour Migration. 1978. "The Global Migration of Labour and Capital." In The Union of Political Economics, ed., US Capitalism in Crisis. New York (January), pp. 102-10.

Selangor Graduate Society. 1978. Plight of the Malaysian Workers in Singapore. Kuala Lumpur.

Short, Anthony. 1975. The Communist Insurrection in Malaya, 1948-60. London: Frederic Miller.

Smith, E. D. 1939. Technology and Labour. New Haven: Yale University Press.

Straits Times (Singapore). 1974a. June 11.

_____. 1974b. September 12.

_____. 1975. November 19.

_____. 1977. "Marriage Between Citizens and Aliens." March 3.

_____. 1978. September 9.

Sunday Times (Singapore). 1976. January 25.

_____. 1977. March 3.

Swift, M. C. 1965. Malay Peasant Society. London: Anthlone.

Ward, Anthony. 1975. "European Capitalism's Reserve Army." Monthly Review 27, no. 6 (November).

8

THE IMPACT OF
LAND REFORM ON WOMEN:
THE CASE OF ETHIOPIA

Zenebeworke Tadesse

Recent studies have demonstrated the need for a comprehensive conceptualization of the sexual division of labor and of the specific nature of patriarchy for understanding women's subordination and the impediments to changes in their status in transitional societies (Deere 1977; Benería 1979). Contrary to earlier studies that pointed to biological and/or sociocultural variables as determinants of the sexual division of labor across countries, these studies have shown that men's and women's tasks in productive activity form a class-specific economic variable that is responsive to changing material conditions of production, and hence has varied over time and space (Deere 1977; Deere et al. 1979).

A historical study focusing on peasant women has corroborated the above observation by pointing out that the sexual division of labor has varied according to the kind and size of landholding, form of rent, and marital status (Middleton 1979). It also points out that since the peasantry was not a homogeneous class, the sexual division of labor was deeply affected by its internal heterogeneity. Middleton argues thus:

> It was not women's exclusion from socially productive labor that determined their subject position but the

Part of the data on this paper is taken from a previous and more general paper (Tadesse 1975). My initial observation was limited to the earlier stage of the Land Reform Proclamation; where possible, I have included more recent data. I am indebted to Alem Habtu for his critical comments and to Lourdes Benería, who raised a series of questions on an earlier draft.

manner of their participation in surplus production and
their relationship with the mechanisms for reproducing
the social formation. It was as landholders rather than
as social or surplus producers that feudal peasants attained a degree of independence and entered the public
domain (1979, p. 165; emphasis added).

It is to the issue of landholding and its relation to women's
subordination in Ethiopia before and after land reform that this
chapter addresses itself. The argument is made that although the
Land Reform Proclamation is in itself undoubtedly progressive,
and has the immense potential of bringing about far-reaching changes
in rural Ethiopia and in the country as a whole, it has failed to
facilitate the transformation of the subordinate status of women.
In spite of its seemingly democratic acknowledgments and rhetoric,
the proclamation has reproduced patriarchal social relations and
politico-juridical superstructures that relegate women to an inferior
position.

This is not to suggest that a proclamation, no matter how
progressive, can in and of itself tackle a complex problem like the
subordination of women, but to argue that it can open the way to
challenge of all hierarchical forms of social relations and their
ideological representation. Contrary to earlier, commonly held
assumptions, recent observations have documented the multiplicity
of issues involved in the redefinition of the role and condition of
women in countries where there have been progressive or revolutionary transformations (First-Dilic 1979; Andors 1975; Croll 1976;
Bengelsdorf and Hageman 1978). Having noted the gains accruing
to women from such transformations, these studies have documented
structural and/or ideological constraints that inhibit further re-
definitions of women's roles. Significantly, Croll (1976) has pointed
out that incomplete transformations in the mode of production and
the reproduction of patriarchal forms encourage the persistence of
certain ideological constraints on the advancement of women, particularly in the rural areas.

HISTORICAL CONTEXT

Since Ethiopia is going through a period of profound transformation, it is difficult to make a definitive characterization of the
present social formation. Instead, I will attempt to provide a brief
historical context for our discussion.

Having been integrated into the world market system much
later than most peripheral countries,[1] Ethiopia remained predomi-

nantly feudal until recently, with subsistence production providing 95 percent of total agricultural output. Over 85 percent of the Ethiopian people are peasants, and before 1974 land was concentrated in the hands of a few landlords. The extraction of surplus from the peasantry took different forms, such as labor service tribute, rent payment in kind or in money, and various forms of taxation by the government and the church. Whatever the form, the peasants had to give up the largest proportion of their produce to the landlords (Rahmato 1970; Stahl 1974).

Incorporation of Ethiopia into the world economy resulted in the creation of a commercial sector that dominated the precapitalist organization of production. Foreign economic interests dominated production, marketing, and processing in the expanding export commodity sector. Following the Third Five-Year Plan (1968/69-1972/73), which stipulated that "progress in the agricultural sector can be obtained only by the rapid development of large-scale commercial farms producing crops for export," the state facilitated the growth of such farms, including large foreign-owned plantations, by providing the necessary infrastructure. This was done at the expense of poor peasants and pastoralists, who were evicted by the thousands (Kifle 1972; Bondestam 1974; Crummey 1976). In connection with this, before February 1974, Ethiopia had a vast number of unemployed, a constantly rising cost of living, and a very serious famine in many parts of the country.

The new production relations, which developed during this period, resulted in the disintegration of the dominant feudal mode of production. In the process the capacity of the state to preside over a new social formation was undermined. This aggravated the contradictions within factions of the ruling class that represented the old and the new orders of interests, as well as between the ruling class as a whole and the majority of the population. These contradictions gave rise to sporadic peasant uprisings, student and intellectual agitation, the emergence of a working-class movement, and the politicization of oppressed nationalities and women. The inability of the state to respond to the interests of the different groups and social classes by means of even "palliative reform," the convergence of this inability with the serious world economic crisis, and the greatest agrarian crisis in Ethiopia's history ushered in a spontaneous movement that began in February 1974 (Hiwet 1976).

The February Movement and the subsequent seizure of state power by the military resulted in some far-reaching reforms—notably urban and rural land reform, and the nationalization of industries (Koehn 1979). The most significant reform is the Land Reform Proclamation, which dissolved feudal institutions at the political, legal, and socioeconomic levels. Although a number of studies have examined the implications of the reform, albeit without any serious theoretical consideration (for instance, Ottaway 1977; Cohen and Koehn 1977; Koehn 1979), the differential impact of the reform on men and women has not yet been dealt with.

This chapter attempts to examine the impact of the land reform on peasant women. It will focus on three issues that are interrelated and reinforce each other with regard to the status of rural women: women's access to the means of production, laws and/or customs that deny or uphold property rights of women, the role of women's organizations.

A word of caution is in order when generalizing on the status of rural women in Ethiopia. Ethiopia is inhabited by people of different nationalities whose cultural heterogeneity is reflected in the many forms of social relations. Therefore, the following generalizations should be taken as a broad representative sample of the country. Furthermore, rural Ethiopia has historically exhibited a high degree of social differentiation. Thus, the status of women has varied in accordance with the amount of land owned, the form of labor extraction, and marital status. There has been a fairly sharp sexual division of labor defining and distinguishing the tasks performed by women from those done by men, particularly the process of transformation of products centering in the household. Early twentieth-century observations of this phenomenon hold true today. Forbes noted:

> In Abyssinia each form of labor is exclusively masculine or feminine. For instance, no male being even on the verge of starvation could be induced to grind grain into flour between the mighty stones employed by his mother or wife. The woman prepares all forms of foods and drinks, but she would not dream of killing the smallest bird or beast for the kitchen (1925, p. 86).

Similarly, tasks are strictly defined in agricultural production. According to a detailed study of decision making in the household, Bauer points out:

> Most restrictions on substitution of personnel among tasks in the production fields are restricted to males, and tasks in the domestic fields are restricted to females. Women are prohibited from plowing and threshing by an indigenous theory that their participation in these activities would decrease the amount of the crops produced. Since weeding, carrying cut

grain from the fields, and substituting for herdboys are
the only areas in which females may be used in place of
males in production tasks, the household must have the
proper number of men in order to carry out such tasks.
The domestic fields are similarly restricted. Men are
thought to be incapable of preparing food. Weissleder
noted that the only man who prepared his own food in
the Amhara town of Ankober was thought to be a physical hermaphrodite (1977, p. 243).

Furthermore, the sexual division of labor is class-specific,
in that whereas women in landless households and those with smallholdings assisted in almost all stages of agricultural production
(United Nations 1973), women in middle peasant strata and above
consider agricultural production as exclusively men's work (often
that of tenants) (Tadesse 1975).
 According to Boserup's (1970) classification of the relationship between farming systems and the sexual division of labor in
peripheral countries, [2] Ethiopia falls in the category in which the
agricultural system is that of extensive plow cultivation and, consequently, women do relatively less farm work than men. More
specifically, Goody (1976, pp. 110-111) classifies highland Ethiopian
society as transitional between his sub-Saharan category, which is
characterized by low class differentiation, polygamy, bride wealth,
and control of women primarily for their laboring and reproductive
capacities, and his Eurasian norm of class differentiation, monog-
amy, dowry, and control of women primarily for their property
rights and reproductive capacities.
 Although useful in some ways, these broad classifications
blur the class-related nature of the sexual division of labor and the
differences in systems of production in terms of specifying who
produces, how the production is organized, how the product is appropriated, and the relations of production within which this takes
place. In addition, the organization of production is partly dependent on the organization of human reproduction. As Whitehead
(1977) has pointed out in her review of Goody's book, these different
relationships to the means of production affect the contours of kinship and domestic domains of different systems of production; it is
in the specific connection between production and reproduction in
any productive system that the root of women's subordination to
men lies.
 Scattered throughout the literature on Ethiopia, one finds con-
firmation of Goody's thesis concerning different modes of inheritance, as well as some correlation between a generally lower status
of women and the spread of a more complex system of production

based on plow agriculture and involving some measure of private property. For example, Trimingham has noted:

> The Galla[3] family is patriarchal and the father has the right of sale and death over his children. . . . Marriage is exogamous and by purchase, the price being generally paid in cows. It is indissoluable once the final sacrificial ceremony (rako-kako) has been performed. The wife has few rights in Galla law, she may not inherit, but her social position is good, she goes about freely, has considerable influence, and travellers have contrasted her position with that of Afar and Somali women. Monogamy is the general practice, but richer men who can maintain separate huts are sometimes polygamous. The levirate is maintained by most pagan tribes and a widow passes to her husband's brother together with her children (1965; emphasis added).

By contrast, Levine (1965), Hoben (1973), and Bauer (1977) point out that Amhara and Tegre women did inherit land. According to Hoben:

> In a limited sense the right to discipline a woman for misconduct is transferred from her father or guardian to her husband at marriage, but with regard to the ownership of land and moveable property and the right to institute divorce the wife is very much the equal of her husband (1973, p. 83).

Substantiating these views with fascinating historical research, Crummey (1979a; 1979b) has shown that Amhara women did indeed hold extensive rights in land but cautions that:

> . . . the possession of rights should not be confused with their exercise. Men and women may have held equal rights in land in Gondarine Ethiopia, but they did not exercise these rights equally. Men dominated and controlled land, where women had it men tended to get it (1979a, p. 8).

He also points out that "Men perpetrated their domination of women" through the cognatic and ambilineal descent and inheritance system discussed by Hoben. Property rights constitute a basic factor affecting women; thus, we agree with Crummey's argument that

. . . while there may not be any direct correlation between property rights and the status of women in other
social spheres, a matter which ought to be capable of
empirical determination, the fact is that the sphere
of property rights is much more important than most
other spheres and assumes a peculiar importance precisely with the arrival of plough agriculture and more
intensive class differentiation (1979a, p. 4).

When inheritance is no longer important—as under the present
Ethiopian system, in which both the rural and the urban land reforms have abolished it—it becomes crucial to determine who exercises the de facto rights upon the means of production.

BEFORE LAND REFORM: INTRODUCTORY REMARKS

To properly evaluate the direct and indirect implications of
the agrarian reform for rural women, it is imperative to have a
brief account of rural women's subordination and their role in production and reproduction, both biological and social. In reality
rural women are so grotesquely underprivileged that it is almost
impossible to capture the magnitude of their oppression.

To begin with, the heterogeneity of the land tenure system and
the concomitant variety of production relations were predominant
in preland-reform agriculture, and have been noted in numerous
studies (such as Rahmati 1970; Hoben 1973). Different categories
of people involved in peasant agriculture have been classified as
poor peasants, middle peasants, rich peasants, and landlords; the
overwhelming majority belonged to the poor peasantry (Stahl 1974,
p. 88). One economic base for the subordination of women in
Ethiopia was the fact that the vast majority of them did not own
their land or any other means of production (cattle or the instruments of labor). This had several consequences.

In the first place, the underdevelopment of the rural infrastructure, coupled with the strict division of labor, rendered
women's work intensive, time-consuming, and monotonous. In
addition, the share of women in the labor process, particularly of
women in poor households, tended to increase with the changes
generated by the penetration of the market into new spheres of economic life, such as cash crop production, male out-migration,
and/or commercialization of agricultural production. But this increase did not relieve women of traditional burdensome tasks.
What Forbes observed earlier this century still holds true for rural
women today:

> . . . to the Abyssinian women falls the hardest of the
> communal tasks throughout a life which prematurely
> ages and destroys her. She is the hewer of wood and
> the drawer of water, and as the villages are always
> distant from either she toils for miles with incredibly
> heavy weights on her back (1925, p. 86).

In a society where land ownership was the primary determinant of political, social, and economic power, it should come as
no surprise that the lack of access to land ownership was also an
important determinant of the powerlessness of rural women. While
lack of land ownership defined the lower-class status of all the
landless peasantry, the prevailing sexual division of labor[4] tended
to place women in subordinate positions. Male dominance was reflected in the politico-juridical superstructure that reinforced
women's subordination. A clear example is the Ethiopian Civil
Code (1960, arts. 635, 647), which states the following:

> 1. "The husband is the head of the family."
> 2. "Unless otherwise expressly provided by this code,
> the wife owes him obedience in all lawful things which he
> orders."
> 3. "Where the husband is not in a position to provide
> his wife with servants, she is bound to attend to the house-
> hold duties herself."

Thus, patriarchal norms that demand the complete submission of the wife to the husband and the denial of her most elementary
rights have been legitimized by law, not to mention numerous other
ideological expressions. Observing this phenomenon, Levine noted:
"Although Amhara women enjoy considerable property and inheritance rights, their generally depressed status reflects the low
opinion commonly held of them. The peasant women's lot is as
hard as that of a slave . . ." (1965). In his more recent work he
states:

> Although in some groups the distribution of wealth and
> power keeps women from a wholly subordinate posi-
> tion, nearly all the peoples of Greater Ethiopia consider
> women generically inferior, express little if any appre-
> ciation of distinctively feminine traits, and harbor many
> idioms of contempt for alleged female attributes (Levine
> 1974, p. 79).

The family is not only an economic unit but also a cultural institution that reproduces the old values of patriarchy and domination. All aspects of peasant life are determined according to the Ethiopian patriarchal family system, which is guided by the principles of domination of old over young and male over female. Thus, it is primarily in the family system that both the reproduction of labor and the reproduction of sexual asymmetry is located. In the socialization of the sexes, for example, a boy undergoes the hazing given a prospective warrior and learns the proper methods of farming, while a girl is taught to care for younger children and assist her mother in all the household chores (Bauer 1977). Women, who are responsible for most socialization in early childhood, contribute to reproduction of sexual role structures and ideology of sexual inequality (O'Laughlin 1974).

Ethiopian women's participation in economic life is high, but has not always been recognized. Recent studies on rural women have pointed out the discrepancy between the high degree of women's involvement in agricultural activity and the problem of underrating their productive roles in censuses and other policy documents (Deere 1977; United Nations 1973; see also chapter 5 in this volume). This is very much the case with Ethiopian women; the latest study on socioeconomic profiles of the rural population clearly underlines this problem. In 1970

. . . The percentage of economically active males was considerably higher than females, 94 percent as contrasted to 33 percent for females. In 1977/78 the percentage of the population that was economically active was 73 percent, the economically inactive was 25 percent. For the total population, the proportion of the economically active, which was 63 percent in 1970, has gone up to 73 percent in 1977/78. The increase is due to the rise in activity rates of females which went from 33 percent in 1970 to 60 percent in 1977/78. This, however, should not be taken to suggest that female activity rates has [sic] gone up since then. Without a re-classification of females from the economically inactive to the economically active . . . housewives that are engaged in agricultural activities would have been treated as in the previous survey as economically inactive (Tesfaghiorghis 1978, p. 20).

For our case what is important about these conceptual problems related to the underestimation of women's productive activities is that

the Land Reform Proclamation was based on the previous survey.
These conceptual problems are reflected in the lack of recognition
of women's participation in economic life that permeates the
proclamation.

IMPACT OF LAND REFORM

As already noted, one of the fundamental changes gained by
the February Movement was land reform, for which the great
majority of Ethiopians had fought under the banner of "land to the
tiller." Accordingly, in March 1975 the state issued the Land
Reform Proclamation, which has since brought about significant
political, legal, and socioeconomic changes. Stating that all rural
lands should be the "collective property of the Ethiopian people,"
the proclamation abolished private ownership of land and tenancy
by denying compensation to former landowners, and assured the
peasants' possessory right over the land as long as they worked it
by themselves (with their family), thereby prohibiting hired labor.
More important, the proclamation established peasant associations
and judicial tribunals within them that were to adjudicate cases involving land disputes and related issues, thus undercutting the
power of the old, corrupt judicial authorities (Proclamation no. 31
1975).
 In addition, a number of other policy decisions since 1975
have given the peasant associations a variety of sociopolitical responsibilities ranging from managing producer cooperatives to
supervising armed self-defense units. At present there is an all-
Ethiopian peasant association that coordinates the efforts of local
peasant associations at the national level.[5]
 The section of the Land Reform Proclamation that deals with
women is chapter 2, number 4, "Distribution of Land to the Tiller
in Provinces with Privately Owned Rural Lands." The following
are the fundamental points, from the point of view of women:

 (1) Without differentiation of the sexes, any person who is willing to personally cultivate land shall be
allotted land.
 (2) The amount of land to be allotted to any
farming family shall at no time exceed 10 hectares
(1/4 of a gasha).
 (3) The amount of land to be allotted to farming
families shall as far as possible be equal. . . .
 (4) No person may use hired labor to cultivate
his holding; provided that the foregoing prohibition

shall not apply to a <u>woman</u> with no other adequate means of livelihood, or where the holder dies, is sick or old, to the wife or the husband thereof or to his or her children who have not attained majority.

. . .

(7) The minister shall determine by regulations the size of land sufficient for the maintenance of a <u>farming family</u> (emphasis added).

The proclamation goes on to state in chapter 2, number 5, regarding the prohibition of transfer of land:

No person may sell, exchange, will, mortgage, lease or otherwise transfer his holding to another; provided that upon the death of the holder the wife or husband or minor children . . . shall have the right to use the land.

The proclamation, which is egalitarian in intent, is internally contradictory when counterposed to the Ethiopian family structure. Let us concentrate on the formulation "Without differentiation of the sexes . . . allotted rural land sufficient for his maintenance and that of his family." We have already noted that in Ethiopian reality and in a concrete, legally accepted sense there is a marked differentiation of the sexes in the family that is literally summed up in "The man is the head of the family." For the phrase "without differentiation of the sexes" to have concrete meaning, land should have been allotted individually, giving women possessory right to land—a right they never enjoyed before—which in effect would have contributed to the elimination of their subordinate position and to liquidation of tenancy from rural Ethiopia, in accordance with the aim of the proclamation. This would not necessarily change the unit allotted to a family, but would have emphasized the economic equality of women. In addition, the ambiguity in chapter 2, number 5 (above), which states that, upon the death of the holder, the wife or husband shall have the right to use the land, could have been made automatic by allotting a piece of land to each partner and registering both partners initially.

Furthermore, to lump together "a woman with no other adequate means of livelihood" and "persons who due to illness, old age or youth, cannot personally cultivate their holding," as done in chapter 2, number 4, is nothing short of a total lack of recognition of the significant amount of agricultural work that women perform in the rural areas. This not only perpetuates oppressive relations of production but also tends to discourage women from participating actively and directly in the land reform movement.

The patriarchal view of women as inferior, in spite of their important share in the rural division of labor, and their being lumped with incapacitated members of society is carried through in chapter 3 of the proclamation, dealing with the function of peasant associations; this function is ". . . to cultivate the holdings of persons, who, by reason of old age, youth or illness or in the case of a woman, by reason of her husband's death, cannot cultivate their holdings."

Thus, instead of changing the self-image and expectations of peasant women, redefining their economic role, and elevating their status in the family and village community by completely breaking the preexisting institutional barriers to women's equality, the land reform program has left women dependent on men and under the umbrella of old patriarchal forms.

The proclamation has left untouched many aspects of male dominance because of the assumptions that women do not participate in agricultural production and that all members in a "family" have equal access to and rights over resources. As indicated earlier, this underlying assumption is contrary to Ethiopian reality and to hierarchical family forms. Thus, the seemingly egalitarian phrase "the size of land to be allotted to any farming family . . ." would be ludicrous if it were not so tragic for women in polygamous areas, where the word "family" loses its meaning.[6] The proclamation, which is based on the assumption of monogamous families, has created immense problems in these areas, where men have been registering one wife and leaving the others without access to land and other resources. Being unaware of their legal rights, and with no organization working on their behalf, women are left out of the direct benefits accruing from the land reform. It is to the issue of the need for women's organizations that we now turn.

WOMEN'S ORGANIZATIONS

Organizations Before February 1974

The first nationwide women's organization, known as the Ethiopian Women's Volunteer Service Association, was formed during the Ethiopian-Italian war. Although the leaders were ruling-class women, their patriotic call was answered by women all over Ethiopia. In the war of resistance, Ethiopian women fought side by side with their menfolk both on the field of battle and in passive resistance against the Italians. As Del Boca has noted:

It was traditional for Ethiopian women to fight side
by side with the soldiers, and many young women of
high birth and girls of the Amhara bourgeoisie played
an active part in the resistance (1969, p. 242).

Their significant participation is barely mentioned, but their major
contribution was nevertheless powerful, moral, material, and incon-
testable. As in all such movements, the ruling-class women were
the only ones rewarded and acclaimed for their participation. After
the war the women's organization remained in the hands of ruling-
class women. Having changed its name to the Ethiopian Women's
Welfare Association, the group can be characterized as philanthropic,
at best. Both before and after the February Movement, the members
of this organization have proclaimed the achievement of the emancipation of Ethiopian women. This is a far cry from the reality.

New Forms of Organization Since the February Movement

The general change taking place in the country, and particularly
the proclamation of land reform, both rural and urban, has led to a
new leap forward, with the emergence and articulation of a new
consciousness among women. Young and militant women defied their
traditional nonpolitical role, and called on their sisters to stand up
and struggle for their emancipation. A small group known as the
Co-ordinating Committee was formed in February 1976. It attempted
to mobilize women by sponsoring seminars, lectures, and political
educational forums for them.
Although the committee, being the first of its kind, has been
able to achieve some political awareness, it has not, for several reasons, been able to have a very strong impact. Consequently, despite
the fact that there are more scattered attempts at mobilization of
women than ever before, Ethiopian women do not yet have an organization that unites their forces, is concerned with their rights and
interests, and, above all, calls for implementation of policies and
decrees regarding equality of men and women.[7] The scattered attempts, however, deserve critical appreciation, since they can very
well be the nucleus for a strong women's organization in the future.
On our initial visits[8] to two rural areas, with the aim of gathering general information on the impact of land reform and the extent
of women's involvement in the movement, we were told that the
women's associations were almost always initiated by Zemecha
(literacy and development campaign) students, particularly female
participants who were conscious of the need to organize and politicize
rural women. The attempts by these students were very positive and

commendable. However, they faced numerous obstacles, and some shortcomings can be pointed out from the long-term perspective of a stable and viable women's organization. To mention a few:

1. Zemecha students, particularly those from the urban areas, were not aware of the magnitude of the patriarchal oppression that rural women faced; their agitation on the need for complete equality between the sexes met with staunch hostility from the men, who still held both economic and social superiority. Hence, not only were men hostile, but many refused outright to let their wives participate. Many peasant women were beaten for trying to suggest that they agreed with the students' agitation for equality.

2. To be sure, Zemecha students tried very hard, in spite of tremendous obstacles, to organize women. In most cases, however, they did not see that rural women's emancipation could come about only if they obtained a direct share of their own land, thereby ensuring their economic independence as a prelude to their social and political emancipation. Hence the peasant women's associations were peripheral to the actual land reform movement, and focused on improving the domestic life of women or on teaching them what can broadly be termed home economics, thereby excluding women from the political struggle.

3. Zemecha students did not stay long enough to create a strong, viable women's association that would have been able to independently sustain the struggle; this is one of the significant drawbacks of not having a permanent and full-time organizational staff. As our second, and particularly our third, visits to the areas being studied demonstrated, when the campaign students left, the women's associations either disintegrated and/or had hardly any regular meetings. Our observations demonstrated, further, that the land reform agents were too busy to pay particular attention to organizing women and/or did not see the need for it. The fact that the ministry failed to appreciate the need for and the importance of women's associations in order to wipe out all remnants of feudalism can concretely be observed from its first publication, "From Yekatit to Yekatit" (a summary of land reform movements from March 1975 to March 1976), in which not a word or a statistic concerned women's participation.

CONCLUSION

In conclusion, then, we can safely state that although land reform has brought important socioeconomic changes to the peasant as a whole, its impact on women has been limited and indirect.

Because of the economic benefits emanating from land reform (Stahl 1977), our observations indicate that peasant women now do not have to worry about where the next meal is coming from, and are less restrained in asking their husbands to buy them new clothes or items for the house. However, rural women are still dependent on their husbands economically, and therefore their social and political position in society is still subordinate to men.[9]

Agrarian reform cannot have a direct and sufficient impact on women until there is an all-out struggle against patriarchal authority. One major solution is a marriage law in addition to land reform that would negate the embedded concept of "head of the family," recognize women's responsibility outside the home, and challenge the existing sexual division of labor. As it now stands, the Ethiopian Land Reform Proclamation perpetuates the legalized, hierarchical family structure, thus excluding women from direct participation in the agrarian reform movement. Moreover, the weaknesses in the proclamation, coupled with the absence of a viable nationwide women's organization, particularly since the start of the February Movement in 1974, have delayed meaningful and long-lasting changes for women, thereby rendering social transformation in the country incomplete.

Recently the government has indicated the immediate need to form a nationwide women's organization. An important issue that need not be neglected is that since 1974, the question of women's subordination has been, and continues to be, widely discussed in public. Such public discussion has become, so to speak, legitimized, albeit in a very mechanical fashion. In the process a growing number of women, particularly the young, continue to voice their discontent and defy traditional norms.

NOTES

1. In a study Habtu (1979) has divided Ethiopia's integration into two major phases: Phase I (1900-35), a period of integration on a small scale, and Phase II (1935-74), a period of uneven yet crucial integration into the world capitalist system.

2. Although some studies have criticized Boserup's overall classification as inaccurate (Huntington 1975; Deere 1977), it is still useful in some ways for the purpose of this section.

3. "Galla" is a derogatory name for the group properly known as the Oromo, the majority nationality in Ethiopia.

4. A broad discussion of the division of labor is beyond the scope of this chapter. It is mentioned here in recognition of its complexity and the multiple levels at which it functions. In an

instructive article Edholm, Harris, and Young (1977) examine the
uses to which the concept has been put, and analyze it as an essential component of the social construction of gender. In addition,
they examine some of the arguments concerning the distribution of
tasks on the basis of sex and the unequal value that is attached to
different tasks, as well as the interplay between the sexual division
of labor and specific forms of the productive unit. See also
Middleton 1979 for a useful discussion of the concept.

5. As earlier indicated, I know of no theoretically informed
study focusing on land reform in Ethiopia. Interesting insights are
provided by Hiwet 1976 and Valdelin 1978, as well as by Stahl 1977.
Theoretical observations on long-term effects of agrarian reforms,
and their relation to accumulation and underdevelopment, that have
been documented for Latin America (De Janvry and Ground 1978;
Montoya, 1978) may have relevance for the Ethiopian situation.
Reference should also be made to Abate and Teklu 1979.

6. A study by the Central Statistics Office (1978) indicates
that approximately 10 percent of all rural households are polygamous. However, in southern provinces like Arsi, Bale, and
Sidamo, the figure is as high as 25 percent with the northern regions showing the lowest proportion of polygamy.

7. The latest study on peasant associations (Tesfaghiorghis
1978, p. 1) notes: "As of March 1977, there were 25,047 peasant associations with a membership of 6,894,320 peasants. . . . On average a peasant association embraces 275 peasants. Peasant associations are formed of male and female peasants without differentiation of the sex. As available data indicates, the participation of
females into peasant associations is insignificant. In Gojjam and
Wollo the proportion of female peasant members is 5.4 and 18 per
cent, respectively." The data on Gojjam are particularly significant because the highest proportion of widowed and divorced females is recorded in the northern regions, including Gojjam (Central Statistics Office 1978).

8. Fieldwork was carried out in 1975.

9. One area in which some progress has been made is the redefinition of rural women's work—observable from recent estimates
of rural labor force mentioned earlier (Tesfaghiorghis 1978, p. 20):
"In 1977/78, the percentage of labor force engaged in agricultural
activities, occasional farming, and off-farm were 76, 22 and 2 per
cent respectively. Occasional farming refers to those who partly
work in agriculture and partly are engaged in other activities, and
these are predominantly housewives and students. While the percentage of the male labour force engaged in farming, i.e., 91 per
cent, is higher than for females which was 54 per cent the percentage
engaged in occasional farming is substantially higher for females,

43 per cent as compared to 8 per cent for males." Accordingly,
"For females the activity rates based on farming only rose from as
low as 28 per cent in the age group 10-14 to as high as 69 per cent
in the age group 45-49, while the combined activity rates rose from
48 per cent to 81 per cent for the same age group. The reason
for the higher combined activity rates is due to the significant
number of rural housewives working as occasional farmers (p. 23)."

REFERENCES

Abate, Alula, and Tesfaye Teklu. 1979. "Land Reform and Peasant Associations in Ethiopia." World Employment Programme
research working paper. Geneva: ILO. (Mimeographed; restricted.)

Andors, Phyllis. 1975. "Social Revolution and Women's Emancipation: China During the Great Leap Forward." Bulletin of
Concerned Asian Scholars 7, no. 1:33-42.

Bauer, Dan Frary. 1977. Household and Society in Ethiopia: An
Economic and Social Analysis of Tigray Social Principles and
Household Organization. Monograph no. 6, Occasional paper
series. East Lansing: Committee on Ethiopian Studies, African
Studies Center, Michigan State University.

Benería, Lourdes. 1979. "Reproduction, Production and the Sexual Division of Labor." Cambridge Journal of Economics 3,
no. 3:203-25.

Bengelsdorf, Carrollee, and Alice Hageman. 1978. "Emerging
from Underdevelopment: Women and Work in Cuba." Race and
Class 19, no. 4:361-78.

Bondestam, Lars. 1974. "People and Capitalism in the North-
Eastern Lowland of Ethiopia." Journal of Modern African
Studies 12, no. 3:423-29.

Boserup, Esther. 1970. Women's Role in Economic Development.
London: George Allen and Unwin; New York: St. Martin's Press.

Central Statistics Office. 1978. Demographic Characteristics of
the Rural Population of Ethiopia. Addis Ababa: Central Statistics Office.

Civil Code. 1960. Imperial Ethiopian Government. Addis Ababa.

Cohen, and Peter Koehn. 1977. "Rural and Urban Land Reform in Ethiopia." African Law Studies 14, no. 1:3-62.

Croll, Elizabeth J. 1976. "Social Production and Female Status: Women in China." Race and Class 18:39-52.

Crummey, Donald. 1976. "History and Revolution in Ethiopia." Paper presented at the Canadian Association of African Studies Annual Conference, Vancouver.

_____. 1979a. "Women and Landed Property in Gondarine Ethiopia." Unpublished manuscript.

_____. 1979b. "The Settlement of Litigation Within the Ethiopian Ruling Class, with Special Reference to the Position of Women: The Bagemder Amhara from the 1750's to the 1850's." Unpublished manuscript.

De Janvry, Alain, and Lynn Ground. 1978. "Types and Consequences of Land Reform in Latin America." Latin American Perspectives 5, no. 4:90-112.

Del Boca, Angelo. 1969. The Ethiopian War 1935-1961. Chicago: University of Chicago Press.

Deere, Carmen Diana. 1977. "The Agricultural Division of Labor by Sex: Myths, Facts and Contradictions in the Northern Peruvian Sierra." Paper presented to the Panel on "Women: The New Marginals in the Development Process," Joint National Meeting of the Latin American Studies Association and the African Studies Association, Houston, Texas.

Deere, Carmen Diana, Jane Humpries, and Magdalena León de Leal. 1979. "Class and Historical Analysis for the Study of Women and Economic Change." Paper prepared for the Role of Women and Demographic Change Research Program. Geneva: ILO.

Edholm, F., O. Harris, and K. Young. 1977. "Conceptualizing Women." Critique of Anthropology 3:101-30.

First-Dilic, Ruza. 1979. "Sex Roles in Rural Yugoslavia." International Journal of Sociology of the Family 4, no. 2:161-69.

Forbes, Rosita. 1925. From Red Sea to Blue Nile. New York: Macauley.

Goody, Jack. 1976. Production and Reproduction: A Comparative Study of the Domestic Domain (1). Cambridge Studies in Social Anthropology. Cambridge: Cambridge University Press.

Habtu, Roman. 1979. "Notes on Ethiopia's Integration into the World Economy." Amherst: Department of Economics, University of Massachusetts. (Mimeographed.)

Hiwet, Addis. 1976. "From Autocracy to Bourgeois Dictatorship." (Mimeographed.)

Hoben, A. 1973. Land Tenure Among the Amhara of Ethiopia. Chicago: University of Chicago Press.

Huntington, D. 1975. "Issues in Women's Role in Economic Development." Journal of Marriage and the Family 37 (November): 1001-12.

Kifle, Henock. 1972. "Investigation of Mechanized Farming and Its Effects on Peasant Agriculture." CADU Publications no. 74.

Koehn, Peter. 1979. "Ethiopia: Famine Food Production and Changes in the Legal Order." African Studies Review 22:51-72.

Levine, Donald. 1965. Wax and Gold. Chicago: University of Chicago Press.

_____. 1974. Greater Ethiopia: The Evolution of a Multiethnic Society. Chicago: University of Chicago Press.

Middleton, Christopher. 1979. "The Sexual Division of Labor in Feudal England." New Left Review no. 113-14:147-68.

Montoya, Rodrigo. 1978. "Changes in Rural Class Structure Under the Peruvian Agrarian Reform." Latin American Perspectives 5, no. 4:112-26.

O'Laughlin, Bridget. 1974. "Mediation of Contradiction: Why Mbum Women Do not Eat Chicken." In M. Z. Rosaldo and L. Lamphere, eds., Women, Culture and Society, pp. 301-18. Stanford, Calif.: Stanford University Press.

Ottaway, Marina. 1977. "Land Reform in Ethiopia, 1974-1977."
African Studies Review 20 (December):79-90.

Proclamation No. 31. 1975. "Proclamation to Provide for the
Public Ownership of Rural Lands." Nigaret Guzeta 35, no. 15:
107-18.

Rahmato, Dessalegn. 1970. "Conditions of the Ethiopian Peasantry." Challenge 10, no. 2:1-49.

Savard, George C. 1970. The Population of Ethiopia. Vol. II.
Addis Ababa.

Stahl, Michael. 1974. Ethiopia: Political Contradiction in Agricultural Development. Uppsala: Raben Sjogern.

_____. 1977. New Seeds in Old Soil: A Study of the Land Reform
Process in Western Wollega, Ethiopia. Research Report no. 40.
Uppsala: Scandinavian Institute of African Studies.

Tadesse, Zenebeworke. 1975. "Condition of Women in Ethiopia."
Unpublished ms. Published in Swedish as Kirnna i Etiopien.
Uppsala: Scandinavian Institute of African Studies, 1978.

Tesfaghiorghis, Habtemariam. 1978. "Some Social and Economic
Aspects of the Rural Population." Paper presented at Institute
of Development Research seminar, Nazareth, Ethiopia.

Trimingham, J. S. 1965. Islam in Ethiopia. London: Frank Cass.

United Nations, Economic Cooperation Administration. 1974.
"Towards Full Employment of Women in Ethiopia." A Report to
the Imperial Ethiopian Government, Annex K. Geneva: ILO.

Valdelin, Jan. 1978. "Ethiopia 1974-7 from Anti-feudal Revolution
to Consolidation of the Bourgeois State." Race and Class 19,
no. 4:379-97.

Whitehead, Ann. 1977. "Book Review." Critique of Anthropology
3:151-59.

9

THE SEXUAL DIVISION OF LABOR IN RURAL CHINA

Elizabeth Croll

Rural development strategies in the People's Republic of China that aimed at establishing the collective as the unit of production, increasing agricultural production, and diversifying rural activities were all planned on the assumption that China is uniquely rich in labor power and that women constitute one of the most underdeveloped of China's resources. In the mid-1950s Mao Ze-dong (Mao Tse-tung) anticipated the role of China's women in reorganization and development when he wrote that they "form a vast reserve of labor power which should be tapped in the struggle to build a great socialist country" (Foreign Languages Press 1957, p. 2).

The economic development of China necessitated the inclusion of women in social production or the waged labor force, but government policy, as in other socialist states, assumed that involvement in the remunerated agriculture labor force was of the utmost importance to the women themselves as a precondition for improvement in their position in society. It predicted direct correlations between women's entry into social production and their participation in the political distribution of economic resources and surplus, and, on an individual basis, between a woman's improved material condition and her new confidence to exercise authority in the household and in the collective.

The incorporation of women into social production or the waged labor force required a new definition of their work that fundamentally challenged the traditional division of labor. This chapter discusses the forms that this challenge has taken in the 1960s and 1970s, and asks what specific policies are designed to alter the sexual division of labor; how far women's role and status in productive, reproductive, and political activities have been redefined in rural China; and what obstacles exist to further changes.

THE TRADITIONAL DIVISION OF LABOR

The traditional division of labor was based on the most important distinction in social, political, and economic affairs for all social classes: that between household (domestic) and nonhousehold (public) spheres of activity. From the earliest times in China, women had been taught that they should be concerned with the former and not with the latter. Codes of feminine conduct ruled that women were to take no part in public affairs and to have no influence on or knowledge of affairs outside the home. "A wife's words should not travel beyond her apartments"; "a woman does not discuss affairs outside of her home"; and "a man travels everywhere while a woman is confined to the kitchen" were all common folk sayings. The mobility of women was circumscribed by the practices of bound feet, segregation, and relative seclusion. Indeed, the word for wife, neiren, literally meant "inside person." In peasant households, however, these customs were frequently modified in the interests of subsistence, and village women customarily had more freedom of movement than their richer counterparts, although their movements were still restricted. Village women were denied participation in any government or local community institution, and all the significant ceremonial roles in society could be filled only by men.

It seems, though, that in some areas of China these prohibitions did not apply to agricultural fieldwork. The most quoted data illustrating the percentage of farm work performed by peasant women before the 1940s and 1950s was that collated by the agricultural economist J. L. Buck in the early 1930s (Buck 1937, pp. 291-92). In terms of work accomplished, he estimated that men performed 80 percent of all the farm labor in China; women, 13 percent; and children, 7 percent. The larger proportion of women might seldom labor in the fields, or what was defined as the productive sector, but these figures also obscure the fact that throughout China peasant women were mainly occupied with domestic production and reproduction performed within the individual household. They primarily reared an animal or two, transformed raw materials for consumption, and maintained the self-provisioning individual household and serviced its members. Thus, any agricultural work was rarely differentiated from the onerous domestic labor and processing of materials for consumption performed within the peasant household; and with no direct relation to production, their agricultural labor was seldom visible or remunerated.

In the 1940s and 1950s the Communist party and government introduced a number of policies and measures to encourage women to take a full and wide-ranging part in the waged agricultural labor force. Policies of collectivization provided for the registration of women members as individual workers on agricultural production teams, the establishment of separate women's work teams designed to provide mutual support and confidence in mastering the techniques of production, and individual remuneration on the principle of equal pay for equal work. Within the collectives, facilities (to be described in some detail later in the chapter) were to be provided to improve women's health and reduce their traditional domestic chores. Finally, to give women the opportunity to acquire new skills, quotas within general and special educational and training programs were instituted for women in rural localities. Since the mid-1950s women have been continuously urged to take up agricultural work; a measure of the success of these mobilization policies is the degree to which women have contributed to the total labor inputs in collective units and the degree to which the sexual division of labor within the village has been redefined.

WOMEN IN PRODUCTION

In quantitative terms the greatest increase in the numbers of women contributing to agricultural production came with the establishment of collectives in the mid-1950s. The establishment of cooperatives providing for an expansion of agriculture and the scope of agricultural occupations was responsible for a sharp rise in the number of peasant women entering the remunerated labor force. It was estimated that the first stage of cooperativization in 1956-57 had increased by six times the contribution of women to nondomestic production compared with that of 1955.[1] The number of women in nondomestic production in 1957 was thought to be roughly 100 million out of a total of 157 million working-age women, 60 percent of their number.[2] During busy seasons this number was reported to have risen to 70 percent.[3] (See Table 9.1.)

The peak demand for women's labor occurred in 1958-59 during the period of the Great Leap Forward and the establishment of the rural communes. The new scope of activities managed by the commune and the removal of men from agricultural fieldwork and into larger projects of water conservancy, irrigation, and capital construction sponsored by the communes created a shortage of labor within the small agriculture production brigades and teams. Most of the reports published during the Great Leap Forward suggest that 90 percent of working-age women in rural areas engaged in agricultural labor, and that there was an increase in the actual number of days worked by women.[4] In 1957 the average number of days worked among all working people in the rural areas was 249 for men and only 166 days for women. In 1959 it was estimated that this had risen to 300 for men and 240 for women.[5] Unfortunately, in the absence of more detailed data, these overall figures must be assumed to mask great regional variations in the numbers of women working full-time, part-time, or on a daily or seasonal basis. (For variations between neighboring production brigades, see Crook and Crook 1966, p. 247.)

TABLE 9.1

Percentage of Women in Nondomestic
Production: Rural China, 1950-59

Area	Year	Percentage of Working-Age Women, 16-60
Old liberated areas	1950	50-70
New liberated areas		24-40
Rural China	1957	60-70
Rural China	1958	90

Sources: People's China, March 16, 1950; New China News Analysis (NCNA), September 22, 1959; NCNA, July 31, 1958.

In the 1960s and 1970s local and piecemeal reports suggest that women were not always fully involved in nondomestic production, and certainly not to the extent suggested by the figures for the late 1950s.[6] There was a drop in the numbers of women who contribute labor to agriculture in the 1960s and 1970s, although there was still an overall rise in the number of women taking part in nondomestic production and in the number of days worked. The characteristic that marks the pattern of their contribution to agriculture since the mid-1950s is the degree of fluctuation, with many women entering and leaving the work force according to local demand. This varies primarily with the labor requirements of the different crop regions in China and according to the range and diversity of economic pursuits or the degree to which nonagricultural activities supplement agricultural production.

Where there is intense agricultural cultivation or a great variety of nonagricultural occupations, women have entered agricultural production in larger numbers, and by so doing have altered to some extent the traditional division of labor, in which women were largely excluded from remunerated agricultural labor. As many Chinese commentaries on the new division of labor have noted, peasant women moved from "an auxiliary to a main force within agriculture."[7] However, the alteration in the relations of production and the specific policies to encourage the direct involvement of peasant women in the agricultural labor force allowed for the visibility and remuneration of women as individual producers, but they did not necessarily challenge the sexual division of labor within agriculture or in the social and political affairs of the village.

THE SEXUAL DIVISION OF LABOR
WITHIN AGRICULTURAL PRODUCTION

The form that the division of labor in agriculture has increasingly taken reflects the dual and conflicting assumptions that underlie all agricultural policies: that women have no physical limitations, and can perform exactly the same labor as men, and that women have certain physical characteristics that limit the type of work they can do and make them primarily responsible for reproductive tasks. Each of these assumptions has affected the forms that the sexual division of labor within agriculture has taken.

On the one hand, policies subscribe to the commonly cited adage of Mao Ze-dong that "anything a man can do, a woman can also do."[8] On this basis women have been encouraged to enter occupations that were traditionally male preserves. There are now women tractor drivers, women fishing teams, women at the plow, and women work teams that drain fields, build dams, and plant forests. These groups are often referred to as March 8 (Women's Day) teams, women red flag holders, or Iron Maiden's teams, and consist mainly of younger and unmarried women of the collectives— that is, those not involved in reproduction. Women have been trained in the new technologies of agricultural production, such as driving tractors and mechanized transplanters, and taught the skills of plowing, raking, mixing seeds, and applying manure.[9] They have contributed to technical innovation by improving certain types of tools, such as wooden-track earth movers, waterwheels, and hand-powered mills.[10] Women's experimental groups have received a share of scientific and technical inputs. On their plots they have been encouraged to use new methods of cultivation, close planting, soil improvement, pest control, watering, manuring, and seed mixing.[11]

In 1958–59 it was estimated that approximately 13 million women took part in these scientific experiments. In Hubei province,

36 percent of all women cultivated 121,000 hectares of experimental land.[12] Very often the new methods proved to be both feasible and successful, and the results of the experimental groups have been popularized in the media since the 1960s.[13] Their entrance into former male preserves, technical and training programs, and scientific experiments has all served to increase the groups' confidence and to prove the ability of women agricultural workers, but at the same time the majority of women are still found in certain of the less-skilled and lighter agricultural tasks because of the second assumption underlying the division of labor: that women have certain physical limitations.

Certain types of work are believed to be more suited to women than to men because of the nature of women's physique, degree of physical strength, and physical characteristics. As one policy statement pointed out:

> Physically some people are stronger while others are weak, some heavy manual farm jobs fit the stronger sex better. This is a division of labour based on physiological features of both sexes, and is appropriate. We can't impose the same framework on female and male commune members alike in disregard of the former's physiological features and physical power. In some kinds of work, women are less capable than men, but in others they do better.[14]

Women are generally to be found tending pigs or poultry, breeding silkworms, collecting manure, hoeing, and transplanting; and they have taken a greater part in the production of certain crops, such as tea, cotton, and rice. These all have been traditionally associated with women's labor, albeit within the domestic rather than the collective sphere of production.

Two examples of the division of labor, in different communes and 21 years apart, give some indication of the allocation of work tasks to men and women in these particular communes. (See Table 9.2.)

There is a tendency for women to be found in the "lighter," though not necessarily less physically demanding, tasks, and this has had the effect of underlining and strengthening the notion of a natural division of labor within agriculture between heavy and light work, on the one hand, and skilled and unskilled labor, on the other. However, there are some regional differences within China. In localities where there are alternative nonagricultural demands on men's labor, women may undertake a wider variety of agricultural tasks, including those normally performed in other areas by men.

Reports in the media would suggest that there is a correlation between the division of labor within agriculture and the demand for men to take part in nonagricultural pursuits. That is, where the opportunities afforded by the establishment of rural industry, projects of capital construction, and the sideline occupations of fishing, mining, and forestry draw men from the agricultural work force, a division of labor has grown up not within agriculture—indeed, women may have had to take up numerous new tasks hitherto performed by men—but between agriculture and nonagricultural pursuits. The peak demand for women's labor in 1958-59 was the result of the strategy to create a shortage of labor by withdrawing men from agriculture, and this pattern may have set a precedent that has become a rather permanent feature of rural China. The first indication that this might be so came in a 1958 document that suggested that "women will gradually replace men in all work suitable to women so as to bring about a reasonable rearrangement of the social labour force."[15]

TABLE 9.2

Division of Labor on Communes, 1956 and 1977

Men	Women
Rice, Corn, Sweet Potatoes, Wheat: 1956	
Heavy work (plowing, carrying heavy loads)	Lighter work
Irrigation, fostering well-grown seedlings	Preparing ash compost
Tilling rape fields	Harvesting rape
Subsidiary occupations	Growing early crops
Double Rice Cropping, Winter Wheat: 1977	
Plowing with water buffalo	Sowing seed
Carrying water	Transplanting rice seedlings
Driving tractors	Harvesting
Driving hand tractors	Carrying manure to the fields
Rural industries	Raising pigs

Sources: Foreign Languages Press 1957, p. 289; Croll 1977a, p. 805.

The result of this policy is that in some areas women have become the mainstay of farming work in the fields.

> Women should shoulder agricultural production. Men's labour power is needed to open mines, expand machine building industry, power plants, cement plants. These all call for new labor inputs. Generally speaking, these departments of industry employ mainly men labourers and provide only a few types of work that can be undertaken by women workers. Thus, up to a certain stage in the development of socialist construction, agricultural production will have to be undertaken mainly by women. Of course with the process of agricultural production mechanized and electrified, agricultural production will follow the pattern of industrial production. By that time women can completely shoulder the responsibility.[16]

This suggests that women have served as a labor reserve to be incorporated into agricultural production as men have moved into rural industries and projects of capital construction. In one commune in Guangdong, a southern province, that I visited in 1977, a more detailed survey of my own contributes to this impression. That is, in communes where there are more alternative occupations, women outnumber men in agriculture. In the village surveyed, the majority of the work force (numbering 79 persons) was employed in the production team, although a number of men worked in nonagricultural occupations, mainly in the small machinery factories, the coal mine, or services run by the commune, the county, or the state. (See Table 9.3.)

TABLE 9.3

Occupations of Working Residents, Jiang Village,
Guangdong Province, 1977

Work	Men	Women	Total
Agricultural production team	27	38	65
Occupations outside team	13	1	14
Total	40	39	79

Source: Croll 1977a, p. 804.

What is particularly noticeable in this production team is that women agricultural workers outnumber men, and that all the women in the village work force, except one, worked on the production team in agriculture. The commune leaders thought this reflected unsatisfactory division of labor, and as a result they were giving some attention to the recruitment of younger unmarried girls into rural industries run by the commune. However, this division of labor between agricultural and nonagricultural pursuits may be a phenomenon particularly associated with the more urbanized and industrial regions of the south, and northern and eastern coastal provinces, and less with the central and more inland rural areas. However, the references to this new division of labor in the media and policy documents suggest that it may be widespread in the former regions.

Throughout China women have entered into new activities, have received a share of inputs, and have acquired new skills, but it is also true that in many areas they are found predominantly in certain of the less-skilled occupations and are de facto categorized as sundry workers. The evidence also suggests, however, that where there is a demand for men's labor outside agriculture, there may have been a degree of feminization of agriculture, with women constituting the main productive workers. In effect this has set up a new sexual division of labor between agricultural and nonagricultural pursuits. These divisions of labor both within agriculture and between agricultural and other activities have affected the rates of remuneration paid to peasant women.

THE REMUNERATION OF WOMEN

One of the main changes within rural society that has directly affected women is that they now receive individual remuneration for work performed within the collective. Since the establishment of rural communes, wages in kind and cash have been paid to them as individual workers rather than, as previously, to the heads of households. The separation of collective production from the domestic domain and the direct involvement of women in social production have made possible the visibility and recognition of women as producers. There has also been a consistent promotion of the policy of equal pay for equal work, and some women have been remunerated on the same basis as the male laborers within the collective. Often they have received equal payment only after challenging the men to a competition in which they proved themselves equal to the men in performance, or the men failed to equal women in the performance of women's allocated tasks. Cases of the reassessment of remuneration to equalize the payments made to men have often been cited in the media,[17] but equal pay is still not a constant feature in the rural collective.

Labor in the collective sector is rewarded according to the system of work points or labor days. Agricultural tasks of individual workers are evaluated according to the degree of strength, skill, and experience required, and quantity and quality of output; then norms are set for the standards and pace of each type of work or worker, and a value is assigned to the labor day. Ten work points generally equal one labor day, but all workers laboring a full day do not necessarily receive ten work points. The number of work points is designed to reward skill and physically hard work, and on both these counts women or the jobs assigned to them normally receive a low estimation. Whereas men are often assigned ten work points for a day's work, women almost always automatically receive less, regardless of whether they are laboring at the same or different tasks. Where individual workers are graded, and for each day's work are allotted a specific number of work points, usually ranging from four to ten points (seven grades), women tend to be distributed among the lowest of the three payment grades. Table 9.4 clearly illustrates this asymmetry.

TABLE 9.4

Distribution of Male and Female Agricultural Workers
by Wage Grade: Sun Fen Production Brigade,
Kungming People's Commune, 1958

Wage Grade	Distribution in Each Grade (percent)			Production in Each Grade (percent)	
	Total	Men	Women	Men	Women
1	12.4	5.8	18.4	22.2	77.8
2	16.0	12.7	18.9	38.0	62.0
3	26.4	21.2	31.2	38.3	61.7
4	23.4	23.1	23.7	47.0	53.0
5	9.5	14.1	5.3	71.0	29.0
6	7.5	13.4	2.1	85.3	14.7
7	4.8	9.7	0.4	95.7	4.3
Total	100.0	100.0	100.0		

Sources: China Mainland 1959; Hoffman 1967, p. 319.

In the preferred method of remuneration, work points are awarded differentially to agricultural tasks, and women always receive a lower number of work points than men. Table 9.5 again shows the discrepancy that has persisted over the years in the number of work points paid to men and women.

TABLE 9.5

Allocation of Work Points to Male and Female
Laborers per Day: Random Sample, 1956-75

Year	Men	Women	Source
1956	10	4-6	FLP 1957, p. 289
1960	10-12	8	Crook 1966, p. 126
1961	10	7	ZF, November 1, 1961
1961	10	8	ZF, November 1, 1961
1964	6-10	under 5.5	Oian Xian, May 25, 1964
1965	10	7.5	ZF, February 1, 1966
1970	10	5	RMRB, March 6, 1972
1972	10	8	Hongqi, February 1, 1972
1975	10	7	CR, June 1975
1975	10	7.5	CR, March 1975

This discrimination has been a major factor affecting the morale of women in the collectives, and several reports in the media describe situations in which women had withdrawn their labor or made only halfhearted attempts to maintain their quotas; subsequent investigation found the cause to lie in their dissatisfaction with the inadequacy of their rewards.[18] Despite the consistent advocacy of the principle and numerous campaigns to implement it, there has been a tenacious opposition to allocating women remuneration equal to that of the men. Their lower rates of pay have been excused by a number of rationalizations. It is claimed that women do not bear the main brunt of agricultural work, for men still do the heavier and more basic work in the collectives.[19] Even when women perform the same tasks as men, they are deemed to be the exceptions to the rule that women just do not match the stronger capacity for labor and the higher technical levels of men. Therefore, until women learn to do exactly the same kinds of jobs as men, they do not deserve equal payment.[20] Moreover, they work fewer hours per day and days per month than men.

Male peasants have also argued that their positions as heads of households mean that they must be the main breadwinners or contributors to the household budget (Crook and Crook 1966, pp. 126-29)—indeed, some feared that because of the particular way in which the value of the work point was calculated, their own levels of payment might be affected if women were to receive more work points or a higher rating for their labor.[21] Generally the lower rates of pay awarded to peasant women are one consequence of the traditional value still accorded to women's labor; another consequence of the traditional division of labor is the lower proportion of women involved in the economic and political decision-making procedures of the collective, a subject discussed below.

POLITICAL PARTICIPATION

It has been forecast that one of the benefits accruing to women as a result of entry into nondomestic production would be access to and a share in the control and allocation of the resources of the household and the collective. As they labored in the collective, they would begin to share in the decision making of the collective, and hence would enter the local and national political arenas. Women were given every encouragement to become members of and active participants in the affairs of political organizations, and political organizations were exhorted to increase the number of women members and leaders. To help women acquire the necessary confidence and experience, the government and local Communist party organizations arranged special literacy and training classes for peasant women. One measure of the success of these policies is the number of women cadres or women who are in positions of responsibility in the Communist party, government organs, and production units. These figures indicate that the expansion in the number of women entering social production was not reflected in the number of women admitted to party membership or selected for positions of decision making in the high-level or government organs. To take the membership of the Communist party and the Youth League as examples, in the 1950s women made up only 10 percent of the party membership and 30 percent of the Young Communist League (Lewis 1963, p. 109). Of the basic-level people's deputies elected in all parts of the country, the proportion of women rose slowly.

Despite a number of campaigns to encourage women to take part in political decision-making bodies, their number remained disproportionately low in the 1970s. True, there has been an increase in the numbers of women cadres since the Cultural Revolution. Of the 6 million new members admitted to the Communist party between

1966 and 1973, 27 percent were reported to be women.[22] At the provisional congresses of the newly reconstituted Young Communist League in 1973, an average of 40 to 45 percent of the delegates were women (Maloney 1976). In Honan province women accounted for 30 percent of cadres of the agricultural production brigades.[23] Several newspaper reports have commented on these figures and expressed dissatisfaction at the continuing low proportions.[24] At the same time, these reports quite rightly make the point that the entry of women into the formal political arena marks a radical alteration in the traditional sexual division of labor that effectively banned women from the political domain.

TABLE 9.6

Proportion of Women Among Basic-Level
Deputies, 1953-63
(percent)

Year	Women	Men
1953	17.3	82.7
1958	20.0	80.0
1963	22.36	77.64

Sources: NCNA, September 22, 1959; Peking Review, January 8, 1965.

Women have indeed entered new economic and political activities since the mid-1950s. In many areas they are now the main producers in agriculture, and they may constitute up to one-third of local leadership positions. They now receive individual wages, and their health and levels of education and training in skills have improved substantially. To the extent, then, that they have entered the waged labor force in larger numbers, there has been some redefinition of the sexual division of labor in the public sphere, but this has not brought with it a correlative redefinition of labor within the domestic sphere. Unlike their male counterparts, women are now required to service the household as before and, in addition, to labor in agricultural production. These dual demands, constituting the "double day," have penalized them in the public domain. For instance, their annual and daily contributions to collective labor quotas have been diminished in order to allow them to undertake domestic labor and service the household. Policies introduced to encourage women to take part in political and collective decision making—many of these jobs are part-time and unpaid—have been jeopardized by the continuing household responsibilities of women. Yet there have been substantial attempts in China to reduce the content of domestic labor and to socialize and equalize the distribution of domestic labor between the sexes.

REPRODUCTION AND HOUSEHOLD SERVICES

Since the early 1950s the government and the women's movement have paid attention to protecting the health of women and improving the methods of childbirth and the health of mothers and infants during the prenatal and postnatal periods. When women first entered nondomestic production in large numbers, there were several reports that commented on the numbers of miscarriages and other casualties due to overstrain and insufficient care and protection of women's health.[25] The national women's organization undertook to report on the matter for the central government, and it circulated memoranda on the problem to its members.[26] Since then production units have commonly implemented labor protection policies, and women have tended to work fewer days per month than men and to be allocated to dry and light work when they were menstruating, were pregnant, or had given birth shortly before.

However, it has also been necessary for the government to continue to remind collectives of the importance of these measures for the health and productivity of women.[27] Policy documents on labor protection blame both the leaders of the collectives for giving the problem insufficient attention and women themselves for disregarding their health and indulging in simplistic physical contest.[28] Apparently some women have felt that the labor protection policies reflect an assumption of physical weakness in women, and hesitate to inform their leaders when they are menstruating or pregnant, and thus in special need of safeguarding their health.

By 1956 it was estimated that trained health workers supervised 60 percent of rural births, thus greatly reducing infant and maternal mortality (Salaff 1972, p. 34). Before the movement to train barefoot doctors and establish a widespread network of local clinics in each production brigade in the mid-1960s, the rural areas had tended to be medically understaffed. The training of paramedical personnel and the practice of assigning to each production brigade a woman barefoot doctor who both worked alongside the women members in production and spread health knowledge generally served to keep a health check and to provide treatment for women workers. The government has established a network of local clinics that have systematized the health services in rural areas and provided facilities for birth control, the treatment of simple problems with herbs and acupuncture, and referrals of the most serious cases to the commune hospital. Indeed, these facilities have been the envy of many international health and planned parenthood bodies.

An important measure designed to enable women to enter nondomestic production was the establishment of collective or communal services to reduce the individual household responsibilities and chores that have long occupied women. [29] These activities were time-consuming and onerous in rural China, where besides the daily washing, cooking, and child care, water had to be drawn and carried, grain had to be ground at a stone or turned by a donkey or by the housewife herself, fuel had to be gathered from the hills, clothes and cloth shoes had to be sewn by hand, and vegetables had to be pickled or sliced and dried for the long winter months. The new policies recognized that under conditions like these, most women would find it impossible to take part in regular social production.

As a spokesman for the government pointed out at a conference in 1958, its main task was to remove the contradictions between nondomestic production and household labor; these contradictions could be resolved only if steps were taken to replace the scattered household tasks by collectivized grain processing, child care, and cooking or dining facilities. [30] Articles in the media have made it clear that what is to be avoided in the process of rural development is the entry of women into the public sphere that results in their merely acquiring dual roles, with ensuing conflict or physical strain, or that women's domestic roles prevent them from fully participating in political processes, many of which in the rural villages are spare-time and unpaid.

In the late 1950s, during the Great Leap Forward, the majority of production brigades could boast a range of services available to women. By 1959 it was estimated that in rural areas there were 4,980,000 nurseries and kindergartens and more than 3,600,000 public dining rooms. [31] The advantages for women were stressed and applauded. One collective calculated that whereas 105 persons were required to prepare meals for 105 households in the past, now 8 persons were sufficient, thereby making it possible to save over 6,000 labor days for the whole year. According to another survey in Honan, use of sewing machines and hand-operated mills helped to cut women's household labor by 40 to 50 percent. [32]

The establishment of these collective living enterprises was initially heralded as resolving the age-old contradiction between participation by women in nondomestic production and the demands of the household for their labor. However, although an impressive array of these services was established, some were soon closed as suddenly as they had been opened. Child-care facilities were closed because of a shortage of trained personnel, dissatisfaction with the level of care, and the widespread availability of grandmothers to look after the children.

The establishment of community dining rooms in rural areas proved to be very expensive, because formerly unpaid domestic labor became paid labor in the public sector. The cooks now had to be paid wages. Whereas members of individual households had formerly gathered fuel for their stoves from the surrounding hillsides, now coal was required; it had to be purchased from the commune station and the collective cart had to be used to transport it. Popular opinion and dissatisfaction with the organization of menus and accounting often led to their closure. Certain pragmatic factors also militated against their successful maintenance. For instance, in northern China it was still necessary to light individual stoves for heating purposes, and since it was the lighting and permanent use of the stoves that took most of the time and effort of individual women, the establishment of communal dining rooms had only a peripheral impact on reducing domestic labor. As a result of a combination of factors, the community dining rooms closed (Crook and Crook 1966, pp. 68-71, 157-58). Perhaps the most successful of the services established were the communal corn-grinding facilities, many of which have remained in operation.

Since this large-scale experiment with rural welfare facilities in the late 1950s, community services have been very unevenly established in rural areas. In the 1970s nurseries and early child care facilities were provided on some of the largest and well-to-do communes located on the outskirts of the urban centers. It is my own observation and that of others that nurseries are usually for children three years and older, and they are by no means universally established in rural villages. Some collectives organize rudimentary child-minding services during harvesting and sowing. At other times arrangements are made among the women within individual households, and grandmothers often retire to mind grandchildren. Ruth Sidel was told that even in communes with many regular nurseries, half, or more than half, of the children stay with grandmothers (Sidel 1972, pp. 84-85, 124-25). Where young mothers can make no such arrangements and there are no child-care facilities, they usually have to withdraw from the collective labor force. For instance, it has been reported that "few mothers with children have the opportunity to work in the fields" (Myrdal and Kessle 1973, p. 239). Although most of the community dining rooms did not survive the Great Leap Forward, in very busy agricultural seasons canteens might be set up by the collective to reduce the labor required by individual households.

Since the end of the Great Leap Forward, policy statements concerning the sexual division of labor within the household have been marked by a certain change. At first, women in the countryside were exhorted to take part in collective production as well as to maintain the household. [33] At the end of the 1960s and in the early 1970s, men and women were encouraged to undertake an equal share of the housework. [34] If women were to move into the collective sphere, surely the corollary was that men should move into the domestic sphere. In the rural villages, meetings have been held to encourage men to undertake their share.

This policy may have had some results among the younger generation, but even in the 1970s policy statements were marked by ambiguity; domestic work should be shared by men and women, but where there is direct competition for men's and women's labor outside the household, it is women's nature that, by definition, better equips her to perform the household chores. An extract from an article published in 1973 juxtaposes the two concepts underlying the division of labor between the sexes:

> Domestic work should be shared by men and women.
> But some household chores, such as looking after children, sewing and others should generally be done by women . . . after a certain phase of farm work is completed during very busy seasons or on rainy days or in winter, women should be given some time off to attend to some essential household chores. [35]

In the main, then, women continue to maintain and service the household. Without the outside agencies to perform household work and to provide labor-saving devices that are available to the urban housewife, rural women must continue to transform most of what the household consumes. Meat and vegetables must be produced and cooked, food salted and preserved, children cared for, and the majority of clothes and shoes sewn. Women within the household usually divide these tasks among themselves, with older women often retiring from collective labor to perform the domestic tasks and care for young children. There may be some sharing between households during busy agricultural seasons, but in rural China women still tend to perform the essential task of maintaining and rearing workers for production.

Peasant women have thus been expected to enter the waged labor force and, at the same time, to continue to service and maintain the household. It seems that the establishment of the communes may not have reduced the demands on women's labor so much as they have led to an intensification of female labor. There has been some redefinition of the sexual division of labor in the public sphere, to the benefit of women, but despite numerous policies to reduce the content of domestic labor and equalize the distribution of the remainder between the sexes, there has been little correlative redefinition of labor within the domestic sphere. The last section of this chapter considers why this trade-off between visibility and remuneration and the intensification of female labor has been made necessary by the development programs themselves, and outlines a number of problem areas that may have contributed to the institutionalization of the dual demands on peasant women.

INTERPRETATION OF THE PROBLEM

As this chapter has shown, the state in China has intervened within the domestic sphere in an attempt to redefine the sexual division of labor. In the 1970s articles in the media continued to draw attention to the problem of domestic labor and the dual demands on the time and energies of women, but the problem has largely been interpreted in terms of ideological conservatism. Since the late 1950s the government has primarily explained the persistence of the traditional division of labor within the household by the "backwardness" of rural areas and inheritance of beliefs such as "Women know of nothing but household affairs" and "The household is responsible for supporting a family while the wife is responsible for household chores," and other equivalent perceptions and customs that underlie the traditional sexual division of labor.

The experience of China in the late 1950s proved to the government that customary norms and beliefs deriving from women's supposed inferiority, physical weakness, and the traditional sexual division of labor can survive quite radical changes in the relations of production and in the material circumstances of women. Their early attempts to introduce women into nondomestic production had suggested that raising the consciousness of both men and women to a recognition of the continuing influence of the traditional division of labor was a very necessary and specific area of reform. Since the 1950s the government has intermittently attempted to introduce programs that both criticize these traditional beliefs and customs and, at the same time, popularize the equitable distribution of household labor. This has been their main approach to the problem. However, it can be argued very cogently that in the rural areas of China there are certain material restrictions that have inhibited the further redefinition of the sexual division of labor within the village.

One of these restrictions is that, despite the policies of collectivization, the structure of the rural economy in China requires that the peasant household continue to function as a unit of production and consumption, and provide a large share of its necessary goods and services. This has determined the substantial content of domestic labor in the rural areas. In the private sector the household is still an important unit for the production of its subsistence. The private sector includes not only private plots, which comprise 4 to 5 percent of the total area of collectively held land and are allocated on a per capita basis, but also the raising of livestock such as pigs and chickens. By providing most of the vegetables and much of the meat for immediate consumption, it constitutes a vital food resource as well as an important cash contribution to the household economy.

In the absence of most community services, domestic labor involving the transformation of produce for consumption—such as grinding corn, preserving vegetables, sewing, cooking, and child care—is an important demand on the labor resources of the household. At particular stages in a woman's life her labor tends to be distributed in favor of the domestic and private sector. It is a common occurrence for the recruitment of a new daughter-in-law or wage earner in the collective sector to result in the release of the women of the older generation to manage the side occupations of the private sector and to undertake, with the help of the younger generation, domestic labor and child care.

As we have seen, there have been a number of attempts to socialize or equalize the distribution of domestic labor, but neither of these policies has been very successful. When community services to share in the maintenance of the household were established, the material resources for providing these services were not always forthcoming. The allocation of resources by the national administration or local cooperative for providing capital expenditure and for establishing local self-financing projects has not been adequate. The emphasis on production and the concentration of investments and allocation of resources to other areas of production, particularly light and heavy industry, caused their diversion from the agricultural and service sectors, where their use might have lessened the demands on women's labor. Indeed, women's unpaid labor in the service and private subsistence sector not only may lessen the costs of consumption for the government, but also may actually subsidize the rural productive and development programs.

The premium placed on women's labor within the household has its origins in several factors. First, because the basis on which work points are allocated within the collective places women at a disadvantage in the collective work force, they are most likely to perform the labor required in the private sector and in the household. Second, the practice of surname and village exogamy, which means that women often remain temporary members of their natal village and become outsiders in their husband's village, has the effect of inhibiting the redefinition of women's work roles. For instance, the "temporary" and "outsider" nature of their position does not encourage any investment by local communities in the training of young women in economic or political skills—and, hence, does not encourage a redefinition of the sexual division of labor. As daughters who are yet to marry out and wives who have recently married in, they are often not encouraged to take up posts in rural industry or develop scarce skills. Men from the production team are much more likely than women to be recruited into these activities. The numbers of women in leadership positions in rural areas also suggest that women have had a much more difficult time breaking into the political decision-making processes, since men are permanent members of the production team and may also be related through kinship ties. As temporary members they may not be sent on training courses, and as outsiders it takes them time to become familiar with a new political arena and build up their own networks of support.

Finally, many of the factors inhibiting the further redefinition of the sexual division of labor in China can be attributed to two underlying assumptions. The first is that any redefinition of the traditional sexual division of labor is assumed to derive primarily from the entry of women into the waged labor force. This was early established as the main theme of policies to do with redefining women's roles:

> . . . the mobilisation of women to participate in production is the most important link in the chain that protects women's own vital interests . . . it is necessary to begin with production for both economic prosperity and economic independence, promote the political status of women, their cultural level and improve their livelihood, thereby leading the way to emancipation (All-China Democratic Women's Federation 1949, p. 8).

The major problem that emerged as a result of this emphasis was the imbalance or lack of attention and resources directed toward women's reproductive and domestic roles, compared with the efforts to attract women into social production.

The second premise underlying policies concerning the sexual division of labor became apparent at the end of the 1950s. In the first decade the government had attempted, and for the most part failed, to establish new and collective institutions in the rural areas that would reduce the dual demands on female labor. Since that time it has identified the ideological constraints, or the "backwardness" and conservatism of peasants in "abandoning the old and embracing the new" social practices, as the primary factors responsible for inhibiting a further redefinition of the sexual division of labor and, especially, the equalizing of domestic responsibilities.

The major problem that has emerged as the result of the emphasis on ideological campaigns to equalize the distribution of domestic labor between the sexes has been the imbalance or lack of attention given to a material base and to practices that continue to encourage the persistence of beliefs discriminating against women. In the rural economy this continues to determine the substantial content of domestic labor in rural China and to structure women's roles within the domestic sphere. Policies to do with raising the consciousness of men and women may be necessary, but it is the incomplete alteration in the relations of production, the household's own production, and the individual transformation of much of the materials required for each family's subsistence that encourages each household to assign its female labor to these domestic activities. In these circumstances it is crucial that China raise questions as to how to conceptualize and integrate domestic labor within socialist strategies of development. Is it to be a visible, recognizable, and remunerated sector of the economy, or a constituent of the unpaid labor of both sexes?

NOTES

1. "Women's Congress and Education in Socialism," New China News Analysis (NCNA), August 29, 1957.
2. "Chinese Women," China News Analysis (CNA), February 7, 1958.
3. "Historic Change of Several Hundred Million Rural Women . . .," NCNA, September 22, 1959.
4. Report by president of All-China Democratic Women's Federation, Renmin Ribao (RMRB), October 7, 1959.
5. "The People's Commune and Women," Hongqi, February 29, 1960.
6. Report of Guangdong Province Women's Federation, Zhongguo Funu (ZF), August 1, 1965; report by Wang Yufeng, ZF, October 1, 1965; "Rural Women Constitute a Tremendous Revolutionary Force," Hongqi, September 30, 1969; "Equal Pay for Equal Work in a Fujian Xian," RMRB, May 13, 1973.

7. Report by the president of the All-China Democratic Women's Federation, RMRB, October 7, 1959.

8. "Work Hard to Train Women Cadres," Hongqi, December 1, 1973.

9. "Women's New Life in Rural People's Communes," NCNA, February 24, 1959.

10. "Historic Change of Several Hundred Million Women. . . ."

11. NCNA, March 7, 1959, and March 6, 1967.

12. "Chinese Women's Achievements in 1958," NCNA, January 4, 1959.

13. Peking Review (PR), July 12, 1960; RMRB, April 14, 1975; NCNA, March 4, 1976.

14. "Equal Pay for Equal Work for Men and Women," Hongqi, February 1, 1972.

15. Cai Chang, report on women's conference, NCNA, December 4, 1958.

16. NCNA, January 1, 1959.

17. "Shen Chilan—Women of New China," People's China (PC), August 16, 1953; report by Yingshan Xian, ZF, November 1, 1961; "Equal Pay for Equal Work for Men and Women," Hongqi, March 1, 1972.

18. PC, July 16, 1957; ZF, November 1, 1961; Oian Xian, May 25, 1964; ZF, October 1, 1965; Hongqi, March 1, 1972.

19. "Li Fang—People's Deputy," PC, January 1, 1954; Oian Xian, May 25, 1964; Crook and Crook 1966, pp. 126-29.

20. ZF, November 1, 1961; China Reconstructs, March 1975.

21. After each harvest the value of the work point was calculated by dividing the total number of work points earned by all the members of the collective into that portion of the total income of the collective set aside for individual earnings. What was feared was that if women received a higher rating for their work, the total number of work points would rise, and by making no allowance for a concomitant increase in total output, it seemed that the value of each work point would fall. This, the men thought, would affect their own levels of payment. See Crook and Crook 1966, pp. 126-29; Peking Review, March 11, 1966; Hongqi, March 1, 1972.

22. RMRB, July 1, 1973.

23. RMRB, March 6, 1972.

24. RMRB, March 8, 1973.

25. "The Health of Rural Women," RMRB, May 16, 1956; RMRB, August 12, 1956.

26. "Forum of Non-party Women," NCNA, June 6, 1957.

27. "Further Liberate Women's Labor Capacity . . . ," RMRB, June 2, 1958; "Bring into Fuller Play Women as Members of the Labor Force," Hongqi, March 3, 1973.

28. "Further Improve the Labour Protection Work . . .,"
ZF, August 1, 1961.

29. "Further Liberate Women's Labour Capacity. . . ."

30. "A New Contradiction Has to Be Solved," RMRB, July
13, 1958.

31. Editorial, RMRB, March 8, 1959.

32. "Further Liberate Women's Labour Capacity. . . ."

33. Reports of the Third Guandong Provincial Women's Congress, Nanfang Ribao, March 27, 1962.

34. "Work Hard to Train Women Cadres," Hongqi, December 1, 1973.

35. "Bring into Fuller Play the Role of Women as Members of the Labour Force."

REFERENCES

All-China Democratic Women's Federation. 1949. Documents of the Women's Movement in China. Peking: the Federation.

Broyelle, C. 1977. Women's Liberation in China. Sussex: Harvester Press.

Buck, J. L. 1937. Land Utilisation in China. University of Nanking.

Chao Kuo-chun. 1960. Agrarian Policy of the Communist Party 1921-1959. Bombay: Asia Publishing House.

China Mainland. 1959. 164 (April 13).

China Reconstructs (CR). 1975. "Breaking Down Male Supremacy." Vol. XXIV, no. 3, pp. 2-11. March and June.

Croll, E. 1973. The Women's Movement in China: A Selection of Readings 1949-1975. London: ACEI.

_____. 1976a. "The Anti-Lin Piao and Confucian Campaign: A New Stage in the Ideological Emancipation of Women." New Zealand and Australian Journal of Sociology 12:35-43.

_____. 1976b. "Female Solidarity Groups as a Power Base in Rural China." Paper presented at Fourth World Congress of Rural Sociology, Poland. Published in Ruralis Sociologus no. 2 (1978):140-57.

_____. 1976c. "Social Production and Female Status: Women in China." Race and Class 18, no. 1.

_____. 1977a. "Jiang Village: A Household Survey." China Quarterly no. 72.

_____. 1977b. "A Recent Movement to Redefine the Role and Status of Women." China Quarterly no. 71:591-97.

_____. 1978a. "China: From Segregation to Solidarity." In P. Caplan and J. Bujra, eds., Women United, Women Divided. London: Tavistock, pp. 46-76.

_____. 1978b. Feminism and Socialism in China. London: Routledge and Kegan Paul.

_____. 1978c. "The Negotiation of Marriage in China." Ph.D. dissertation, University of London.

_____. 1979. Women and Rural Development: The Case of the People's Republic of China. Geneva: ILO.

Crook, I., and D. Crook. 1966. The First Years of Yangyi Commune. London: Routledge and Kegan Paul.

Davin, D. 1976. Woman-Work: Women and the Party in Revolutionary China. Oxford: Clarendon Press.

Diamond, N. 1975. "Collectivisation, Kinship and the Status of Women in Rural China." Bulletin of Concerned Asian Scholars (January-March):25-32.

Foreign Languages Press (FLP). 1957. The Upsurge of Socialism in the Countryside. Peking: FLP.

Hoffman, C. 1967. Work Incentive Practices and Policies in the PRC, 1953-1965. New York: State University of New York Press.

Hongqi (Red Flag).

Kristever, J. 1977. About Chinese Women. London: Marion Boyars.

Lewis, J. 1963. Leadership in Communist China. Ithaca: Cornell University Press.

Maloney, J. 1976. "Women, Ladies and Junior Level Leadership in China." Current Scene 13, no. 3-4:15-22.

Myrdal, J., and G. Kessle. 1973. China: The Revolution Continued. London: Penguin.

New China News Analysis.

Peking Review.

People's China.

Renmin Ribao (RMRB, People's Daily).

Salaff, J. 1972. "The Role of the Family in Health Care." In J. R. Quin, ed., Medicine and Health Care in China. Washington, D.C.: U.S. Department of Health, Education and Welfare.

Schram, P. 1969. The Development of Chinese Agriculture 1950-1959. Chicago: University of Chicago Press.

Sidel, R. 1972. Women and Child Care in China. London: Penguin.

Weinbaum, B. 1976. "Women in Transition to Socialism: Perspectives on the Chinese Case." Review of Radical Political Economics 8, no. 1:34-58.

Young, M., ed. 1973. Women in China, Studies in Social Change and Feminism. Ann Arbor: University of Michigan Press.

Zhongguo Funu (ZF, Women of China).

INDEX

Abate, Alula, 218
Abdullah, A., 112
Accumulation, capital, 4, 24, 30, 31, 179
Active labor, concept of, 127-34
Activity rates, by region, actual and projected, 124, 125
Agnikulakshatriyas, 17; capitalist relationships among, 21-22; pauperization of, 20
Agrarian reform, 203-22
Agricultural implements, women and, 78
Agricultural laborers, distribution of permanent and regular casual, 42-43
Agricultural production, 34, 50, 227-31; sexual composition of labor force, 72-82; tasks associated with, 69
Agriculture, surplus population in, 53
Algeria, 123
Amhara women, 208, 210
Amsden, Alice, 88
Andean region, 79, 125; sexual division of labor in, 68-82
Andors, Phyllis, 204
Animal production, activities associated with, 69
Anker, R., 125
Arizpe, L., 168
Association of the Lace Manufacturers of Narsapur, 14

Bangladesh, 112
Bauer, Dan Farry, 206-7, 208, 211
Beechy, V., 130

Benería, Lourdes, 66, 95, 112-13, 114, 124, 133, 141, 203
Bengelsdorf, Carrollee, 204
Bennholdt, Thomsen, V., 141
Benston, Margaret, 88
Bhalla, G. S., 58
Bhalla, S., 38, 39, 44, 46, 57, 58
Bienefeld, M., 140
Biki, 99
Billings, M. H., 35
Biological determinism, 1
Blauner, Robert, 192
Bonded labor, 51, 52
Bondestam, Lars, 205
Boserup, Ester, 66, 120, 141, 207, 217
Boulding, E., 141
Bracero program, 157-58, 160
Bride price, 106
Briggs, Harold, 181
Briggs Plan, 181
Buck, J. L., 224

Cabrera, G., 152
Caceres, Ingrid, 89
Cajamarca, 66, 67-68, 78, 79, 84-86; agricultural fieldwork by women in, 71; labor market participation rates, 82; sexual composition of labor force in, 72, 77
Capital, internationalization of, 183
Capital accumulation, 4, 24, 179; in agriculture, effects of, 31; and female migration, 179; and patriarchal relations within peasant households, 30; and subsistence production in rural sector, 179
Capital-intensive industries, 183

ABOUT THE AUTHORS

MARIA MIES is Professor of Sociology at Fachhochschule Köln, West Germany. From 1979 to 1981 she worked on a visiting assignment at the Institute of Social Studies, The Hague, Holland, where she developed a program on women and development. She has lived and worked for many years in India. Her research has concentrated on rural and urban women in India, on women's and peasants' movements, and on theoretical and methodological questions related to women's studies and feminist research. She is the author of Indian Women and Patriarchy, Concept Publishers, New Delhi.

GITA SEN is an economist at the Graduate Faculty, New School for Social Research, New York, and currently at the Centre of Development Studies, Trivandrum, India. She has been working on conceptual and empirical issues in the links between gender and social class, with particular reference to changing agrarian relations in India.

CARMEN DIANA DEERE is Assistant Professor of Economics at the University of Massachusetts, Amherst. From 1975 to 1976 she conducted field work on rural women and peasant economy in northern Peru and then took part in the national level Colombian rural women study as a research associate.

MAGDALENA LEÓN DE LEAL is a researcher affiliated with the Colombian Association of Population Studies (ACEP). She is primarily interested in the study of women's work and the relations of production and reproduction and in the evaluation of action projects for women. She is the editor of La Mujer y el Desarrollo en Columbia (1977) and Mujer y Capitalismo Agrario (1980).

RICHARD LONGHURST is an agricultural economist with a doctorate from Sussex University, England. He is currently a visiting fellow at the Institute of Development Studies, University of Sussex.

KATE YOUNG studied social anthropology as a mature student at the London School of Economics, gaining her Ph.D. in 1976 for her study of the social setting of migration in an indigenous community in Mexico. She is currently a fellow of the Institute of Development Studies, Brighton, England, where she coordinates a program of research and dissemination on aspects of the link between development and women's subordination.

NOELEEN HEYZER is a Singaporean sociologist working in the Social Development Division of the United Nations Economic and Social Commission for Asia and the Pacific. She obtained her Ph. D. at Cambridge University and has published material in England, Singapore, the Philippines and Geneva on trade unions in Singapore, and on the development strategy and women workers in Singapore and Peninsular Malaysia.

ZENEBEWORKE TADESSE is a sociologist from Ethiopia writing her Ph. D. dissertation for the Department of Sociology, State University of New York, Binghamton. She is a founding member of the Association of African Women for Research and Development and is currently working at AAWORD's headquarters, Dakar, Senegal.

ELIZABETH CROLL, a former fellow at the contemporary China Institute, University of London, has been a full-time consultant for the ILO and the United Nations Institute for Social Development in Geneva. Her books include Feminism and Socialism in China, Women and Rural Development in China, and The Politics of Marriage in Contemporary China.

LOURDES BENERIA is Associate Professor of Economics, Rutgers University. During 1977-78 she was in charge of the Program on Rural Women within the ILO's Rural Development Branch. She has carried out empirical work on women in Spain and Morocco; and is currently doing research in Mexico.